Being The Other Woman

Being The Other Woman

*Who we are, what every woman
should know and how to AVOID us*

MICALLE A. CULVER

authorHOUSE®

AuthorHouse™
1663 Liberty Drive
Bloomington, IN 47403
www.authorhouse.com
Phone: 1-800-839-8640

First published by AuthorHouse 01/27/2012

ISBN: 978-1-4520-0798-4 (sc)
ISBN: 978-1-4520-0799-1 (hc)
ISBN: 978-1-4520-0800-4 (ebk)

Library of Congress Control Number: 2011908741

Printed in the United States of America

CONTENTS

Dedication

For My Daughters
You are the spirit in me behind all that is good.
May you always do as I say and not as I do, because;
I often give myself very good advice,
But I very seldom follow it ~ Alice in Wonderland

Acknowledgments

My Mother and Father; Who shall now be convinced that I did in fact "hear" your wisdom from time to time.

My Sisters; You are more than sisters, you are my best friends and a large sum of my purpose, the totality of joy. Particularly the one who spent all of her free time between projects editing for me.

My Brother and Son; Because you remain in my heart unconditionally, the few of the great men who inspire truth and authentic love.

My nieces and nephews; Because Towey would rather play in your sunshine than do anything else. Therefore, you are my inspiration.

And last but far from least; To "Sasha" and "Janet"—My father once told me that if I died with the ability to count true friends on each finger of one hand, I would be truly blessed. Because of you, I could survive without the other three.

I should not go without mentioning thanks of sorts to the man who inspired this book. Because so many other words in these pages will speak to you, I leave you with this;

> *"For every moment of triumph, for every instance of beauty, many souls must be trampled"* ~ Hunter S. Thompson.

My God, sometimes "we" still cracks me up!

All names have been changed to protect the not so innocent and, my ass from a law suit.

Part 1

The Story of My Affair

We are inclined to judge ourselves by our ideas,
others by their acts

—Harold Nicolson

Introduction

Perhaps it was my father who first said to me, "Never judge a man until you've walked a mile in his shoes." Whoever it was, I doubt that his meaning was that I should walk a mile in every shoe I've judged.

Most of us have been privy to office or neighborhood chatter about who is committing some sleazy act of adultery. We have all been exposed to soap operas or movies that create the image of those involved in sinful circumstances. When a married man is creeping off to hotel rooms, back alleys, or broom closets, we immediately visualize the one accompanying him as the Great Babylonian Whore. Whereas the man is viewed simply the shameless, arrogant dog, or worse—the innocent victim of the devilish siren who possessed his mind and drew him away from wife and children. Were he to hold title of Supreme Ass, then the other woman is in fact Queen of the Kingdom of Ill Repute. Ironically, if it is a married woman who gives in to the temptation of an affair, she still is Queen of the Kingdom, while the trespassing man is either the sorry victim of her scheming lies or the son of a bitch the woman's husband has labeled him.

It seems apparent that the DNA of Eve still runs strong in all who contain a double X chromosome. But what has perplexed me, even as far back as my first experience of Sunday school, is why it was Eve who suffered the greatest of consequences when listening to the lying snake. Was Adam not responsible for his own broken pact with God? Eve may have offered a bit of the forbidden fruit, but Adam had a choice as to whether he would bite and swallow. As God walked up and down in the Garden of Eden in search of his hiding subjects, Adam was called to the carpet with regard to his sudden interest in hide and seek. "The woman gave it to me," he explained with pointed finger.

So it has been since the beginning of time.

One night several years ago, I sat at the dining room table of Sasha, a woman who would later become one of my dearest friends. She had

3

just finished unpacking her belongings after moving into her new condo following a devastating breakup. Sasha had spent more than eight years of her life with a man who could never seem to bring himself to marry her. In many ways, she had created her now former partner's career. She had inspired him with idea and moved cinder blocks for him to step upon as he climbed his way to success. They had built a home together in which she had poured herself into creating atmosphere and comfort. She had hopes and dreams of little blond daughters in pink dresses and patent leather shoes, piano lessons and dance recitals. But he wouldn't commit, and she was still feeling "not good enough." The inability of her former love to make Sasha his wife had cost her years of longing for more than just a shiny rock on her finger, years of wasted effort in continuing to try harder to accomplish perfection. She was like any other woman. She had an overwhelming desire to feel loved, to have an impact in the life of a man who would find her to be the center of his universe and adore her. Sasha simply wanted to be special and unique to that one person she could share her life with.

This extended beyond her romantic desires, for should you be blessed to be called her friend or lucky enough to be family, she will do almost anything to bring you joy. She is one of the most giving and thoughtful women I have ever known, the kind of woman who sets herself aside and consoles your heart until 4 a.m. if necessary, regardless of her 7 a.m. meeting. She is the middle child of a rather large family that has suffered circumstances and dramas unavoidable to any family so large. More often than not, Sasha is their rock or savior in time of need. She takes charge in any crisis when the rest fall apart. She is well known throughout the community. Never did she and I go anywhere without someone stopping her to say hello. She takes careful steps to always search for ways to improve herself and to understand and extend herself to people.

But that night as we sat together at her table, as she sat with slumped shoulders, mascara running down her face and swollen nose, she told me something that shocked me beyond comprehension. "I have been having an affair for two years," she said. I looked at this stunningly beautiful friend of mine who had the world to offer any man. She had a distinct sex appeal, her attire was always perfect, her sense of décor was elegant. She had the silliest of personalities that kept you in constant stitches and a distinct ability to communicate in profound ways. She was fun to be around—the life of the party. When the party ended, Sasha could reach inside the spirit of anyone before her and extract from them the deepest parts of their heart. Why on God's green earth would she settle for so little for so long?

As I listened to her speak of the two years she shared with a married man whom she had met through her business, I could not find an ounce of understanding as to the allure of lunches in hotel rooms and the sacrifice of valuable time and responsibility in order to jaunt off at the ring of a phone for an hour's worth of sex. I imagined a relationship where, as quickly as he'd drop his seed, the man would pull his pants back up and leave. It cheapened her in my eyes and I wondered how she herself did not feel cheapened. She referred to his wife as "that bitch" so often during the course of our conversation that I could no longer contain myself and had to point out the very obvious fact that "that bitch" was suffering an invasion of the deepest kind and the fact that she was bedding "that bitch's" husband removed her of all dignity. I was quite appalled that the wife would be spoken ill of at all. She was in fact the victim of these two shameless, inhuman asses. I wondered if I had missed the signs of serious defect in Sasha's character.

This was my first close look into the heart and soul of the "other woman."

Until I became one myself.

Chapter 1

A Harmless Flirtation

One lazy summer weekend, I was visiting a friend watching the sun set from her back deck. She received a phone call from another friend inviting us to stop over for a glass of wine. It seemed the perfect thing to top the day.

We entered the friends home anticipating the casual setting where I was introduced to Blake, a neighbor who had dropped in before our arrival. Blake had been conversing about his travels to many countries which quickly drew my interest in speaking to him.

We quickly found ourselves in a delightful conversation that lasted for hours on topics in which both of us shared deep interest—travel of course, then mythology, religion and history. It has long been a dream of mine to travel around the world and explore every culture possible. I had never encountered someone who could mentally stimulate me to such capacity. As one glass of wine became a bottle, we debated over the taboo topic of religion while mixing Biblical scripture or famous historical quotes into comical conversation. We were both surprised on several occasions that each or the other were familiar and knowledgeable about the topics our chat seemed to haphazardly lead to, and became engrossed with testing each other to see if either would "get it" when using word play. He had intrigued me and I sensed the feeling was mutual. A surge of attraction overpowered me while we were in the middle of an excited debate. I leaned in closer to him while I was in mid sentence.

Whatever words of wisdom that were about to fly out of my mouth at that moment were halted by his lips and the talk turned into a heated kiss. Quickly sobering, I realized that no matter how hard I attempted to rationalize the connection I felt, this man was married with three children. But I had liked him instantly, and so my mind raced with questions to justify or excuse the attraction. Were there problems in his marriage? Were they separated? I hoped to find justification but quick review of thought determined that it didn't matter, he was married nonetheless. My friend and I left the gathering shortly thereafter and I avoided seeing Blake for several months.

When I met Blake, I had been single for some time. I had dated here and there, but I had not found the man or dating circumstance that fit within my life. For almost two years I had been teaching Sunday school to fourth-grade girls, many of whom suffered incredible dysfunctions in their daily lives that ripped at my heart. I was a single mother to two beautiful, growing girls of my own. As the oldest of eight children, I had such a strong sense of responsibility that I put many other people high on my list of priorities. I ran a business with demands from clients that stretched far beyond nine to five and I was also studying to earn my degree. I had little time to offer just anyone, and so few men came close to meeting my long list of requirements and earning a second date. It was unfortunate that the one who finally caught my attention was not available.

My friends soon began to inform me that Blake had been inquiring about me. Due to the nature of my profession, my contact information was very public and easy to obtain. Eventually he called me, and we shared many long conversations. Mostly, however, we maintained our intriguing chats through e-mail, which became the secret high point of my day. He would send me little challenges at night while I was studying on my computer. *Pop Quiz: If I am a poet and you are my muse, sing to me your name. What is your name goddess? Which muse are you?*

This e-mail led me to study the muse Erato and goddess Eris which inspired me to respond my answer with a cleverly written poem in an e-mail about this goddess and her mythological golden apple. Eris, the goddess of strife as she was called, became enraged after being refused attendance to a wedding of the gods. In anger she threw a golden apple inscribed "for the fairest" amongst three goddesses and in their fight to claim it, brought about the Trojan War—a war fought over an affair.

As I was exchanging these e-mails, my thoughts drifted to a prominent businessman in my community whom I had dated briefly a year before the fateful day I met Blake. The other man was handsome, warm and intimidating in that way that makes your mouth open but words hesitate for fear they will fall from your lips in discombobulated jargon. My whole body shook when I was in his presence, and this freaked me out because I could not control my physical reaction even when I thought I was not nervous. But alas, he was "separated" though still living in the same residence as his soon-to-be-former spouse. Despite my wishes that a clear path might exist on which I could explore the possibilities of this relationship, the path did not exist to me. Regardless of my infatuation I rejected his seemingly sincere defense and ignored him when he said "Do you think that because I am legally married that I cannot fall for you?" I immediately broke off what seemed to be the beginning of an emotional affair, only to soon learn that he had, in fact, moved out of his home and had divorced his wife a short time after. Because his divorce was so recent, my next thought was that he needed to "get out there" and dabble in the single life. I feared that after having been married for so long, he would be enjoying his new-found freedom and have the desire to date around. I was not interested in being a transitional relationship and getting hurt in the process, so I kept him at arms length for quite some time. Finally, his calls ceased when he met a woman he is still with today. I have always wondered what might have become of things between us if I had not clung so hard to my convictions and worried so much about the public concept of right and wrong. I decided I had missed an opportunity to connect with a really great guy because I was too rigid. I allowed my thoughts to tempt me into pondering if perhaps my encounter with Blake would lead to a similar scenario.

Soon communication between Blake and me became nightly conversations online, plus random text messages that always brought a smile and burst of laughter. Then there were the ever-so-welcomed phone calls. I saw him on only two occasions during those months. Once, at a lakeside restaurant, he boarded the boat I was on. Suddenly inspired by Coors Light, Blake begged me not to leave with my friends. "Step off the boat, Blake," the irritated driver demanded while putting the watercraft in reverse and almost disposing of the pest in the lake. Another time, at an evening business function, he approached me with a question: "If you could go to one place in the whole world, where would you go?" I thought about it for a moment, replied, "Italy," and promptly went back to socializing with my associates.

Not long after, Blake read a notice in the newspaper that announced an event I would be attending. He dropped in and asked if I would join him for dinner. Even though my head clearly told me to flee, I was intrigued and wanted to explore our developing friendship.

This marked the beginning of my own two-year affair.

Chapter 2

The Slippery Slope

We had dinner that night. Before now, I had always rested comfortably in some form of electronic communication or larger social gathering. I had never been alone with him before. I was feeling unsure of myself and I was immediately on guard and began to bombard him with questions about his marriage. It was far from the fun, casual flow of conversation that we had become accustomed and looked forward to.

Alone that night, Blake seemed to me to be a very sad and lonely man. As we talked, I learned that he had been living a solitary life. His wife had ceased showing him love and affection for what he said was the last five years. He said he had done everything in his power to rekindle their romance, planning exotic vacations, which she refused, and buying her extravagant gifts, such as jewelry that she never wore and fur coats that she threw to the floor. Their communication concerned only business, her complaints about his family, and her demands that he accomplish tasks she felt necessary for her lifestyle and the children's needs. They were disconnected. He had an aura of dejection, and his eyes seemed to convey his belief that he was unloved and unable to do anything to be needed, loved and appreciated. He appeared to be hiding insecurity in himself. He seemed to be trapped in a prison of a lifeless marriage. Still skeptical, I continued to drill him for details of his marriage as each response he gave only elicited a suspicious and sarcastic reply from me. I tested him by roping him into conversations so that I might dissect his answers. I spoke of a couple I knew who were having troubles with their sex life and commented that the wife had told me she had lost her sexual desire. "I would never put up with that," he replied, then quickly switched gears and implied he suffered from his own wife's lack of interest. "Oooh," I shot back. "Catching yourself so you can lie to me later?" I was so hard on him that I am amazed he ever sought my company again.

I poured several chardonnays onto my nerves, leaving me in no condition to make the hour and a half drive back home. Blake had a cabin on a nearby lake and insisted that I stay to sleep it off. I agreed, but said he had to make my bed on the couch. An awkward kissing session resembling my high school days occurred until I pretended to fall asleep and he left me alone. In the morning, I woke by myself on the couch. When I called for him to wake up and drive me back to my car, Prince Charming arose and tossed a *Cosmopolitan* magazine at me.

"There was my girl last night!" he said, indicating it was the girl in the photograph, not I, who was successful at bringing him to orgasm.

In that moment I was overwhelmed with relief that I had not succumbed to the pig. We soon got into his truck, which was piled with garbage he had forgotten to take to the dump. The stench of dirty diapers almost caused me to add the previous night's chicken wings to the mess. I rode back, feeling incredibly ashamed of myself for having gone to dinner with him, not to mention our drunken suck face session. I was grateful that my fascination with the man had passed in the nick of time, along with any attraction I might have had for him.

Then the large bouquets of flowers with "For the fairest" sentiments began to pour into my office and the phone and e-mail conversations began again. I think it was all of a week before I somehow ended up back at his lake house, this time in the bedroom. Blake was restless that night and after we made love and went to sleep, he jolted awake several times. I believed this was because he was experiencing anxiety over what had just happened, figuring this was a clear sign he had never strayed from his marriage before. Somehow this helped to convince me that he was not a playboy, that we were different from others who had crossed the line, and that what was happening was due to something special and magical between us. This reaction made me believe he was trustworthy and I then persuaded myself to throw every caution to the wind. My intelligence went on screensaver while he seemed at the same time to become more alive.

Our affair began as I suppose most of them do—creeping off to odd places at stolen moments to have sex. Finding strange places to park in the city, working late in the office, and . . . well, hell . . . in my profession, I've had access to every vacant model home in the city for years and as the question will now be asked of me—yes.

We spent a substantial amount of time together during those first few months. Blake stopped by my office often just to brighten his day and mine. We phoned each other hourly, sharing each miniscule happening, from gossip to strange bumper stickers seen while driving along the road. During business meetings, when our thoughts would drift to one another, we would shoot off silly or seductive texts or leave e-mails filled with inside humor. Neither of us could miss an opportunity to share a thought with the other. We spent most lunch and dinner hours together, and we talked endlessly about our children, our childhoods, our family members, our hopes and our goals. To the world, Blake was a wealthy and shrewd businessman, but I came to know Blake as a tortured soul who lived in the shadows of doing and being what he thought others wanted him to do and be, never feeling free enough to discover or develop into the person I could see he was inside, the real him, the one I was growing to appreciate and accept more intimately. It wasn't just his wife that he blamed for causing these feelings inside him; he seemed to also struggle with seeking approval from his father, who found nothing in him but things to criticize. Blake longed to hear the words, "I'm proud of you," fall from his father's lips. He despaired over feelings of rejection from his mother, who was neither expressive nor sentimental, and wanted to connect with her, even though she always seemed to close the door on him. Blake's parents seemed strange to me; they were so different from him. He did not fit in with such emotionless parents, who were raised in the Great Depression and had a primary focus on business. All his life, Blake had been surrounded by cold individuals who were distant and self-seeking, always in pursuit of their own interests. It was as though the only connection, acceptance and love he received came from the innocent embrace and total acceptance of his children. It was with his children that he felt bonded and most whole. His wants were simple, and thanks to his financial freedom, seemed easy to meet. Blake wanted to laugh and enjoy his life.

Because both of us were self employed and our businesses were complementary, our lives began to entwine regularly while we referred clients to one another and shared successes. We found refuge in his home on the lake and spent many days and nights boating or riding jet skis. Blake had beautiful blue eyes and there was something seductive to me about the way he looked when his hair was wet. I could watch him water ski for hours and when the hours were up, I was a puddle myself. Some nights we simply watched movies or went over blue prints and made interior selections for the home he was building on the adjacent lot. What kept us most connected was our shared interests into whichever study we chose to pour ourselves. I could talk to him about anything, like one of my closest girlfriends. Even when I was spilling my deepest fears or hurts, he found the right way to comfort me, often cheering me with some humorous metaphor. Our deep and open conversations always seemed to center on our future "happily ever after" together.

I recall taking my little brother to the state fair sometime during those first months of my affair with Blake. My brother begged me to ride the daring "Zipper" with him to which I declined several times due to the substantial age difference between us, feeling a little too old to be whipped and whizzed around. But suddenly I jumped up "OK! Let's do it!" I said. Seeing the look of horror cross his face, I realized I had just called his bluff. This added to my excitement and now he was forced to climb into the rickety cage with me. The contraption was secured by what appeared to be a metal clothes pin and we were lifted high above the crowd. I began to rock the cage until we were spinning round and round. The sound of my brothers giggling hysteria beside me caused me to laugh with the same joy I'd had at age twelve, the last time I was on this ride. After the rocking subsided and we were still hoisted above the crowd, I breathed in the crisp air. My chest filled with the sensation of Blake and I thought "I have never felt so alive." At the same time, my smile fell as I thought "there will be a price to pay for this." As I think about it now, that ride on the Zipper is symbolic of the two years that were to follow. As soon as I felt alive with joy in spinning glee, I also felt a painful sorrow in stillness.

Though I had moments of lucidity in the beginning of our affair, they were seldom and far enough apart that I was able to ignore them and carry on with things in the spirit of fun. Blake and I were getting dressed after one afternoon romp, when his wife called his cell phone and he answered. I listened as they had a casual conversation about who she had voted for in the local election that day and who else was on the ballot. When he hung up, I was struck with reality. I said to him in shock, "I don't know what I am doing! I'm gonna get hurt in this deal." I then called it off for the first time and began the run for my life.

This would never work for me, I told myself; I was not this girl. I needed it to be over before anyone found out. I was sick enough knowing about it myself. My daydream came with a big problem.

But he wouldn't allow things to end so easily. He kept calling me over and over, attempting to convince me to stay. Then he pulled off the convincing when he slapped tickets to Italy down in front of me.

Chapter 3

The Adventures of Falling in Love

A saint I am not, nor will I ever be because frankly, it doesn't sound fun and as far as I know, I've only got one shot on this planet. I've always been very noncommittal when it comes to promises of boredom. Perhaps not every woman would have taken the bait, but can anyone say that she would not have been tempted to take the vacation of her dreams with a man she adored and loved sharing every minute with? At least for a millisecond? Or is it only me and my trampy-tramp friends who understood this dilemma? Honestly, I was very apprehensive, but the temptation was easier to yield to than the regret I thought I'd have if I didn't go.

Just before we left my friends threw me a huge thirtieth birthday party. Blake was one of the many guests, and I thought that I did an excellent job of working the room and not focusing too much attention on him. In fact, I thought I had barely paid any attention to him at all. I was corrected the day before we left. My friend, who hosted the party, confronted me and let me know that he was on to us. But I danced around his implications, saying "It's not what you think." I am a horrible liar, and to tell my friend that I was not dating Blake would have been worse than trying to dodge the topic. I avoided my friend thereafter and, though today he seems to have forgiven me, I am still unable to hold his gaze before I hang my head with lingering feelings of shame.

I don't think that I ever really believed that I was going to Italy until I arrived at the airport. One never knows what to expect of plans while having an affair. Plans are always subject to change at any given moment, and so I never took in that I was for sure traveling. I kept myself on guard for cancellation. Because of the secretiveness of the ordeal, I wasn't even able to brag to friends or acquaintances that I was going abroad. I was able to share my anticipation only with my best friend and my family, but they were concerned with my decision making and only sucked the wind out of my joy. So I internalized most of my anticipation, choosing not to listen to well meaning advice. This wasn't normal but, what the hell, I was going to Rome!

At the airport, we pretended not to be accompanying one another. It was pretty lame, actually. What kind of lovers' holiday is this? I asked myself. We can't even wait for our flight together in giddy anticipation? I think my original fantasy of traveling to Rome had something to do with a Cinderella-style poufy white dress, a horse-drawn carriage and public displays of affection at an airport filled with rice throwers. Instead, we sat in distant seats for three hours until we reached the lay-over in Seattle, which was also spent on nerves' end, with Blake constantly looking over his shoulder. Before we boarded our international flight, Blake spotted someone he knew, and I was then forced to delay boarding so as not to be seen climbing into the aircraft with him. I chose to spend my time in the restroom, popping a half surfaced zit on my forehead that was irritating me. I became so fixated in diverging my frustrations by my attempt to burst it that I almost missed the flight. I heard the final boarding call and scrambled to the gate, unprepared for a final search before boarding. I was then faced with having to unpack my carry on while being pressured to hurry, as I was holding up departure. Perhaps this was my final notice from God to throw me off the primrose path, but the devil on my shoulder looked like Caesar and was shouting "To ROME!" I quickly jumped onto my chariot.

All passengers had boarded while I walked down the aisle shaking and sweaty. I had fingernail gouges in my skin and blood oozing at the top of my eye from the zit I had attacked. In between Blake's on and off freak outs about where his acquaintance was seated, he looked at me aghast for the damage I had done to my face while poking fun at me. The awakening from my fairy tale pissed me off but the humiliation made me wish my seat would swallow me. Eventually, as passengers began to snore, the redness went down, the blood stopped and we resumed our fun and laughter—and accomplished admission to the Mile High Club. The farther we flew from the U.S., the farther we flew from the troubles of our reality.

Words will never convey how I felt arriving in Rome. I had never been out of the country before and everything was surreal to me. While claiming our bags, I watched the most beautiful young Italian couple retrieving their Louis Vuitton luggage and wondered what lovely things they could be saying to each other in their romantic tongue. For all I know, she could have been chewing his ass, but the language itself sounded like sweet-talk. The bus ride from the airport to the hotel was worthy of thirty journal entries alone. As we drove, I was tossed so thoroughly all over the cabin that a whiplash law suit in America might have covered the expense of the trip. At each stop light I began to fear that I might be a passenger in the movie *Speed*. I stared at my surroundings as if they were movie sets. My senses were in shock. It was as if I had landed on another planet experiencing life for the first time.

Blake was mesmerized by my excitement. He loved giving this to me, loved watching me take in the experience. His face softened every time he looked at me, which he did constantly—almost to the point that I felt discomfort in his gaze.

Our hotel had been built in the 1800s as the residence of a noble Italian family. Marble architecture and paintings filled every vista. We were perfectly positioned near the Piazza del Popolo, the Trevi Fountain, and the Spanish Steps, where hordes of people gathered to rest after shopping at the pricy boutiques that surrounded us. That night, after Blake fell asleep, I wrapped a sheet around myself and followed the moonlight to the thick, antique, double wooden shutters of our grand window and leaned on the brick ledge to watch two Italian men yell, "Arrivederci," to every mop head or car that passed by. To say that I was swept away is an understatement.

Everything in Italy is better. Tomatoes (which I formerly hated) were eaten like apples. Real cream is used in cooking. We do not know true mozzarella in America. Every second, it was as if I were taking my first breath. Every bite was tasting food for the first time. I was present in Vatican City for Pope John Paul II's anniversary. We did not miss a ruin or museum within the city—the Square of Augustus Caesar, the Coliseum, the Pantheon, Mausoleum of Augustus and St. Peter's dome are priceless memories. Yet they are not the things that touched my soul the most.

What reached inside the depth of me was a sort of connection I had never shared with anyone before. It was not the fact that I had traveled to such an exotic place, though I'm sure it helped the amore, but that Blake and I had studied Roman culture with the same like mindedness all while no one was able to interfere with our falling in love. Who could resist falling in love in Rome? We walked cobbled streets hand in hand, dined in romantic cafes and drank wine by ancient fountains, usually the Trevi, where we tossed our pennies each night to make our wishes come true.

Blake had asked me if I could go anywhere in the world, where would I choose to go. He delivered it in splendor. He gave to me Rome. Not only did he give me my own dream, but he also shared his with me. Our trip did not end in Italy. After two weeks there, we went to Istanbul, Turkey.

I was apprehensive, to say the least. Actually, scratch that. Scared shitless is the proper term. A year had passed since 9/11. America had already declared its intent to go to war with Iraq. Vacationing near Iraq's boarder was not my idea of a romantic time! I figured I had already lost my mind. Perhaps I could keep my head.

I knew I was leaving the comforts and romance of Italia when the flight attendant set a sliver of raw fish, a boiled egg, and a piece of golden cheese on my tray. The airport at Istanbul was empty and stale, and all I saw were walls of large stainless steel doors, which (I was certain) were there so the blood of unveiled and disobedient women could easily be cleaned. Blake sent me to have my visa stamped while he exchanged our money, and a turbaned, rifle-carrying man behind glass peered over his large pointed nose and demanded to know with pure hatred why I was in his country. I was asking myself the same thing! I obediently said, "Holiday." If it were possible, he might have punched a hole through my passport. Blake returned with a fistful of Turkish money and we grabbed our bags. At the same moment, the steel doors slid open, a hundred angry rioters with black hair and beady eyes came into view and began to violently grab my luggage from my hands, obviously intending to pillage my belongings. I clutched at them in panic, wondering how Blake would protect me. This is it! This is where it's all going down, the day I dreaded—my death, I thought while deciding to be religious again and beginning to pray. "Give the cab driver your bag," Blake said, his voice filled with irritation as he pulled my white-knuckled fingers from the handle of my suitcase.

I was completely on edge during the nerve racking ride to our former prison, now hotel. I was expected to feel excited like Blake was and to ignore the minivans unloading men armed with weaponry I had only seen in Wesley Snipes movies. I lost all trust in my traveling companion. He seemed to be totally naïve in believing that we were safe. I thought, holy shit, I've traveled with an imbecile! My attitude was pissing him off. Thankfully our converted prison was now a four-star hotel. I began to relax in luxurious comfort, and though many might have died gruesome deaths in the courtyard our room overlooked, the overgrowth of floral hid the despair. From my window I could see the towering minarets of the Haghia Sophia Mosque and hear the calls for prayer that bellow every hour.

The next morning, I decided to embrace my experience and vowed to trust Blake as my guide as we explored several historical sights. Blake did not like to travel in any traditional fashion. He said that a person could only truly embrace culture by getting in with locals. Men running small shops (in order to create a bond) claimed to have family in our home town. They invited us into their homes, where Turkish rugs were rolled out for us in hopes we'd buy one and apple tea was forced down our throats. I was reluctant to drink the poison until Blake had finished his. My mama did not raise a fool. Seeing that he still functioned normally, I went ahead and sipped more culture. It was quite good, actually, something like warm, liquid Jolly Ranchers. The rug ordeal took up half of our first day and got old fast. We had found a lot of extended family that day, and I was itching to get onto the streets where I could stare at women wearing black wool tents in 98-degree heat. So I hurried to surrender to my great uncle twice removed and chose a rug to purchase. I didn't like the traditional styles and pointed to a more modern, hand-woven, hand-died rug. Blake insisted that one should never leave Turkey without a rug and, saying that someday it would lie in our new home, he purchased it.

Later that day, we met backpacking college kids from all over the world who were experiencing life with reckless abandon. They gave us the idea to do some abandoning of our own. We booked several adventures to fill the remainder of our week.

One day at lunch, Blake insisted that I should have a Turkish *donor kabob* (something resembling a gyro). While ordering our food, he instructed the vendor to load his with peppers. "Are you sure?" the man asked. Blake confidently replied, "Some like it hot," with a cocky chuckle. Later, as we were walking through a city lined with political flags and viewing goat heads available for purchase, I turned to realize that Blake was not behind me. Backtracking through the crowd, I found him leaning against a light post near a trash can with snot running down his nose, tears streaming down his face, and his arms hanging limp as if they were paralyzed. He could not answer my desperate pleas to tell me what was wrong, and it appeared to me that he was in cardiac arrest. I must have looked to the non-English-speaking pedestrians around me like a chicken flapping around, warding off prey of her young. How was I to communicate my need for an ambulance? I looked frantically over his body for what might be causing him this near-death experience. In his right hand he was clutching something. I was able to pry his fingers apart and released the pepper filled *donor kabob* into the trash receptacle. This was my first experience of having deep concern for his well being. This also was my first experience of pee-your-pants laughter. Those kinds of experiences would continue through much of our relationship.

As Blake came back to life, we decided to take a boat tour along the Bosporus and into other parts of Turkey that offered us yet more culture shock. This land has such beauty and rich history, it was a glorious trip. There were historical homes, along the river, one of which took my breath away. "I would love to design a home like that!" I said. Blake went quiet. Then spoke sadly "But I'm building you a house." Just before we met, he had begun construction on a large lake home he anticipated someday retiring in. He had shared his plans with me and asked for my input, which I had enjoyed giving him. Now he had revealed his secret heart.

As we neared the harbor, the captain slowed the boat and began to ask each of us a question. This caused a forty-five-minute slow down in docking, as it seemed we were anchored. While the captain was making his inquiry of a Dutchman, Blake began to agonize in pain and was unable to speak. The captain approached him with his question, and while Blake struggled to understand what was being asked of him, the Dutch couple began to make conversation with me, complimenting Blake and me as a couple and remarking on our obvious "soul mate" relationship. (In fact, everywhere we went, people commented on what a delightful couple we were or how connected they observed us to be in our wordless communication with each other.) The Dutchman was tall like Blake, and I realized at that moment how attracted I was to Blake's height. Each time something like that happened, I found new appreciation for him, and my heart would go deeper. I looked at the Dutch couple, who also looked very much in love, and thought of Blake and me growing old together, imagining we would be the same. I began to be very distracted by my conversation with the couple, though I could still hear Blake's frustration in trying to understand the captain's question while he was doubled over in pain. I saw the captain holding a Turkish-English dictionary and he pointed to an entry. Blake looked up at me and said in disbelief, "He's asking me, *Do you feel heartfelt?*" I was genuinely confused until I saw Blake reach into his pocket and hand the man a large tip while holding his abdomen (the peppers were acting up again) so that the captain would pull into the dock. I'm unsure to this day how much that poop cost him.

One evening, we found another interesting place to dine in the row of shops and restaurants built on a bridge across the Bosporus. The waiter arrived with freshly slaughtered fish (eyes and all) lying across a platter and asked which fish we would like to eat. We pointed to our best guess, and later our fish stew arrived (not what we had guessed) accompanied by a group of men carrying acoustic guitars and xylophones. We left in the "spirit" and as we walked along the moonlit bridge, we noticed that some of the shops were vacant and exposed to the elements. The moon was full, into the river. We crept into one of the vacant shops, climbed a spiral iron staircase and began to make love in the little hiding place we found at the top. The romantic scene was like a movie, and it became one of a different sort as I turned my head and was instantly transported into a Humphrey Bogart film. A man in a top hat was standing beneath a street light, leaning against the wall, smoking a cigarette, and watching us. As we scrambled to grab our laundry, the man began to yell at us to not be bothered by him but to pay him to watch for the police. We ran down the spiral staircase as fast as we could and along the cobbled bridge with him chasing after us yelling, "Policia! Policia!" I stepped into the path of an oncoming cab and when he screeched to stop, I grabbed the door handle and we jumped in. I do not know what the laws are in Turkey, but rumors of Turkish whores being beheaded were worth the risk of a broken leg.

One of the studies that Blake and I made together was on Homer's *Iliad*. It was only right, therefore, that we took a tour to what may be the site of the Trojan War. To our surprise, the cheap tour consisted of our own Mercedes bus with a personal driver and also a private tour guide. We visited several ruins, had lunch, and stayed overnight in a town called Assos. Actually, many of the places we visited by chance seemed to have double meaning and correlate to our studies, even as far back as our initial meeting. (Funny, but I just realized so did Assos, pronounced the way our Mexican friend Alex said assholes.) This we took as a divine affirmation from the universe that we were meant to be together. After our visit to Troy, we stopped at the edge of the Black Sea for lunch and I began to get acquainted with our tour guide on a more personal level. We spoke of his Muslim upbringing, his culture, political passions and his life. He shared with me a story of old Turkish women and their belief in reading tea leaves. His grandmother had taught him how to read them himself. I decided to test his fortune telling skills and ordered a cup of tea. After finishing my tea, I was instructed to turn my cup upside down on a saucer, spin a penny around the top and then flip it right side up again. When I turned my cup over, the image inside looked like a man with a hunched back slumping over a cane. Behind him, was a depressed blob resembling a woman with long hair and three small remnants of sludge were behind her, as well. To the other side, the man with a cane faced something that looked like a shapely woman standing tall with visible breasts and holding her hand out, cupping a ball. It looked like she held the world in her hands. "It looks like three people." The tour guide said. Blake and I looked at each other with freakish shock and decided it was time to move forward with the tour. To this day, I can still see with clarity the vision in that tea cup. I have always wondered which of us is the woman who held the world in her hands.

Assos was just across the ocean from Greece. It was a stony little town and we felt we had stepped back in time. Our bus hurled down a dirt road and, seeing us approach, a woman scooped her child up along with a handful of rocks to toss at the sheep blocking our path. We drove up a mountain side to something resembling a bar, passing old men sitting in rocking chairs, smoking pipes and playing backgammon. We also passed a man pulling his donkey with straw piled on its back. When we arrived at our hotel we found another mesmerizing, romantic scene. We sat overlooking the ocean just in time to watch a Mediterranean sunset. In the morning, we dined outdoors by the ocean and watched the Greek Air Force fly drills across the waters. Feral cats surrounded us, taking grabs at our fish breakfast. One actually bit Blake's finger in retaliation for his attempt to scare them away with hissing.

We walked through many bazaars while fighting off venders who would yell "Hey you, American!" while promising "Special price for you today." Broadening my cultural understanding, as well as paying money for each square of toilet paper at potty time, bonded me with Blake in many humorous ways. Every day in Turkey was a life-changing experience and to this day we remember each minute of that trip with humor and nostalgia.

After we left Istanbul, our flight laid over for one day in London, a perfect place to acclimate ourselves for our return to America. As we walked the busy city, looking for a place to dine, Blake suddenly dashed into a shop. Confused by what had startled him, I followed after him, and he informed me that he had spotted the same man he had seen in the Seattle airport three weeks before. I had just spent three weeks having the experience of a lifetime, falling in love, believing a home was being built for me, buying Turkish items to put in that home, and being told and shown that I was "the everything." I had not a care in the world as to the disagreeable details of our relationship. Yet the moment that he saw someone who knew him, he hid in fear of being found out. I said not a word while I digested this brutal reality.

We ate dinner in silence that night, then decided to lighten up at a nearby pub. It seemed to me that American girls receive a lot of attention in London. Perhaps it was only this one particular pub, but the men all seemed to be sure that I was Sandra Bullock, Courtney Cox, or some other actress with dark hair. The absurdity of it flattered me and lifted my spirit, but Blake became very insecure and jealous and attempted to drown his feelings in cocktails. This did not relieve the internal chaos already churning inside us, and during the cab ride back to our hotel, our tension ignited as we argued over the directions to give to the cabbie. Adamant that I was right about how to get to our hotel, I got out of the cab and walked there. I fell asleep leaning against the door while waiting for him to arrive back from his long detour. I awoke as he slipped the card in the door and pushed it open, breaking my back support. I looked up at him from the floor and he made a snide remark (something about having a key in my purse) that caused me to react stubbornly and grab my luggage. I headed for the "tube" to return me to the airport and was halfway to the train station before Blake caught up with me. I saw that he was crying. "Is this how you want this to end?" he asked. It stole my heart in an instant. That night, as Blake confessed his undying and hopeless love for me, I sank like lead to the bottom of our delusion, the delusion of a powerful love.

Chapter 4

Spoonfuls of Sugar

Arriving home from our three-week vacation would give me another dose of cold reality. Blake was scheduled to leave the following morning for Hawaii with his family on their annual trip. After all we had just shared, I was devastated that he would be leaving with his wife. According to him, he was, too. But refusing to go and dropping such an unexpected bomb on his children would only hurt them unfairly. He was gone for two weeks, which I spent remodeling my home and keeping my mind occupied and my broken heart safe in hiding. Each time logic told me that the situation I had allowed myself to enter was ludicrous, he would phone or send an e-mail or text message. There were even handwritten letters in my mailbox almost every day. He did everything he could to show me that being away from me was a living hell for him. His anxiety engulfed him when he realized he was coming home a day later than he thought.

I am so ready to feel you, he wrote, *and hold you and kiss you and just be with you that it's making me crazy. When I discovered that I had another day away from you, I lost all blood pressure and nearly passed out. This has been a rough two weeks for both of us. I was able to deal with the few hard days that we had earlier. That was nothing compared to having to deal with being stuck away from you for one more day. It's like being stuck on a Bosporus tour and the boat driver doesn't speak English. I want to get off of this boat and into your arms for it is you for whom I am truly heartfelt.* The night he flew home, he drove straight to my house with anticipation and stayed the night with me. We felt like long-lost lovers finally reunited. His ability to be front-and-center enabled me to trust that his marriage was not at all a connected one and convinced me that neither husband nor wife cared much for the other.

Things continued between us as they had in Europe and, having had a taste of freedom, we soon found ourselves forgetting to be careful and beginning to behave as a normal couple would in public. His desire to include me in his life brought introductions to friends we naively thought would accept our relationship. Our naïveté helped me to sell myself the fantasy and forget that a real marriage existed. Blake's wife, Beth, was a figment, a bothersome backdrop to the play that was *my* life and what was otherwise a normal partnering.

A month after Blake's return from Hawaii, I flew to New Hampshire to be with my sister as she gave birth to her son. Most of my family had also flown in for the event, but instead of spending time with them, I spent most of the visit in a withdrawn and somber state of mind in the spare bedroom, reading the books Blake had given me, or calling him or sending him poems in e-mails about vacationing in a little town I called Norman Rockwell hell. I was miserable without him. I wanted him there with me, enjoying my family and my events. After being swept off my feet by romance, I was beginning to see some of the shortcomings of a relationship like this. Depression overtook me.

Shortly after my return home the holidays began, and now I learned more about why an affair leaves one so lonely. I spent Thanksgiving with my family as Blake spent it with his. I understood this, of course. The children, the in-laws, his parents—none of them were ready to be affected by what we had created in darkness and family holidays were certainly not the right time to "out" our affair. Nonetheless, my own holidays were miserable, lonely and empty. We sent beautiful letters to each other each night we were forced to be apart, longing for one another and anticipating the time when all of this would be behind us, when we would be free to openly be in love. We were eager for the day when we would be able to comfortably express our love to others and walk arm in arm in public without second thought. Stuffing reality to the back of my mind didn't help me. No matter how much I tried to enjoy those days with those closest to me, inside I was dealing not only with pain but also with shame as I looked at those I loved and knew that I was hiding an ugly truth from them. Though a part of me was happy and very much in love, a larger part of me wouldn't shut up about how wrong the whole situation was.

Blake's wedding anniversary was also near the holidays. In effort to prove to me that the date was not significant to him, he spent the day with me, until it was time for him and Beth to go to dinner together. I was assured that she had made the reservations without his knowing. But what was he to do? To reassure me that nothing physical would transpire between them, he made love to me before he left and called me several times from the restaurant bathroom. He sent text messages from his phone he held under the table while they dined speaking of how much he missed me at that moment and expressing all of the love he held in his heart. After he got home that night, he went right to the computer and stayed there until well past three a.m., sending notes to assure me again that he had never climbed into their bed.

We just had to get through the holidays. Then we would talk about the next step.

As I write this, a key moment of total and utter self-disgust for the situation I had allowed into my life strikes me. One evening, my friend Sasha shared with me that one of her male friends had reacted in surprise that I, of all people, would allow myself to be involved in an affair. I realized then that others thought more highly of me than I had thought of myself. I resolved to end things before more people learned what I had been doing. In fact, I intended on ending things almost every day for the first six months of my involvement with Blake. I am not a hypocrite so I resigned right away as the fourth-grade Sunday school teacher at my church. After going to one of the ministers privately to speak about the circumstance I had involved myself in, I quit attending church altogether.

I had also placed the college courses I was taking on hold to fly to Europe. When a paperwork error caused my student loan to be called in, I stopped taking classes at all. I was not this person, I told myself. Why was I handling my life this way? Why, when I knew this affair was completely wrong, did I continue to stay in it, as if I were not in control of my own person? I began my collection of the Barnes & Noble self help section and read everything that I could about affairs. I wanted to understand myself. I wanted to understand Blake. I wanted to understand what we were doing. In a sick hope that together we might figure out the twisted psychology of our relationship, I even began to share with him my findings as to why he was involved with me. We would actually lie in my bed at night discussing various types of affairs, the dynamics of each type, and the effects an affair has on each party, that is, the affects for the husband and the wife. I was finding a serious lack of information for the woman in my position.

I suffered much difficulty in trying to let go and simply walk away due to the fact that we shared such immense joy. It was beyond chemistry, beyond addiction. There was a unique like-mindedness between us, a fascination with the same topics and intellectual stimuli. We laughed constantly and developed our own private language so that almost every word we spoke had double meaning that only the two of us understood. Our communication resembled, in fact, those high school crushes that had kept me on the phone from three in the afternoon until I was forced to hang up at midnight as my father screamed, "Get off the damn phone!"

Nothing was left unspoken between us. We shared the same passions for travel and adventure, the same hunger for constant new experience, the same fascination with the same things. Almost every day was filled with fun, excitement, exploration and entertainment. I had never experienced someone so into me. It was as if I were in his constant thoughts. I was the girl he had always dreamed of but had come to believe never truly existed. It was as if at my arrival he woke up from the dead. Even his jealousy flattered me because it appeared that he thought everyone else might discover his find and might steal me away because he was already married. So he responded in desperation, so much that I wondered if I had missed some secret power I possessed within myself, a power I believed he found in me. He seemed to be consumed by me, and thus he consumed my life. I had idealized him and thus I spent most of my time thinking of him and reminiscing on all that we shared. He became a top priority to me in every way. I wanted to make up for everyone who had left him feeling abandoned and hurt. I wanted to make him know that he was loved for exactly who he was.

As ridiculous as this may sound, I loved him most for the family man that he was, how naturally playful he was with children, how relaxed and understanding he was with the chaos of family drama, how warmly he accepted life's little imperfections. I remember being on the phone with him during his daughter's birthday party. His yard was filled with children. I could hear them screaming in the background as he bombed them with water balloons. Blake was a big kid. He hadn't forgotten how to be a child. He loved to do fun things with children and watch or make them laugh. As a single mother, I have found it highly difficult to meet a man with a love for family, a man who would comfortably and naturally blend into the sort of atmosphere I desired. His affection for children was one of his most enduring qualities. It was what made him most unique and irreplaceable. I felt that I could be myself with Blake, that I did not have to maintain perfection. At the same time, however, there were certain areas where I feared I might fall off the pedestal, and so I fought to keep up with what I believed his expectations of our love was and all of the ways he told me he was impressed with me.

There is a unique passion and perceived honesty that encumber an affair, an intimacy at a level unexplainable to those who have never experienced being in one. I became the one to whom he told all his secrets. He shared intimate and finite details of his marriage with me.

As he searched within his own confusion, he laid his vulnerabilities and emotions before me. I knew about every lie he had ever told Beth, perhaps his previous indiscretions, too. Feelings he had, feelings he doubted—they were all laid bare. Deep emotions that he refused to share with his wife for fear of upsetting her spilled from his lips, along with his compassion and fear for any hurt that I might be feeling while in "this mess." But his honesty only made me love him more. I become his counselor . . . with the added bonus of having a vagina. Believing that we were best friends, I took his need of me as deep intimacy. He needed me, and the feeling of being so deeply needed was powerfully addictive to me. He shared how he met his wife, how he came to marry her, how she changed. He was sad and hurt. He felt neglected, unappreciated and rejected. She was cold and didn't seem to need him enough. He was brow beaten, abused and (in my own opinion) constantly manipulated.

Beth was portrayed in a way that made it seem that she had no idea how lucky she was to have a man like this. Especially to someone like me who had been single for a good length of time and had dated my fair shares of duds. But I knew it! I knew how difficult it is to find a man willing to be as open, honest, and vulnerable as Blake, someone as giving and loving, someone who wanted to share all of his time with me. I longed to give him everything he deserved and shower him with enough affection for a lifetime.

He was my lucky find and so I enjoyed all of our time together. Any worries that existed united us as a team. We were Romeo and Juliet. The world was against us, and it was us against the world. It's like that with affairs—until the day they are discovered.

Chapter 5

Exposure and Inner Conflict

Despite what Blake told me about his wife, my guilt held me to the vision of Beth as a sweet, innocent and very boring mommy. Blake had a friend who he confided in about our affair early on. One afternoon the friend phoned me at my office to talk to me about the situation between me and Blake. I shared with Dave my feelings of guilt and the vision that I had of Beth. Even though Dave was telling me to cease and desist the affair, in response to my vision of Beth being sweet, he asked "You don't know Beth do you?"

In some ways, I perceived myself to be superior to her because I was out there in the business world, whereas she was a stay-at-home mother. But at the same time, she intimidated me as a homemaker. One of the things Blake loved most about her—and even bragged to me about—was her ability to cook. I serve three kinds of meals: microwavable, dine-in and take-out. I was afraid he would miss her domestic ability and that later my lack of skill would be disappointing.

I felt sorry for Beth and guilty, guilty, guilty because I believed that she had gotten too comfortable. She'd wrapped her life in her children and neglected her husband, carelessly taking him for granted, so much so that he fell out of love with her. I pictured her learning about us and being destroyed. I saw her in total despair. I myself have felt the hurt of being cheated on, and in no way did I wish to hand deliver that pain to another person. My compassion led to understanding this "stuck" place Blake and I were in and his not wanting to "devastate her."

At first I did not want to see her, did not want to know what she looked like. I assumed that I was more attractive or Blake would not be with me, so I had no desire to "size her up." Knowing I was sleeping with her husband, there would be no way that I could look this woman in the eye. I feared that if I saw her, my guilt would consume me. I would be sickened with myself and, being unable to turn back time, I would feel trapped in the body of a blackened soul I couldn't sever. The thought of hurting her constantly drove me away from Blake emotionally.

At times Blake, too, would be so guilt-ridden that when he said things like, "She is a good woman who puts up with a lot of shit" or "I feel bad, she is trying so hard to be cool, but I just can't do it, I can't be with her anymore," it caused the sweetness to thicken around my vision of her. This paradox created insecurity inside of me. Because he was soft and sensitive to his wife's emotions, I was left to question where I stood in things. But at other times he seemed vengeful, as if he wanted to hurt her. For example, after she found out about us, she wanted to believe that I was unattractive. Several times, she told Blake that she thought I was ugly. His ego would have no part of that conversation, however, no matter how it might help her to feel better. He always insisted that I was not ugly, which enraged her and led her to demand to see what I looked like. This led to his rifling through my photo album one evening until he stumbled across an old set of boudoir photos in which I had posed for a photographer to use to market her business at a bridal fair. He asked if he could have the photos. Flattered, I said yes. A few days later, he told me that Beth had "found" the photos and "spun out of orbit," tearing them up as she "went all crazy." I realized then what he had done to both of us.

Another example; Beth purchased a parking space that was auctioned off in a fundraiser at their children's private school. She was proud of the parking space because previous year's ownership of said space had belonged to some prestigious names in the community. The delightful front row of cement in the front of the children's school parking lot now displayed her name, and she would seethe if anyone used it for passenger drop-off or pick-up. Blake said he wanted to park in her precious space and have sex in the car. It would be his private "ha-ha" on her pompous attitude. I declined to participate in his revenge plot. Putting such energy and focus onto hurting her and wanting to use our love making as means to express hatred, hurt me.

I started to feel like Blake's feelings toward me were tainted because I was willing to be a part in victimizing Beth by being his lover. Blake always trusted Beth. His guilt made him blind to her manipulative tactics, and eventually he began to question my deepest honesty. He made slighting comments that let me know that in some ways he wondered if he shouldn't share Beth's vision of me as "the evil one." The signs were not always simple to read, of course. When someone is showering you with love, it is difficult to see where he can simultaneously think ill of you just for loving him back. The relationship became convoluted and the emotions went back and forth like ping pong balls. He loves her. He hates her. I was the best and the worst thing that ever happened to him. His attitude confused me. But then I began to persuade myself that it was obvious that *she* was an awful person who created hatred in him and that it was the goodness in *him* that caused him to feel guilty for breaking his marriage vows. He suggested that we do many hateful things to get back at her, but at the same time he also said he did not want to hurt her or "shove things in her face." Seeing his wife as the enemy I became hungry to hear and see ugliness in her. I needed to justify my actions, lest Blake and I become total shits. As he griped about her unpleasant characteristics, I clung to them and hated how she used their finances and children to hold him captive in a loveless marriage.

As time went on, I heard stories from Blake and even others about Beth screaming at him in public, tales of dinner parties where the guests were taken aback by the way she spoke to him. These events happened before we became involved, and they supported what I was being told of their relationship and her character. Hearing the stories, I opened my heart to trust and receive him. She sounded like someone to be greatly disliked and I began picturing her as a haggard bitch. I was blessed with the removal of a large part of my guilt after his wife discovered the affair and staged an angry confrontation. Seldom does the wife take the broken-hearted approach. She is usually insane with rage. Jackpot! Beth's hostility showed me why Blake would want out of a relationship with such a hateful person. It didn't matter to me if it made sense that Beth would lose her mind and spew hatred at me in words or flying objects. I didn't really want to consider how the shoe would feel on the other foot. Ugly confrontation is what was needed to firmly convince me that Beth was just an awful person. I was off the hook. I didn't have to understand her hurt any longer. Everything I looked for to justify our behavior was handed to me through her hostel actions. I held tightly to these "facts" of his wife being a bad person and reminded him of them when he had a moment of confusion about what direction our affair was moving. Her display of poor character offered me help in pleading our case of a better life together and showing him the light. I then simply wanted to help Blake end his marriage. I personally believed that Beth didn't really love Blake—she loved the ease of her lifestyle. She just didn't want things in her life to change. I believed deeply in my heart that I had something in this guy that I wouldn't find anywhere else. I didn't want to give that up for what someone else might feel. What about how I feel? I love the man! Why should I care about her? I don't want to be hurt myself! He wanted love. If it wasn't me he found love in, eventually he would find love in someone else. Why rob myself of my soul mate for someone who didn't love him enough anyway?

35

It was an anonymous letter that revealed our affair to Beth and prompted her to drive Blake to my doorstep. He was instructed to end the relationship just three weeks before Christmas.

He had been at my house for less than an hour when Beth called him several times frantically on his cell phone. When he eventually answered, she cleverly told him that her mother had been rushed to the hospital. He darted out of my house in a flash, but I intuitively knew something wasn't right. I phoned my sister, who picked me up and drove me by their house so my vehicle wouldn't be spotted. We passed Blake's car, parked on the side of the road about a block from their driveway. I could see that an intense conversation was taking place. Blake later described it to me as Beth luring him away while he was oblivious to the hammer that was about to be dropped on his lap. They began driving to the hospital he thought, and she tossed a letter at him, demanding, "Read this!" Seeing this was a serious matter, he pulled over and began reading the letter. His hands started to shake halfway through the letter, which described in detail the affair that was taking place behind her back. While his heart was racing, she beseeched him to tell her the truth and, under duress, he confessed.

After seeing them in conversation off the road side, I drove home. Shortly after I arrived back at my house, I heard a knock at my door. Seeing his lifeless expression, I knew in that instant what had happened. She knew.

He stepped inside and spoke in an almost still voice. He told me that someone had written an anonymous letter to Beth, informing her that I had been to Europe with Blake and that we had been having an affair for at least six months. We had become too public. Someone had informed his wife. "I already know where she lives," Beth had apparently told Blake, and she'd ordered him to drive to my house and break it off immediately. The fool bought it and had just led her right to my home.

I had tried to prepare myself for this day. Knowing the statistics, I tried to expect that if Beth were to ever find us out, I would most likely face the brutality of being cut when he was presented with losing what had been his "life" for so long. I tried to remind myself to not cling to his words and promises in case the worst happened. I didn't want to experience the shock of rejection. I'm a "pessimist with such negative thinking," Blake often told me when I expressed concern that we would be discovered and I would be tossed.

We walked into my bedroom and closed the door for privacy from my children, then Blake began speaking to me. I hardened anticipating the verbiage I had always expected would come should we ever be caught. I am a strong woman and have always preferred straight talk. I have always found it insulting when words are prepped to not crush the fragile as if I don't know what is really being said. When I told Blake to give it to me straight, he could not speak. Standing pensive, all he could do was grab a pen and write "Wait for me" on a piece of paper sitting on my night stand. Are you out of your freakin' mind? I thought. Then Beth honked from my driveway and he scrambled out the door like a child caught smoking. She had sat in their car and waited for him while he entered my home. At first I felt for her and agonized about what she must be going through but later I took that as a power play, and not a step to save her marriage. At least that's how I read into it as he told me how the event played out. In the end, all I saw in her action was a game that she was playing against me, a game I vowed to myself I would never play. I had decided that I would never try to manipulate Blake. Whatever was real and pure would be the final outcome.

He left, and I sat on my bed for what must have been an hour staring at the wall feeling numb. It was a day later that he called from a pay phone down the street (so the call could not be tracked from a cell bill) and asked me to pick him up. When I went to him, I saw tears streaming down his face as he began desperately trying to explain his predicament in not knowing what to do the night before. It was so sudden, he told me. He'd been thinking his mother-in-law was in danger, and then he was broadsided by his wife and the anonymous letter. He hadn't seen it coming. He couldn't think anything through. He panicked. That's not entirely unreasonable, I thought. "The clutch is pushed," he told me. He was going to leave her and move into my home while we searched for a new house, as he felt mine to be too small for his comfort. And this is when I discovered what must be lurking in the subconscious of a large percentage of other women: an overwhelming fear of commitment. It engulfed me. Had enough time passed for me to determine who this man really was? What if we do not work out? What if I have cost him his marriage, his children and his savings? It was all happening too much too fast. Do or die! Did I know enough about Blake to take things to this next level? And what about his wife? Now that she knew about us, things were sure to get ugly. It would have been different if he had asked for a divorce and then she had found him dating, none the wiser that it had begun before they split. That is the way I had always imagined things would go down.

I was certain that I was not prepared to move so quickly, but I was also overwhelmed by a sense of obligation around what I had participated in creating. How could I reject him at a time like this?

I said nothing at the time. I just listened to him speak frantic while he laid out the plan. I decided to allow things to play themselves out. Luckily, what he was saying was just the chaos coming out of his mind. He decided very quickly that Christmas was not the time to pack and move. This sounded reasonable to me. I have children, too, and I would not wish a Christmas to remember of that negative magnitude on anyone. Besides, the delay would give me time to breathe and sort my thoughts. It also gave me the luxury of not having to share my own panicked concerns with him. Were I to do that, it would only have made him more afraid. All I needed was a moment to digest the news and think things over.

So instead of shifting the gear while the clutch was pushed, we simply hit neutral and coasted downhill for the next eighteen months, sometimes breaking to allow life to pass us. I started to realize how much intensity was in our relationship. I saw that when a "normal" couple begins dating, there is the slow process of getting to know one another. There is no unnatural pressure on them, they are able to easily find out what they like and dislike without heavy consequences. In our affair, however, everything occurred at warp speed. Choices had heavier weights.

After Beth discovered our affair, I thought for certain that we would end at the risk of losing his family. I thought that getting caught would change how he felt about me and our relationship. I was prepared for him to tell me that it had all been a mistake. In a sense, I expected to feel relieved that what was troubling my conscience had come to an end, that the ordeal would be ended before it got further out of hand or to a point where there would be no looking back. In my mind, this was still a quiet and private matter.

Instead, he reaffirmed his feelings of love for me and I learned to trust that his love for me was real. Instead of Beth's discovery of our affair ending it, in many ways it ended up helping it grow. I was amazed that someone could love me this deeply. Within two days of Beth's receiving the anonymous letter, I received this letter from Blake:

> *I'm sitting here like an animal that has just taken a bullet, slumped over and wheezing. Feeling like I am going to die. I know I am human because I have emotions of a tidal wave right now. Feelings that I have never felt, and amplified feelings of newer feelings since I met you. You are such a wonderful person. I am fortunate to have met you. I don't want to lose you. I want to run away with you. I just need $100, a machete and a thong, and I'm in business. I need a partner. You are the archetype of the perfect woman. You are the most wonderful woman I have ever met. I have been most pleased with you as my lover, partner, travel buddy, and friend. We have been dealt a low blow by bad people, but I want you to know that I am certain that we can work through this unfortunate episode of our classic novel story. I know of no other love story more awesome than ours. You truly are the best. I miss you so much.*

Christmas was ruined that year as we adults forced smiles and painfully feigned joy for the sake of our children and our social obligations. I could not wait to tear the tree down and lock it in the basement as a forgotten piece of the past. Christmas has forever been scarred for me as every year that has passed brings memories of those feelings on each new Christmas morning.

For New Year's Eve, some friends of mine rented several rooms in a nearby ski resort town. The plan was for the adults to have their space and for all of our children to have another space where they could enjoy a supervised children's celebration while we hit the grown-up festivities. Blake's plan was to stay in his condo near the resort, but he surprised me by renting a chalet. He planned to leave his condo and spend the night with me. He surprised me again by arriving early at the party we were to meet at. When I spotted him I was talking to an acquaintance, I jumped up with glee and ran to him. I was so excited to just be together and ring in the New Year and our new life. I was immediately disappointed, however, when he accused me of being flirtatious with the acquaintance I was talking to. I had been speaking to the on again, off again boyfriend of a friend who had been inquiring about the friend. I disregarded this because I thought it was Blake's nervousness at stepping into the unknown, a passing moment of insecurity. I was able to convince him that no foul play was at hand, and we resumed our loving behavior toward one another.

That evening, a large group of Blake's and my friends entered the establishment. With them was a woman who was a close friend of Blake's wife. Of the party, one of the men, who was slightly inebriated, approached Blake and chastised him for being seen in public with me. The entire group of businessmen had determined that the affair itself was not a bad thing, but being on public display was. This blew me away. It was not the *sinfulness* of the affair that was being judged, but the fact that it was "flaunted." What's worse, several of the men in the group were known to be philanderers themselves. All of this "public" concern increased my belief that Blake's marriage was a mere social arrangement.

Blake told the man that he was in love with me and that it wasn't an "on the side" kind of thing. I believed that this was because Blake was different from the businessmen and their shallow lifestyle. But his defense inspired the inebriated ass to become irate and call me a whore. As Blake jumped to my defense, I also came to his defense when I told the rest of the group, "I love him." With that, Beth's friend who was with them, pushed me to the floor.

Blake and I left immediately, and when we arrived at our chalet I had a full-on anxiety attack that lasted all night. I had never experienced anything like it. I couldn't breathe, couldn't settle my nerves, felt like I was on the verge of throwing up any minute. I had an overwhelming feeling of impending doom, as if something had happened to my children or to a family member. Someone was hurt or in danger, and I couldn't get to them. I could not be still, could not stop shaking. I felt trapped and imprisoned, as if the walls were closing in around me.

The next morning, our group met for breakfast. When Blake finished eating, he said that he was going to go back to his condo to deal with the mess he knew was imminent. He promised to meet me back at the chalet in about an hour, where we were to stay an additional night with my children. I waited for him for a long time. When I didn't hear from him, I phoned him out of concern. I could hear that he was driving, and he told me that he was back in the city almost home. He said that when

Beth had heard about the previous night, she had lost her mind and had been screaming horrible things at him and their children. Chaos was exploding on the home front. He had to get home to calm things down and remove his children from exposure to their mother. I was shocked that he had not phoned me to inform me of what was going on. Why had he just left me there to wait for him? I tried to take advantage of the rest of my rental time with my children, but this incident, in my eyes, signaled what the New Year would entail, and it consumed me.

Blake had done a splendid job of winning me over. He had met all of my needs. Except for one thing: he was married. His marriage seemed to be a sliver in his finger that he wanted to remove, but he couldn't get it out. It was as if subconsciously he asked for help. Nurturing him came very naturally to me. I likened my help to bringing my tweezers to a child, *this will hurt for a second, but once it's out, things will be quite better and heal rapidly.*

I thought that because he loved me as much as he did, it was inevitable that we would share our lives. I believed that our deep relationship would drive him on its own to start the life we had planned and dreamed of. I never thought for one moment that we were not in forward movement. What seems to be the most difficult to convey as I write this is that our relationship was very real to me. Others don't understand how that is possible in an affair. Blake was everything that I had ever wanted in a partner. I was willing to surrender my life to him. As our relationship grew stronger, I began to realize that this man was the man that I was willing to endure all things with. As we were meeting one day, an involuntary thought flashed through my mind:—I could easily spend the rest of my life with this man for all of the right reasons. The most compelling reason was that he was my best friend and most intimate confidant. I had contemplated marriage before in my past, but I had never in my life been so sure until that very second. He was the meaning of comfort to me. I had never felt a greater or more intimate closeness to anyone before him because of the openness we had in communication.

Blake was consistent in his assertion that I was "the one" and that he was just having a difficult time with his guilt and figuring out how to do things right. He hurt for the hurt that he was causing Beth. I understood his guilt—I felt guilty, too. Certainly not on the same level, but I did feel it deeply. Blake had met Beth right out of high school.

She had expectations. She had stuck by him through some hard times, hoping that he would marry her, which he did five years later. She gave him three beautiful children for whom she wanted nothing but the best, which included having their father as an active participant in of their lives. She expected to live out the rest of her years with this man. But he had sideswiped her in every sacred place. I sideswiped her. It is difficult for me to witness someone in emotional pain. It is unbearable to me when I am the cause of it.

My former husband was an alcoholic. I stayed miserably married to him far longer than I should have because I knew that my leaving would devastate him. It is a hard thing to get around, and so I understood. Probably to my own downfall I understood emotional pain, and I did not want to make Beth miserable any longer. I wanted no part in additional pain, heartbreak or divorce. I did not want to hurt Blake's children or rob them of their right to a two-parent home. I had experienced being cheated on myself and wished it on no one. I was willing to get out of the way, especially if he had doubts, but he begged me not to leave him and fought vivaciously to keep me in his life which kept me in a constant state of emotional and mental turmoil.

Finally, I suggested to Blake that he take some time to himself to really think through what his heart was telling him. Go away someplace alone, I told him, away from guilt, sadness, etc., away from others who were pushing their opinions on him. I believed that if he were able to just be alone with his thoughts, the answer would be clear. I wanted him to realize that the grass was not necessarily greener on the other side, that every relationship takes work, and that I was not without faults of my own. I did not want the pressure of being thought his life saver. I wanted him to be sure that he was leaving because he was no longer happy in his marriage, that he believed in his heart that he could never be happy in his marriage, that he had no desire to put effort into making his marriage work. I told him he needed to be certain that he was out of his marriage not because he had created a grandiose vision of something better without problems or argument but because he was sure that he did not feel he owed it to his wife and children to work on the marriage. I wanted him to be sure that he wanted to leave, regardless as to if I would be there waiting in the wings or not.

Blake agreed that getting away would be good for him. He said he was going alone to his condo at the ski resort for a few days.

Blake spent several days in seclusion and we kept our contact minimal. I received a call from him one afternoon where he sounded desperate. He asked me to drive down and see him. He had things he needed to talk to me about, feelings that he had come to realize. He also had a serious topic to discuss. Fearful and hopeful at the same time, I drove to his condo.

When I arrived, Blake set in front of me a contract that Beth had prepared for him to sign. It seemed that Beth had also been spending time reading self-help books on affairs and had come across a book that suggested separating under agreed-upon terms and in writing. It seemed absurd to me that she would put any faith in his agreeing to a contract that ordered him to stay away from me, when their very marriage license which he also signed did not cause him restraint. One condition of Beth's contract was that Blake would refuse to see me. Another was that he would not live in their lake home (which she referred to as our "love nest") during their separation. I told Blake that I didn't have a problem with any of the terms to the contract, except for the condition barring his children from seeing him unless she was present. I felt that was blackmail. If he were to really have time to think and feel out the life of a divorced man, I thought, then he should experience it realistically, which included having full responsibility for his children while they were with him.

Blake was not pleased with my response to the contract. He was hoping that I would protest the whole thing. Then he said he refused to sign it, as he would not lie to her and lead her to believe that I was not still in the picture. With that, he threw the paper away, and said that he did not need anymore time away from me. What he needed was time away from her. We continued to discuss the contract for several days until Blake had the brilliant idea of requesting a contract from *me* specifying our expectations and needs from each other. He thought that our relationship was the one that was starting to slip because of all the mess surrounding us and that we needed to clarify and define things to each other. So I prepared a short contract that asked him to create a visitation agreement with Beth concerning his children. I did not stipulate a no-contact clause for either Beth or I, but I thought it would be better if he spent his evenings alone in thought so he could determine the direction he wanted for his future. At Blake's request, I agreed to place my faith and trust in the here and now, promised to be confident regarding our relationship (my insecurity of the situation bothered him) and agreed not to discuss our relationship with friends or family members who he felt influenced and affected my thinking and my emotional state. Though he said he agreed to my contract, he never did hand me a signed copy. I can only assume he did the same with Beth's. Still, the contract between Blake and Beth gave us more uninterrupted time together because he now lived full-time in another home that was a much easier commute for me than the lake house she had banned us from.

This may sound odd, but my instincts with Blake were very intense and accurate. While he was spending his time alone, one night I suddenly had the sensation that he was not in the state. I just knew that he was not nearby I could feel it. I sent him an e-mail saying, "Hope you're enjoying your trip," and a little while later, my phone started ringing repeatedly. I knew then that my instinct was correct. I was so devastated that he'd travel without telling me that I couldn't find it in me to answer the phone. He left me several voicemails "confessing" that Beth had booked him a trip to San Francisco to get away and think. She had then decided to go herself, he said, changing her motivation into a post-anniversary trip so she could make things right and work on their marriage. He said he didn't know what to do. He'd been afraid to tell me because he knew I would be upset. It wasn't his plan, he protested; she'd just shown up.

He was right, of course. I was upset. I refused to speak to him. I was of the opinion that he had made a choice, and I was determined to hold him to it. If he was not going to have the balls to stand by his choice of one or the other, then one of us was going to have to take control of our lives. I could not be the "other woman" forever. I could not continue to disgrace myself like this. I could not live with the guilt and the embarrassment. I could not hurt another person in this way anymore. I had allowed myself to accept less than I deserve, and now I was disgusted with myself for becoming an "on-the-side tramp." I had lost my self-respect. After telling me that he did not love her as he used to, he had left me to take a "repair-the-marriage" trip with his wife. He had told me that he wanted to spend his life with me, that he had made a commitment to me during the time he had been alone with his thoughts. I concluded that he was lying, that he had made a choice he wasn't telling me the truth about. I was devastated. And I was forced to accept the facts he had shown by his actions.

My refusal to take his calls only landed him right smack in my office lobby, begging for an opportunity to be heard. Fearing we were drawing attention, I took him to the building atrium and sat with him while he tried to explain away his trip to San Francisco. He told me he had not made up his mind to be with Beth. That was not what he wanted. He had been tricked. She was trying to come between us. She was putting forth great effort to make me go away and he argued that I was letting her win. He began to paint her as a deviant; my love now became a challenge to win him away from a woman who did not love him but just hated to lose anything, I thought it was all just her ego. Beth was the villain.

At that point, he took out a pen and wrote out a contract to me:

From this date forward, he wrote, *I promise to always speak the entire truth, no matter what the truth may be or how reluctant I am to tell it for whatever reason. Not only will I tell the entire truth, but if additional or supplemental information becomes known, the whole truth will from this time forward include this additional information."*

He promised that he would see an attorney, and he said he wanted me there with him so I would know he was being proactive in what he was telling me. He also promised that he would never take a vacation with Beth again and that he would separate from her within an allotted time. The minor delay was due to his masterminding the details of his plans to dissolve the marriage by finding ways to work around many financial complications, so that she could not ruin him financially or destroy his relationship with his children. Our big concern was Beth holding a power of attorney to all of his business dealings. He needed to remove that concern. He told me he believed that by dealing gently with her, he could forestall potential disaster. "Trust me, I know how to handle things in my marriage," he said. "This is going to work."

He wanted to "get away from all of this," he said. He wanted us to take another vacation together. The last month had been hell on both of us, and he wanted us to decompress and be happy together like we had been before. He bought tickets to Aruba and the Dominican Republic, with a one day stay over in Puerto Rico, with the idea that we would have a three-stop tradition following on from our trip to Europe. He wanted us to get our magic back, to save what was slipping from our fingers. "I need this," he said. "We need this. You'll see. Let's just go be us and have fun," he begged.

So I went, but this time my thoughts were far from being a non-saint as they had been when leaving to Rome, they were on my love for a man who clearly did *not* want me out of his life. This vacation together was about holding on to my last ounce of hope that I had truly found the love of my life, my hope that he truly had found his love. I couldn't remember why I had thought about giving that up! I just wanted to be alone where we could lose ourselves in each other again.

We went together to meet with an attorney, a woman reputed to be a tigress, a few days before leaving for this vacation. She prepared him for what was to come: a 60/40 asset division and joint custody. While counseling him, she told him how Beth would be responding to the divorce because he was leaving her for "that whore." We sat there listening to the attorney give us examples of what to expect from Beth as she use the "whore" innuendo to the point of an obvious emotional attachment to our situation. It was apparent to us that she too shared the belief that Beth had about me being a whore. We paid her $375 per hour fee to insult me; Blake gave her his income and asset documentation and then told her we would contact her upon our return. We were both unsure of her ability to represent him to her fullest capacity, as we suspected this case might be a personal issue with her that she had negatively prejudged.

Common sense flies out the door in situations like ours. The other woman hears frequent warnings, like "Once a cheater, always a cheater," "You'll be in her shoes as soon as a younger model appears," and "He'll just keep trading in the car." The other woman grapples with facts that contradict her lover's actions.

It's like preparing for a hurricane. We batten down the hatches and close ourselves off from the outside. We board up our windows and imprison ourselves, all the while believing we are protecting ourselves from what should be a temporary storm. Our hope is that we will emerge and restart our lives in an unchanged environment. As the storm nears and the warnings sound, we cling to our loved one, believing that all that matters is what is here in our shelter. Vulnerable and unable to control what's happening outside, we pour out our hearts to one another and try to say everything we want each other to remember. But we are unable to predict precisely where the storm will hit, and so we are left with nothing but hope. We close our eyes, and as the wind starts to beat against our sanctuary, we cannot ignore it. We are being attacked. Such is the war within the heart and soul of the other woman. As the weather forecasters predict the fate of the house on the shore, so do those who judge us predict what will inevitably happen to us. What they predict, of course, is disaster. But we numb ourselves to their warnings. We fight to prove them wrong. Victory is now our only choice.

Chapter 6

Reality and Fantasy
Struggle to Connect

Our first week in Aruba was shared with a friend of Blake's who flew in from Colorado. This turned out to be yet another phenomenal "sign" to me. My sister and I had rented a home for a few years and regularly received mail for a man with a unique name and a variety of interests. We had been receiving Rocco's mail for so long and so regularly that we joked about our missing friend who we had never met. Rocco was Blake's friend and our roommate on the island.

We became fast friends and the three of us had a blast together. We enjoyed dancing almost every night, attended elaborate carnivals, and took up windsurfing and kite surfing. We ate fabulous meals and made friends with several locals, which resulted in gatherings and barbeques on our patio and, of course, we also made time for the mandatory beach bumming. A few of the locals had come to know Blake from previous trips he had made to the island and they expressed their approval of me, saying that I was a joy and a pleasure to be around, whereas Beth was rude and bitchy. This, again, fed my developing image of Beth and ability to reject feelings of guilt. I had won his friends' approval. Everyone was saying that Beth was an intolerably selfish person. He and I were the couple that everyone recognized and supported, not he and Beth. Those who truly cared for Blake were glad to see that he was happy with me. They encouraged him to leave his miserable marriage and embrace the loving woman beside him. They supported us and helped to solidify everything about us that I had come to believe.

I became a certified diver while we were visiting Aruba and enjoyed exploring several aircraft and shipwrecks under the sea. Blake was right—being here together was what we needed. We were having fun. We always had fun. My life was always expanding and I was continuously being exposed to new interests. During our second week on Aruba, Rocco left and we were alone like newlyweds.

We ventured off to a remote beach location late one afternoon. We were all alone for miles around so, we decided to check "sex on the beach" off our list. When we returned to our car, however, we discovered it buried beneath a few feet of wind blown sand. Forced to hike out, we headed toward a distant lighthouse. It took a few hours to get there, and as we walked it became very dark and possibly dangerous, as we had no idea what we were stepping on. Arriving at the lighthouse, we found that it had been converted to an upscale restaurant. Covered in dirt and sweat, we were not welcome guests and were forced to wait outside for more than an hour until the car rental company came to dig us out. We named that area of the beach "sacred ground" because it was a place on the island Blake had never been to before. We spent another romantic afternoon at a butterfly zoo, and later we hiked the only mountain (really a large hill) on the island. Almost everywhere we went, we threw in adventuresome sex. One evening, for example, we tried driving down the highway while otherwise engaged. This was a part of our silly "us."

As I look back now, as happy as I felt on Aruba, I still could not embrace deep contentment. I was able to enjoy myself because I chose to overlook things. The delusion that all would be well stayed with me, but the tension of knowing I was with a married man was also present, and I was never able to fully let down my guard and relax. I never knew what tomorrow would bring because things always seemed to change once we were back home and he was faced with having to choose between me and Beth again.

Blake was a night-time Houdini. The man could creep out a bedroom with stealth. I, however, suffer from the serious childhood trauma created by a mommy who tricked me into believing that she would snuggle with me all night in order to get me to sleep. As a young girl, I would doze off in full trust, but then I'd feel my mom's arm move and wake up feeling betrayed and enraged. I am thus hypersensitive to the "arm move." Blake pulled the arm move maneuver several times while we were there. I pretended to sleep, but I kept one eye half open and focused on the door. Somehow he could still get out of the room without my seeing him. One evening, I sat on the top step listening to him rustle papers and use the fax machine in the room below us.

The next morning I noticed papers in the trash and pulled them out. I had found a letter he had faxed home. It contained the words *I miss you.* When I inquired about this, he recovered smoothly. The letter was written to the entire household, he said; what's so bad about telling his children that he missed them? I also found a purchase contract for another condo at the ski resort. Huh? We had just met with an attorney, and I thought the idea was to divide assets not accumulate them. "Business doesn't stop, baby love," he told me. He was buying the condo to flip at a large profit. Incidentally, they still own that property to this day.

Every time I was pulled out of my fairy tale illusions, I made the mistake of running my thoughts and feelings by him, which always gave him an opportunity to tell me what I wanted to hear. If I were to voice my feelings about actions I perceived from him to say that he had no intention of divorcing (adding to their financial portfolio and marital assets), he would argue that he had shown many actions to me that should reassure me that he did plan to divorce (properties he had sold to release assets and begin dividing funds between them). If I responded emotionally, he said I was "crazy"; if I was matter-of-fact, then he said I had "too much mind."

We spent two weeks in Aruba and then departed for the Dominican Republic. As we arrived there, we were joined by several of Blake's windsurfing friends. The trip to the Dominican had originally been planned as a "guys' trip," and so I was concerned about being the only woman in the group and worried that his buddies would see me as an intruder. When the guys headed out for their sporting events, Blake always stayed behind, wanting to spend time alone with me. It wasn't long before I started to feel that the guys were seeing me as the nagging girlfriend who kept him away from his guy time. Time after time, therefore, I encouraged him to go with them. He wouldn't leave me, however, and every time he declined to go, the tension inside me grew. I could see that the guys were growing irritated, and I felt that I was being blamed for his lack of participation. I could feel their thoughts of blame toward me, and this made me very uncomfortable and insecure. Eventually, I pushed him so hard to leave me on the sand and head off with the guys that he finally went.

After lying alone for far more hours than I had anticipated, I went out to search for him through the bars along the beach. I found him seated in one of them with a girl he had met on a previous visit to the island. He had told me about this girl, saying she was someone he "almost didn't go back home" after meeting. When I met her in person, I was surprised that this was the *she*. This girl did not rival me (or Beth) in looks, personality, or intelligence. Further, as she began to join us regularly, I learned that she was currently living with a boyfriend from Holland and had a heroin problem. This is the competition? My insecurity began to build and her presence in our group elicited a snotty attitude from me toward Blake.

I tried to interact with the guys as much as possible and assure them that I was not there to wreck their good time, (or prostitute quest) but just as they started to accept me, Blake began to display bizarre jealous behaviors himself, always accusing me of being up to something that inevitably meant cheating. Instead of noticing the unfairness in his expectations of me to be his partner exclusively while he could not offer the same, I poured myself into reassuring him that I was faithful and devoted to him. One evening, after far too many "Cuba librés," Blake began to accuse me of being too interested in one of his buddies. Then he started questioning my reasons for wanting to stay with "our friends." Completely frustrated, I left and headed back to the hotel, walking alone along a dark and dangerous beach.

As I walked, I heard rustling in the bushes. My heart started racing, but a minute later a stray dog walked around a bush and began to walk alongside me. Holding my sandals and purse, and unable to hear much beyond the crashing waves, I kept going. Suddenly someone grabbed me from behind. Startled, I dropped my things and turned around. It was Blake. The dog growled and barked at him, Blake instantly began to hate the animal. But like a guardian angel, the dog stayed by my side, watching him. The animal followed at my side, all of the way to the hotel courtyard. I went inside and grabbed him a Twinkie from the vending machine as a thank-you for being my protective knight. Blake became more irate at my affection for my new little friend, thus our argument escalated.

Not wanting to speak to him while he was in that mood, I went right up to our room, then went out on the balcony to call home and check on my children. I spoke to their father, who told me how my girls were doing. While I was assuring him that all was well and that I was enjoying myself, I suddenly heard a loud noise behind me. As I turned around, I saw foam pouring down the balcony sliding door. Blake had thrown his beer at it. I struggled to keep my voice calm and not cause any concern on the part of my family. When I hung up, Blake came out. We continued to argue but I turned cold and refused to speak to Blake after telling him he had too much to drink that night and I was not going to talk about things until both of us were completely sober. My unwillingness to address our issues only caused the fight to escalate until I went inside and started to pack my things, telling him I was going home. While we were yelling at each other, the room phone rang. I assumed it was the hotel operator phoning to ask about the noise, but as I reached for the phone, Blake shoved me away and ripped the phone out of my hands.

I did not understand the reaction until I learned that it was Beth calling. Blake had never given her telephone numbers and room information in the past, we had never been bothered before and so I never suspected she would be calling now. Not wanting to put up with Blake being an ass anymore, I determined then and there to go home. But when I opened my purse, I discovered that Blake had removed all the cash from my wallet and hidden my passport. This gave me my second panic attack. I was angry that my free will had been forcefully removed, that I was under his control, and I began to scream and cry.

Trapped in a foreign country with no passport or cash, I scurried to leave anyway, but Blake grabbed around my waste, sat on the bed and held me down. This only increased my panic and hyperventilation. Eventually, he promised to leave me alone for the rest of the evening if I promised to not go and talk in the morning. I tossed and turned that night on the couch getting minimal sleep. I didn't really want to go. I wanted us to be like we were in Aruba and I didn't like the tension that was building between us on the island. I fell asleep both sad and angry.

The next morning, I woke up to find him kneeling on the floor beside me, crying apologetic tears for losing his mind the previous night, saying all of the tension was a manifestation of his fear of losing me. He said he had never felt so much love for a woman before and didn't know how to trust me, he needed to know that I was always going to be there for him, that I wasn't going to bail if times got tough. So, again, I reassured him of my undying love and comforted him.

We decided we needed time alone to reconnect and resumed our adventures without the guys and set out to explore other parts of the island. Toward the final days we spent in the Dominican Republic, we had dinner once more with our group. I was determined to set things right with them and wanted them to like me as much as his friends in Aruba had. It felt important to me to have fun as a group so they would get the right opinion of me. After we finished eating, the group strolled off, separating along the beach, investigating the nightlife. As Blake and I walked, I discovered a bar which offered one-dollar piña coladas. I wanted to find the guys and share our fortunate find. Aren't piña coladas mandatory for tropical vacationing? I darted off, but ended up face-down in sand under a volleyball net. When I looked up, Blake was crouched above me. A crowd had gathered and all I could hear was a woman screaming, "That's a bad man, that's a bad man!"

Before I could move, Blake was hoisted away by men I assumed were the police. I realized he had knocked me down. It took a minute for my head to clear, and then the screaming woman came over to comfort me. I thanked her and began to walk aimlessly, unsure of where I should go or what I should do. I didn't understand what had just happened or why. I soon spotted the guys, however, and let them know the night had ended for us. I told them what had happened and they tried to lighten the drama by encouraging me to stay with them awhile so Blake and I could both cool off. I was standing near one of the bars when one of the men handed me a cocktail. But as I reached for it, Blake reappeared. Accusing me of kissing his friend, he shoved me. His friend, now pissed at being dragged into the drama, grabbed Blake and dragged him away from the bar. As they stood outside yelling at each other, the other guys asked me to leave and take our upheaval with me.

Blake and I did sit down together the next day to discuss our troubles. We decided that alcohol was a large factor. We needed to step away from the vacation night life. We were pouring alcohol on unresolved emotions and it was causing the emotions to be poorly expressed. Also significant was the guys' lack of understanding of the dynamics of our relationship. The stress of Blake's unresolved marriage was taking its toll on our relationship. It was destroying our beautiful love story and filling us both with insecurity. We agreed to disengage from the group and stay away from the party scene and anyone who sought to destroy our relationship.

That afternoon, we were thrilled to discover cannoning, and we rediscovered each other all over again as we swam through tunnels and slid down waterfalls. When we left the mountains, tears filled Blake's eyes. "I am such an ass," he told me. "You deserve for me to be the best that I can be to you. I'm going to try to be the best man you have ever had in your life. I just want to show you how fortunate I am to have you in my life and how much I really love you." He was filled with remorse for the craziness we had gone through on what had begun as a beautiful lovers' get away. Upon leaving the Dominican Republic, we decided it was full of "bad juju" and vowed never to return there again. Spending the next day alone together in Puerto Rico, we were very quiet and a little distant.

Chapter 7

One Dysfunctional Family

Shortly after our return home, Beth left for a two-week vacation. She left their youngest child with Blake, thinking (I suppose) that he would not be able to spend time with me while caring for the toddler. Instead, this opened the door for Blake to invite me into the world that I had not been able to share with him. He begged me to come to his home, to share the side of his life that I had been denied. I was apprehensive. Was I ready to see how he lived while apart from me? I liked my fantasy world, a world where Beth did not exist. In this world, I could ignore the fact that he shared his life with another woman. But it was important to him that I see his home. He wanted me to know all of him, to share his whole life. Wanting him to have what he wanted, and also wanting to be privy to trinkets from his childhood, I reluctantly agreed.

I had an eerie feeling when I went into Blake's house. Walking through it I was struck with many slaps of reality. Children's toys scattered the floor. There were left-over dinners in the fridge. Every wall I looked at had a family photo or piece of artwork done by the kids. There was a piano with the keyboard open, as if someone had just stepped away, and a blanket tossed on the couch that said the same thing. The bedrooms had freshly folded clothes on top of the dressers. In the home office, his and hers desks sat with the files she had been working on still open. Entering the master bedroom, an unmade bed on her side, and a book she was currently reading sat on a night stand with her glasses set beside it. There were artistic hangings of their wedding day on the bedroom walls and her towel hung and toiletries in the master bathroom.

I was extremely uncomfortable. I hated being in that home. It was *her* home, and *her* presence was everywhere. Everything in the house said, *"I'll be right back."* I could not be in that house without feeling that I was invading the most private parts of her space. I was suddenly afraid of karmic repercussions. I felt my real intrusion. Being there made the fact that we were having an affair very real to me. It didn't feel like him, or us, in that house. This was a life that was foreign to me. I was in the home of a stranger, sneaking about like a thief.

Every second I spent in that house left me thinking about how I would feel if I were her. How would I feel if I discovered that another woman had been in my home, let alone in my bed? It was an ugly, disgusting feeling. I felt tainted and dirty. Being in her house made me see Blake in a negative light. He couldn't even honor this space. How could he be capable of finding comfort with me in his wife's house? How could I live with myself for staying there?

I tried to understand why inviting me there was important to him and pushed my feelings down deep when he brushed over my upsets. I allowed him to show me their photo albums and memorabilia from his youth. I spent our time feigning enjoyment while internally on egg shells. We played with his son and even brought my children to the home to squash their questioning about why we never went to his home in the city. I helped care for his little boy, which allowed me to build a bit of a relationship and a quick love for the child. He would climb up next to me and cuddle with me, calling me his "nuther one Mommy" not understanding who the mommy imposter was. I rocked him to sleep when he woke up at night and brought him into "our" bed to sleep beside us when he was being restless. I myself was restless every night that I spent there. I felt like throwing up the whole time and hardly slept the entire two weeks.

One night during that week, we attended a potluck dinner together, for which I prepared a dish in Beth's kitchen, moving uncomfortably in search of pots and pans. In my nervousness about intruding and the insecurity over being compared to her superior domestic skills, I flopped the dish altogether, which increased my humiliation. Everything I had believed about myself was beginning to crumble. We also took our children—his son and my daughters—with us to a dinner party. His son's neediness gave me a feeling of what our family life together would be like and made me long for it to be "right" all the more.

At the end of our pretend family time, I helped Blake wash the sheets, clean the house, and erase any evidence of my being there. I departed with deep-rooted hurt and confusion. I wanted space to digest what I was feeling and couldn't get out of the driveway fast enough. Why was I continuing to just "go along" with things when I did not feel good about them? I felt certain that what I had seen in her home would backfire on me later in life if he and I ever married. I was hurt to see the easy "turn over," the casual "changing of the guard." I was confused by his apparent ease in bringing me into her home and his lack of guilt. Or was it that he cared for me so much more than her? Was she really this much of a non-issue? Was she really *this* bad of a person?

Before I drove away, Blake pled with me, "Don't ever let me forget how good I felt these last couple of weeks." He had gotten much more out of this time than I had. He got to see me in the circumstance of a "normal" life. I had witnessed the lack of compassion and honor he was capable of, and his total disregard for how I felt about participating in this time together. I was feeling the sickening evil of what we were doing.

While Beth was gone, I went to church to sooth my empty soul. While I was waiting for my children's Sunday school class to end, one of the assistant pastors approached me. I was staring out a window and my misery was probably transparent to him. He asked me if I was all right. I looked up at this tall, incredibly built man, who shone with strength and kindness, and suddenly confessed that I had been having an affair with a married man for over a year. He suggested a counseling session with a minister. I agreed.

When I met with the church counselor, it filled Blake with anxiety. He was afraid the minister would persuade me to end our relationship and give me the strength I needed to walk away. The minister I met with, however, was not the man to whom I had originally confessed. The minister I met with seemed to be a very angry man. I had just begun telling him my story when he interrupted and started with what appeared to be his own agenda. I wondered if what I was saying reminded him of anything in his own life. "He doesn't love you," the minister said in a snide voice. "He doesn't love her, either. The only person he loves is himself." This seemed to be a pretty bold judgment of someone he had never met. He refused to hear about Blake's struggles. As a result, instead of feeling any need to repent, I felt more protective of Blake. Blake loved me. I did not doubt that. He also had love for Beth. The one he didn't love at all was himself, I decided.

Irritated at the minister, I changed the subject and asked a Biblical question to test the value of his advice. "In the Bible," I began, "it says that the only way to heaven is by believing in Jesus Christ. Unless you are a Christian, you are damned to hell. Right? As children raised in the Christian religion, this is pounded into our thinking, and therefore we are closed out of fear to any other belief, just as other religions have similar fearful thinking pound into them. "What," I continued, "about the children being raised in other cultures? The ones who have had the Muslim religion shoved down their throats? The ones who are not allowed the choice of believing in Christ or something different, having the same fear of our religion as we do theirs or any other belief. If they refuse to believe in anything different from what they were told they must believe with similar fears of damnation being the cause of their refusal, will they go to hell?" To which my counselor replied, "That's what the Bible says."

I thought about the beautiful little brown haired children I had seen in Turkey and about our tour guide who I had shared several deep conversations with about his Muslim culture. I had developed a quick affection for our guide who was a warm and passionately spirited man. The children were as innocent, carefree and playful as Christian children; would an all loving God really send them to hell? I left the church that afternoon and I have never been back since. I drove to Blake's house where he had been waiting for me, holding his breath. I told him my counseling session was a waste of time and that the man had angered me. Blake sighed relief so hugely that I could see his muscles loosen as he dropped to the couch. We spent that afternoon comforting one another. I felt all the more love for Blake because he would have been hurt by the churchman if he knew what he had said about him and I felt sorry for him as if he had heard it. All I wanted was to shower him with affection.

When Beth returned, she promptly booked a girls' trip to Hawaii with a new friend with whom she had been commiserating. A few days before she left again, Blake had phoned me with the news that he had discovered a motor home for sale and bought it to fulfill an adventure idea I had shared. I had always thought it might be fun to drive across the United States in a motor home, exploring each state along the way. I wanted to fill in the stickers of every state in the U.S on one of those maps of America pasted to the back of some RVs.

After Beth left again, we decided to test the idea on a small scale. Loading up all five of our children, we drove to several remote towns and campsites. We stayed in an old remote mining town on the trip. It was a strange place, an era forgotten. The area lacked many modern conveniences and a large family of seventeen called "The Pilgrims" seemed to be talk of the community. Their lifestyle was much like the Amish. Using livestock to pull trees they lived almost completely off of the land. The family sent their children into various parts of town to play the fiddle. The fiddle was one of their only sources of income along with home baked goods they tried to sell to the occasional tourist.

During the day we took all of our children on a hike through old gold mines and the children scavenged rundown abandoned buildings collecting scraps of copper and antique tools left behind. Spotting an interesting shack with a pulley line, Blake's oldest daughter and I went off to investigate. Climbing a steep hill we became trapped at the peak while the rest of the kids and Blake teased us for not paying attention. After our hike, we found a dining hall and the seven of us ate lunch. Afterwards, we realized we were too tired to walk all of the way back to the motor home. The Pilgrims had parked a covered wagon, pulled by two horses, at the dining hall entrance and offered us a ride back to our campsite. Blake, myself and our five children laughed hysterically for almost the entire duration of our ride. The pilgrims handed to us, in the back of the wagon, a plate of odd looking fudge for our children. Not looking like your typical Nabisco treat, our city kids made poop jokes for most of the ride. And terms like "Oh, fiddle sticks" became regular comments during our adventure. At other spots we camped along the way, our kids ran off to build forts in the trees and collect odd items left behind by previous campers. The children all had bonded quickly and had a blast together. Blake's middle child fought to be let into the club of my younger and his oldest who kept sneaking off to their little retreats to tell secrets. My teen became the loving older sister and caretaker. At the end of our adventure, we collected photographs of everyone together, created a scrapbook, and titled it "Dysfunctional Family."

Because Blake was so present in our home and lives, I had told my children that Blake was in the middle of an ugly divorce and that his kids were too young to understand all that was going on. This was to forestall discussions of our relationship and to explain why Blake and I slept apart on that trip. My younger child fell head over heels for Blake, and my heart melted as I watched the way she looked at him. It broke when she said, "I wish he was my daddy." His participation in their lives to the extent he did was so natural as if he had always been there.

My domestic feelings did not, however, prevent me from thinking about the risks we were taking by involving our children in the lie we were living. Our children were vulnerable to potential hurt. I didn't know how we were going to eventually explain things to his kids. I figured it was something he was working out in his own thoughts. As for my girls, Blake promised that he loved me and my children and soon we would all be together in one home. They would never be any wiser. He assured us that his affections ran so deeply that if anything were to happen to me, he would always take care of them like a father. I believed him. I tried not to abuse myself with guilt for being such a horrible mother for exposing them to our relationship.

I didn't have a backup·plan for if the relationship didn't work out between us. For one thing, I had no idea what kind of future I would face. My reputation was beginning to be pounded to the ground. My friends had been pushed away for not "wanting my happiness." Whenever they saw me, the negative aspects of my affair were always the first topic of our conversation and their reason for rejecting any acceptance of it. The only person I had left in my life who wouldn't condemn me for my relationship with him, was him. The more friends we lost, the closer our friendship became. He was the only one who understood why I was willing to sacrifice so much. And I was the only one who understood his complications.

I remember once speaking to Blake on the phone, lamenting, "What the hell am I doing? There are three people here who are sure to experience torment and pain. In the end, one will be forced to leave. Here I am, knowing I will be that person and still doing this." I was trying to push my way through the powerful persuasion of fantasy. I knew the statistics. The odds of our relationship ending in marriage were slim to none. If we beat those odds and got married, the odds that we would have a successful marriage were even bleaker. Blake detested my lack of faith.

Like every woman I picture walking in my shoes, I believed in my heart of hearts that *we were different. This was my soul mate.* The world did not understand what he and I shared. My rational, logical mind experienced a sort of astral projection. It hovered over me, watching my foolishness. I was like a teenager acting out the Sleeping Beauty myth and singing "someday my prince will come." If I had a dream about him or if I were to pass him on the highway or coincidentally run into him at an unplanned location, *it was fate.* He assured me we were doing the right thing and these "signs" convinced me.

In many ways our relationship *was* different. The difference was in the particulars. Blake's lifestyle provided advantages most married men do not have. He had multiple homes and changed location regularly. His wife was very active in their children's school and bore the sole responsibility of getting them there, and often other children as well. Each home they owned was at least forty-five miles from their main dwelling, so to stay at one of the other houses meant packing bags for all of the children and waking up much earlier than usual to drive them to school. Beth refused the added effort and Blake refused to participate in helping her, which allowed Blake and I to live a very "regular" relationship where we could spend our nights together freely. Since I spent so many nights a week with him in his home, or he in mine, it was easy for me to believe that he was "separated with complications."

Eventually as we stuck by one another, others began to open to our relationship and accept us.

We often traveled together. Three weeks would pass with only e-mail communication to and from home to "check on the children and the business." We threw large parties, attended functions, and blended our five children with events and slumber parties. For all intents and purposes, we spent more time together than he spent with the woman who bore his last name. Our similar careers melded us into a potentially powerful team. The business he started, which also held his wife in title, we began to dabble in together.

I believed that Blake was my partner for life. He shared in my family events. My mother, who had originally opposed our affair, grew to love him and build a bond of her own with him. My brother-in-law made business connections through him, and even years after our break up invited Blake to my sister's birthday party instead of the man I was dating at the time. But like the other woman in any affair, I still spent almost every special occasion or holiday alone. Gifts that I purchased or tokens of affection were stored in "his drawer." The photo albums we created together were kept in my home. Because his wife now began to read his e-mails and study his cellular bill, we created a secret e-mail account and purchased a cell phone we called the "love line."

She knew I existed, and he had told her he was in love with me. Or so I was told. The secret "love line" was to not rub it in her face and cause her additional hurt. Though I knew his children and spent a considerable amount of time with them, I was unable to create the bond that I desired. If Blake had divorced Beth and married me and if I were the step-mother, then I might have been able to be with him without creating psychological damage to the children, but as his mistress, I was simply a friend the kids could play with. But it's the children who are often the rope in their parent's tug-o-war. Beth felt her life slipping out of her hands. She responded by also involving the children in ways that an adult who understands desperation and temporary insanity can find forgivable, but the children are still damaged. She told her children that I was trying to take their daddy away from them and the oldest became very guarded and aware. She was frightened of me.

Seeing my role in Beth's breakdown and what Blake and I had exposed our children to, I had to step back from his children for fear of doing more harm and creating long-lasting negative affects. I was living in an illusion—actually a delusion—that Blake and I were moving forward. Establishing a relationship with his children seemed natural to me. As insane as it may seem, not being able to have a relationship with his children, especially after getting a taste of one, was a terrible loss to me. I had grown to care for them deeply. As a mother myself, I could understand the fury that possessed Beth when she thought about "that woman" coming into the lives of her kids. I wanted them in my life. Though we naively and irresponsibly tried to share our children with one another, the sickness of what we were doing to them became undeniable, tragic and unforgivable.

One of the last times I saw his children, he had brought them out to the lake house. I had fallen asleep naked in his bed after lovemaking. In the early morning they opened the door and came into the room to wake their dad. I woke when I heard the bedroom door open and quickly tried to roll off the bed onto the floor. It was too late, his oldest daughter saw me. I woke Blake after she left the room and told him what had happened and in his sleepiness, I was never sure if he took it in. I kept repeating my concern to him but he seemed to dismiss it. I took it in, however, and knew we were at an important cross roads. To this day, I still worry over her psyche. I've run into his daughter a few times since, once in a restaurant bathroom and a couple of others at our children's mutual school. Each time, her eyes became filled with horror and darted down as she scurried away. She knows, she remembers, and she is scarred.

I was also unable to meet Blake's parents, who were a central part of his life. Blake idolized his father and quoted him so regularly that I longed to meet the great Max. I also ached to show his mother how much her son was loved. I believed that once she saw how happy her son was, she would come to accept me.

My own family was close, and when I discovered that Blake and his mother did not talk freely about their lives and feelings, I was confused. I did not understand how his mother could be neither aware nor interested in how poorly her son was treated at home, how sad he was living with such a cruel woman. To me, getting his parents to understand his predicament was simple: just tell them. I could not comprehend why it was so difficult to speak from the heart. I didn't understand how anyone could fear the judgment and rejection of their own parents so keenly that they told the parents only what they thought they wanted heard. I truly thought that Blake's mother would come to understand and want only happiness for her son. He shared with me the hurt and rejection he felt from his parents when they learned of our affair. He said he had never spoken about me to his father, who turned every visit into a business meeting. He said that his mother had disowned him over our involvement.

I couldn't accept this. I was sure it was only a misunderstanding on his part. I thought they would realize how he had been living before he met me. I understood that they would be angry and disappointed by his behavior, that they would be hurt for Beth and have concern for the children. I even understood that they would feel fear of losing Beth from their life. Blake's affair would make them uncomfortable and change the way that they all lived. I expected that, with their love of Beth, they would not want anything to change.

One summer when they visited Blake, he told me that he'd had a conversation with his mother. She talked about witnessing Beth's ugliness to Blake and his children. His mother agreed Beth was acting unkind, he said. He had briefly spoken to her about our affair. But I came to feel that Blake had missed an opportunity to take the conversation deeper so that his mother might have come to understand how unhappy he really was. If he only could have opened to her about how he felt for me, maybe she would have begun to accept things. Still, I began to hope that she would open her heart to us because she had seen a bit of how her son was treated first hand.

Chapter 8

Let the Games Begin ~ Bitch

Spring was upon us and Blake's parents arrived from their winter home to spend their summer nearby. Emotions were high. Blake's family ruled his financial life. He was a private investor who used his father's pool of funds and connections in every facet of business. During their stay, Blake's mother received an anonymous Easter card in the mail that commented on her son's "hop-hop-hopping around." Blake accused me of sending this card to his parents, which I found absurd. Up until that day, it never crossed my mind to tattle on a thirty-seven-year-old man. I never thought such a thing would affect him. It seemed juvenile and ludicrous. But he was coming to mistrust me, and now I realized the game playing I was up against. Beth was using manipulative tactics to make me seem either crazy or childish.

Because I hadn't sent the card, I emphatically denied his accusation. I also tried to convince him to use logical thinking. There was only one person who could know the catastrophic affect such a stupid card would have on him, and it wasn't me. But he still doubted me. I was beginning to feel that he was seeing me as Beth saw me. She was pounding the image of me as malicious into his mind.

For the first year of mine and Blake's relationship, I had no contact with Beth. I only heard second-hand what she thought about things and what she said about me and my children. Blake kept telling me that she was a constant angry bitch, that she was mean to him and the children all the time. When I explained why she behaved that way, he always assured me that it wasn't entirely due to our affair. He said she had been like that for years and nothing had changed. He said she brought up the topic of our affair in front of family and friends, even while the children were present, just to humiliate him, paint him as the asshole, and make herself the victim. But, he added, this only caused others to see her for who she really was.

I never could understand why she did not contact me, if for no other reason than to say, "Stay the fuck away from my husband." How was it that she never wanted to ask me questions? Why wouldn't she want to know the truth about what he told *her* versus what he was telling *me*? I could only assume that she did not want to know the truth. Knowing the truth meant she would have to act to preserve her self respect. But I also thought maybe, as long as she did not have to divorce him and leave her lifestyle, she did not care or want to know. Never once during that time did I see real evidence that she cared about him, only concern for loss of finances and social prestige.

There were times when I felt certain that he was telling Beth that he was not seeing me anymore, but we were still together everyday. It was obvious that I was still in the picture. She knew we had always stayed at the lake house. Why did she never show up to catch me there when she knew he was there but wouldn't answer the phone? Even well after she knew we had alternative methods of contact, she was still snooping on his e-mail and phone records, constantly looking for evidence of our relationship. I thought the woman was insane or down right wearing the crown of fools. Now I have to wonder, though, if he wasn't painting a picture of me as an ugly person out to get her. By not contacting me, maybe she thought that she was winning the battle against the "crazy woman." Otherwise, it didn't make sense for her to choose to search in places she was sure to be convinced we did not have contact, rather than taking action to search in places where she was sure to find real answers. It reminded me of the saying "A fool would rather be deceived than disturbed."

I think that about a year's worth of suffering might have been saved if she had called me. I would not have been able to bear hearing the voice of a broken woman when I was a major cause of her pain. I am certain that if she called me, crying, spilling her heart, begging to know why I would wreck her family and damage her children, I would have felt obligated to end the affair. If I wouldn't have ended it, I would have suffered tremendously every day that I continued. It would have killed me to hear her despair. I would not have forgiven myself for aiding in causing it. Wanting to get out of a relationship with him would probably have been reinforced had I been told all of the dishonesty that was inevitably told about our relationship or all of the lies he told me about theirs. When she did speak to me for the first time, she didn't seem to come from a broken place, however, but expressed concern only about her finances. This made me believe him all the more. It justified my fight for my true love. I saw her as pure selfish evil.

I guess I don't understand her behavior because I have never been someone's wife for fifteen years or more. Maybe what she really did was focus on her family, and I was the outsider who didn't matter in the larger scheme of things. What mattered to her was what took place in the confines of her home, and that was where the problems needed to be addressed. If preserving her family was in fact what motivated her, then there is a redeemable quality there. I might admire her ability to handle things. I would not have been able to handle things as she did. I would have not rested until I had gotten to the bottom of it all.

Before Beth and I had our initial confrontation, I envisioned her as this dear, sweet woman whose life was wrapped around the domestic needs of her family. I tormented myself with this vision so much that it was a relief to me the day she became "that bitch." I had phoned Blake an hour after a delightful breakfast together and was feeling mushy. I called him to share my happiness, only to be stunned when Beth answered the phone. She said some harsh words to him and I heard an incredible amount of chaos in the background. So I said to her, "Beth, why don't we just talk?" I was thinking that at this point, there should be no more secrets. I had told Blake that I would never lie to her, so if we ever spoke, he should be prepared for the truth to be laid out. I had assumed that eventually she would contact me. If I had been in her place, I would have contacted the other woman a long time ago.

But her immediate response to me was, "Bitch, you will never have my money." Forever changing my view of her reason for remaining in the marriage. It also gave me a way to justify our affair. As Beth felt challenged to win the war between us, she informed me, "I am powerful." Then she started screaming at me and threatening to ruin him financially, destroy his relationship with his parents, take his children away, or move next door to wherever we lived. She promised to make my life a living hell. Unable to calm her, all I could say was, "Take the money. I only want him." She mocked my comment and I surrendered to an inability to communicate, by hanging up.

The only time that I ever heard any affection from Beth about Blake was when I listened to Blake's voicemail. The first time he played them for me as he retrieved them in my living room. I saw a tear fall from his eye and asked him if everything was all right. He played the messages back and groaned for the sadness and hurt she was feeling. I heard a woman in pain, but what she was saying always confused me and I still thought she was playing games. One time she said, "Are you over there because I can't have sex right now?" Weren't they not having sex long before I came along? He was "over there" every day.

He had told her he had feelings for me and that our relationship was clearly not just sexual. So what did she mean? I often wondered just what it was she thought was going on. There were a lot of crazy voicemails that made me ask him what he was telling her, but he always said, "I don't know. Baby, the woman has lost her mind. She's trying to mess with you, I told her I would be here, and she knows that we are together right now. She's just trying to mess up our night."

Other times when I heard him checking his voicemail, she would be saying something like, "Blake, I just found a generator for the motor home and there's a coupon in the mail for thirty percent off." Her voice sounded like everything was fine at home, like our relationship did not exist and they were moving forward with their marriage. I couldn't figure it out. Hearing her made me furious. He and I were together so much, when did she have the time with him to be convinced that things were ok between them? How could she have come to that conclusion? How could she sound happy? The only explanation was that she *was* trying to mess with me.

Other times I spoke to her, I heard no emotion. It was almost as if I were a bee swarming her picnic table. No big deal. Something she tolerated that otherwise annoyed her. I told her things that he told me, such as their never having sex, and she just replied, "That's not true." But she never offered up anything to support what she believed was true. She never revealed that he was manipulating both of us. When he told me that she was only trying to get at me, it was easy to believe him. She never had an answer to my questions or said anything to expose him. His explanations made more sense.

I fought to maintain my sense of self even as I understood her hatred of me. In fact, I came to know intimate things about her and even developed an honest caring for her. Whenever I was thinking she was an ugly person, Blake shared a voicemail she had left him, knowing that we were together. I would listen to her cry and say things like, "Do you just want me to drive off a cliff and get out of your way?" I realized that she really was broken hearted, and almost every time I spoke to her, "I'm sorry," was all that I could say. But I could never offer reason for why I couldn't stop hurting her and thankfully, she never asked. All Blake had to do was walk away. But he refused to do so and said that he would rather be shot. His actions kept me in emotional turmoil and a constant state of confusion.

To me, Blake's emotional state showed his desire to be here with me. But he would not formalize an end to the past. He would not divorce Beth. Soon I began to question myself. Was I making too much of a deal about a piece of paper? I had him. We shared everything. Is any relationship perfect? Perhaps this divorce limbo was the one imperfection of my relationship.

As the battle between two women who were both determined to come out victorious with her prize (Blake) in tow, I realized that both of Blake's relationships added up to a "tripod." All three legs were important to keeping the relationships together. When I pressured Blake to act on his decision to divorce Beth, thoughts of the past flooded his mind, and all he could think of were events of his fifteen-year history with her. Suddenly, all of her faults were forgotten, and all that he could see or recall were the beautiful things within her that had made him love her from the beginning. He became overwhelmed with guilt. He tried to make amends for the hurt he was causing her by doing more to help her in their home, staying home more often, and planning alone time together. He bought her gifts and took her on trips. This is when he started lying to me, most often using his children as his excuse.

The dynamics of our relationship changed. On one occasion, I received a phone call from my friend Tony, who said that Beth had been visiting one of his coworkers showing off her new wedding ring with its rather large stones. Freaked out, I immediately called Blake to check on this. He had stopped wearing his wedding ring some time ago and we were working on the whole division of assets thing. There must be some mistake, I told myself. She must be playing more of her games. He became pissed off that I would even buy the story from Tony and hung up on me, then later sent me an e-mail;

> Beth's ring, was biggie sized long ago. I don't know who your caller is, and it doesn't matter. Diamonds don't mean shit. What does seem to mean something is her ability to weather this storm with relative ease. It's hard to chill when I have based my whole existence on something that the other person doubts from me. It's pretty unsettling and I feel pretty vulnerable right now. Thanks for the reassurance.

When I insisted that Tony had specifically said that the ring was new, he replied that he stopped buying her jewelry a long time ago because it didn't get him anywhere. She never appreciated the gifts that he bought her, he said, and gifts only increased her expectations for what she felt she deserved. He implied that either Beth had gone to my friend's office on purpose, trying to make sure the tale got back to me or (what he believed) that Tony just had the hots for me and was making up stories to disrupt our relationship. He had, in fact, told me to end that friendship before because my friend was vocal about his negative feelings concerning extra-marital affairs. Now he was putting his foot down. Thus my loyal friend Tony became a constant bone of contention between Blake and me. Blake said that my questioning him about the matter at all displayed my lack of trust and faith in our relationship. (Incidentally, I learned just a few months ago that Blake had in fact "biggie sized" the ring just days before Beth showed it to Tony's co-worker.)

Blake and I were together so often that I began to get calls from friends when they spotted him out on the town with Beth, as if he were cheating on me! As I began to see his dishonesty, my confusion and distrust grew. Enraged, I threatened to end the relationship. Every time I made that threat, however, he suddenly saw all the things he found dissatisfying in his marriage. Every time, he returned to me with tears and promises, profound realizations, and the desire to move forward with our future.

This created a vicious cycle, as Beth became more determined to put effort into the marriage and be less hostile. She cooked three grand meals a day, she was always cheerful when she spoke to him and she tried extra hard to look nice. She went shopping and purchased many new clothes, she got a breast lift, and she even developed a sudden fondness for the spa. In competition with her, I also tried to look my best, I made the sex we had three times a day more exciting, and I gave him hour-long, full-body massages almost every day. Poor guy! He had things pretty friggin' bad.

The three of us kept both the marriage and affair alive because Beth and I were always at war. Neither of us would throw in the towel because we both were afraid the other would not only win but gloat, besides.

One afternoon, when Blake and I had returned from a boat ride at the lake house, I was sitting in the boat at the dock while he went to his truck to retrieve his cell phone. I could see him engaged in what appeared to be a heated conversation. After waiting in the boat for more than thirty minutes, I went to the truck and climbed in, only to hear Blake assuring Beth that things were OK between them, that I was not at the house. Why, I asked him when he hung up, were we continuing this game if he was playing on both sides? Why not just let me go? He said that he didn't know what to do. She was "a devastated mess" and all that he could do was lie to make her feel better. I grabbed my purse and started to get out of the truck, but he stopped me with "Why do you always push the snowball back up the hill?"

This back-and-forthing continued for the rest of the month. We had some wonderful times together but soon I suffered devastating blows when I learned that on the evenings when I could not join him, Beth and the kids were up at the lake house that she had previously never inconvenienced herself to go to. "I miss my kids," he always said, accusing me of trying to keep him from them. I resented him using that excuse. I never encouraged him to neglect his children and often asked him why he didn't bring them up to the lake to spend quality time with them.

The thing that made me angry was when he broke his promise to never spend an "overnight" with Beth again. Time and again, he broke this promise. "It's her house, too," he always said. "What can I do? I can't keep her out of her house." I was infuriated by his inability to bring about a legal conclusion to the marriage and split the assets and custody so that she could not force herself between us. Then he started telling me that she was using the children as a way to control him. My bitterness grew. As I saw it, he lacked the balls to demand his right to see his kids without her being present. But I was stuck. I wanted him to enjoy his children and I wanted them to spend regular time with him. I was hurt and jealous that his failure to formalize his divorce left me out of the experience and allowed her to interfere with our life.

We discussed the matter in depth one afternoon while driving out to the lake. Blake told me that after he finished "this whole divorce thing," we would need to get away and be alone together for awhile so that he could deal with the loss and the changes. Getting away was the only way that he thought he could handle it. He wanted to take his motor home and go for a long trip. After boating that day, we returned to his truck to find it covered with sticky notes. Beth had apparently visited the truck while we out on the water. The notes were filled with demands. One of them, WE WILL CONFRONT HER TOGETHER, caught my immediate attention. I held it up to him. "If you ever—" I began, but he interrupted me. "No way," he said. "There is no way that I could. Stop it! It's NOT going to happen."

Beth and I fought our war over Blake until something happened that I thought would end our relationship forever. He and I had been discussing plans to attend Sasha's birthday party together in a few days. After dinner, he left me to visit his parents. I didn't hear from him for the rest of the evening, which was highly unusual, and soon began to worry that something was wrong. When I still didn't hear from him the next day, I became filled with anxiety. It occurred to me then that if anything ever happened to him, I would never know. I would never be notified, never be able to visit him in a hospital, and, God forbid, if he died, I would not be welcome at his funeral. I realized that the relationship that was the center of my existence would never be recognized or acknowledged in a time of grief or emergency.

I began to check every place that I could think of to find out how he was, even looking for signs of an accident along the highway. I drove forty five miles to his condo at the ski resort and then drove another one hundred miles from the condo to the lake. I was up all night, frantically calling his phone over and over, pulling over on the side of the road to vomit. My voicemails ranged from desperation to hostility—"If you are telling me to fuck off, then have the courtesy of calling me to do so. Don't leave me to worry that something has happened to you." I left in one voicemail that was a crying fit. I ended up on my mother's doorstep in the wee hours, fearing the worst and seeking comfort. Later that day, my cell phone fried and I went into hyperventilation. I raced to buy a new phone behaving hysterically toward the poor kid behind the counter at the electronics store. Just about anything that could happen to toast my nerves, did. It was an unforgettable day in hell.

Eventually, I received a call from Blake. He had just escaped from his family. His voice filled with anxiety, he told me how his family had just performed an intervention on him. Using "tough love," his parents and Beth had sequestered him in his childhood home and bombarded him with threats of ruin. Beth had taken his cell phone away from him and was clearing my voicemails in front of him while taunting him with evil laughter. "Ahhh, Blakey," she said, "she's worried about you," or "Poor thing. She's driving all over the state looking for you." She played my messages to his family then deleted them, he said. It's funny, I just now realized that when he told me that story, I always pictured him being tied to a chair.

His family told him that he had to make a choice that day and announce it to the family by a set deadline. Leaving Beth meant that he would be cut off from the family bank, which would ultimately destroy his livelihood. He would lose millions of dollars.

Summer solstice, when he and Beth had met years before, was approaching. Somehow, he secretly called me and assured me that he'd made his choice: he was going to spend his life with me and there was no better day to end his marriage than on the anniversary of the beginning of their relationship. Beth had shown a side of herself that he never knew existed, and it only gave further reinforcement for him to end the marriage. That same solstice evening was Sasha's birthday party at a popular restaurant. Blake and I had already RSVP'd to attend, and he had assured me that only death would keep him. In my anxiety to see him after so much emotional trauma, I spent the day buying gifts and cards to give him when he arrived. My heart was aching. I missed him to my core. I was counting the minutes till I could hold him again. Every second felt like an hour. At the restaurant, I sat with my nerves on edge, the only empty seat in the room next to me, awaiting his arrival.

A friend who was not a part of the celebration but seated in the bar next to the restaurant, came to our table and whispered in my ear that Blake and Beth had come in. Instantly recalling the day of the sticky notes, I knew what this meant. I got up and went to head them off in the restaurant entry. Horror crossed his face as he saw rage fill my eyes. My joining them in the entry left us exposed to both the restaurant and the bar. Before everyone, Beth said, "Blake, you have something to tell her." I challenged him to speak. Putting one arm around her shoulders, he said, "I'm sticking with Beth." He spoke robotic and used hesitant body language to attempt to convey that he didn't really mean what he was saying while trying to mouth something to me without sound.

My world spun as I searched for a way out of the room. I became dizzy and slipped, catching my self by the wall, aware that Beth was enjoying the brutality of this very public moment. I was able to stand up again, and as Blake flopped down on a chair, Beth and I began an exchange of heated words that lasted until my friends came to pull me away. They left together arm in arm and my friends spent the rest of the evening pouring drinks down my throat while dragging me to several night clubs until I was inebriated. I ran into a man who I had entertained dating years before I met Blake. He was a very handsome man whom Blake was always jealous of, and that night I went home with him like a drunken bar floozy.

I woke up sober and sickened with myself the next morning, crawling around his floor retrieving my cloths and trying not to wake him. Succeeding, I quietly crept out of the house. When I returned home, I found my e-mail inbox filled with excuses and statements from Blake that he was in pain and that the ordeal had only occurred because I had failed to "roll with things." They had come to the restaurant "to talk it out together," he claimed, but I forced the issue by greeting him with an angry look on my face. Blake said that he was not the one who chose to do the confrontation at Sasha's birthday party; Beth had made some phone calls and was somehow able to gather information about where I would be that night. And that was the moment that I hated her for succeeding in humiliating me publicly.

A few days later, I learned that Blake and Beth left on a long vacation in his motor home. This was what he had told me we would do when he left her. I began to receive postcards from him wherever they stopped. He later said they were his way to show me that I was constantly in his thoughts, but to me they were just his way to rub the situation into my face. Bitter and mind screwed, I phoned one of my closest friends, Janet, who is the most selfless and nonjudgmental woman in the world. When she heard how I sounded, she immediately booked a flight for me to her home in Florida. That's what saved me from a nervous breakdown.

I did not see Blake for two months. I was at Sasha's company's annual party, while I was mingling with business associates, I saw him out of the corner of my eye. He made a point to stand near a particular woman for most of the night and speak loudly to her on topics he and I had found a common interest in. This was too much for me! He was pursuing this girl and intentionally rubbing it in my face. He made sure he was in earshot of me while he spoke to her on the very same subjects that had drawn us together. He was using the same lines that he had used to lure me. I kept moving to another part of the room, and he kept following me. He would not let me be. I knew that he was attempting to break me down with jealousy, and I tried ever so hard to not allow the tactic to work. I couldn't understand why it would please him to hurt me like that. Wasn't I hurting enough?

After the woman left, he sat down beside me, the emotions I had kept bottled up exploded and I began to cry. "Do you want to just kick my ass?" he asked me. "Yes," I said, and we agreed to go outside so we could talk privately. He egged me on to "just let it out" and hit him, and I finally pushed at his chest. He pushed me back, thinking that by adding "humor" to the situation, my pain would lessen. But now we looked even more foolish than before. It looked like he was abusing me to our peers who could see us through the window. This made me think, again, that we "got it" but no one else did. I still felt that he was the only one who understood me and I, him. But I was much too wounded to speak to him very often.

Eventually, I began to date for the sake of my pride, and in my attempt to move on, a new friend and I decided to spend the weekend at an out-of-town carnival event. As luck would have it, the hotel we chose was hosting a weekend seminar that Blake was attending. I saw him walk through a door. He stopped in his tracks, then went on, pretending not to have seen me. My heart stopped. I regained my composure and tried to pretend I was having a good time with my new companion for the rest of the evening, but as I lay in bed that night, my heart broke again and I began to wonder if Blake too was feeling the same things I was. The next morning my friend and I went for a walk to find a coffee shop. From the corner of my eye I saw a familiar little boy bouncing and running down a hill toward his mother. I glanced at his mother who stopped in her tracks, looking fear stricken. It was Beth, and she seemed to recognize me, too.

Blake denied having seen me there, but soon the e-mails and letters began to flow again.

Chapter 9

The Sun Sets,
Even on New Horizons

Two months after seeing him at the conference, I finally agreed to meet with Blake. He bared his soul to me and made what seemed to be new promises, new horizons. It was easy for him to persuade me to reconsider our relationship because one thing that still held me to Blake was his open display of emotions and desperation at the thought of losing me. The man was relentless and willing to drop all pride. Pride ruins love for many, but Blake would never allow it to come between us. If I refused to speak to him, he showed up or called seventy-two times until I picked up the phone. He refused to let me go. He fought tooth and nail to keep me. No one had ever shown me love like that before, I conned myself, forgiving him the brutal way he had let me go already.

Blake poured out his feelings again. He said he had been fear stricken and confused when faced with the years he had spent with Beth. He was petrified that his choice to leave her would some day cause him to suffer penance for making the mistake that his family and friends had cautioned him so deeply against. If he and I were not together, if I were to ever leave him later in life, he would be left to regret his decision to leave Beth. He would be disinherited and left with nothing, alone. Thus he had turned back to his marriage and given one hundred percent effort to make it work. He had bought her gifts, spent more time with her and the kids, cleaned the house, cooked dinner, sought couples counseling. He had done everything possible to be present in his marriage.

And after all that, he had discovered during our summer apart, it was really finished and he did not want to live another moment married to Beth he said. Without a doubt, the marriage was in fact over, he said, and any question or hesitation he would have previously had was now removed. He could walk away with a clear conscience. He had given his all and in doing so he had confirmed all of his reasons for wanting out. All he had gained were the grief and loss of me from his life. Once Beth had him back, he said, it was as if nothing had ever changed. Things went back immediately to how they had been, the same chronic problems and her unwillingness to work on them. He told me that our separation had only "pushed the tether further." He was willing to contact the attorney again and get the divorce in motion if only I would give him the one chance he knew he did not deserve. We agreed to seek couples counseling together so that I could release the hurt he had created in a healthy way and we could move forward without our relationship suffering permanent damage because of his mistakes.

We began seeing a therapist about our issues. I also wanted to deal with the mental stress of his divorce, which was certain to take time due to the amount of assets that had to be divided. We jokingly referred to this as "extra-marital counseling," though, in all honesty, I could find nothing credible in the words of the therapist simply because she agreed to see us at all under the circumstance as a couple. I explained to her that while I was deeply in love with the man, I could not handle the stagnant place we were in. I wanted to move forward with our lives, to stop all this negativity. I wanted us to be free! I wanted us to be able to sleep next to each other in our own house, not a home that belonged to Blake and his wife, without worrying that I would wake up to a pickaxe one morning. I wanted us to do family things together without all of the risk. I wanted it to be OK for us to be together like "normal" divorced couples who blend their children. I wanted to participate in the lives of his children. I wanted to feel comfortable with him participating in the lives of mine without worry of what I was leading them into. I wanted us to travel together in comfort both with and without our kids. And though we were attending functions and parties together, I wanted to do so without feeling that eyes were stabbing me in the back. I was tired of being viewed as a big dramatic mess or asshole by my associates. I wanted to be "allowed" to attend his gatherings with friends and family. I wanted to LIVE.

The counselor asked him direct questions, but he danced around answers until she named him "the spin doctor" and scolded him on the jokes he made about issues that were not funny. I became immediately protective of him when she was harsh and couldn't stand to see the look in his eyes when they were sad. The "jokes" were how we handled things, we knew how each other really felt about each issue. Jokes spoke real emotion, that was our "us." She wasn't "getting it." She set separate appointments for us, and I soon began to notice that what she was really starting to help me with was finding acceptance in how to live with the situation as it was. In other words, she was telling me how to continue being the other woman. She shared with me that she had talked to him about how to "cut the puppet strings," but she did not see him doing that. She based her belief on his finances. How stupid and shallow, I thought. She misjudged. She also (unprofessionally) told me that while they were in session, Beth had called Blake's phone and our therapist heard their conversation as he hid the fact of where he was. She said that Beth sounded worried about him and kept asking him if he was OK. Based on the brief conversation our therapist overheard between Blake and Beth, she told me he wasn't going to leave her. I left that session seething but didn't tell Blake the therapist was repeating things to me she shouldn't. It took every piece of strength I had not to tell him, so that I wouldn't screw myself out of any future information from her. I was convinced that if I shut up about things, she would probably divulge more.

Blake also used the couples counseling time to spring on me the news that while he and I had been separated, he and Beth had purchased tickets to Aruba for Christmas, choosing the same home to rent that we had used on our trip together—a place that was supposed to be special and sentimental to us. Not only had this stabbed my heart but it also robbed me of a precious memory. He said he only rented it again because he had gotten a good deal. It was to be their last vacation together, and he begged the counselor to help me deal with this emotionally while he was gone. He offered to do everything possible to help me endure the holiday. He even offered to fly me and my children to the island and put us up in another house. The very thought disgusted me. He was suggesting that I stay hidden off in (what I called) the "slut hut" that he could escape to at will. My children would certainly be confused and I was beside myself. The counselor seemed to side with Blake or was wishy washy at best. She seemed to think the vacation idea was reasonable. This left my self-esteem on the floor. I was being made to feel that I was the one being difficult and uncooperative. Agreeing with the idea was a flaky therapist.

As his version of the "twelve days of Christmas," Blake had a gift delivered to me for each the first ten days that he was gone. He had given the packages to my secretary with instructions to place one envelope in my inbox per day. The little envelopes contained three movie tickets for me to treat my children to a feature, a gift certificate to Denny's for a $20 breakfast, a free movie rental at Blockbuster, a bag of microwavable popcorn, a bag of M&M's, a $30 gift card for Home Depot for more remodeling supplies, $30 gift card at the local grocer for dinner items, a punch card at a nearby coffee house, and left over Halloween coupons from McDonald's. Each gift had a silly handwritten note inside that brought a smile to my face. I waited for a grand finale gift on Christmas but nothing else came.

During the first few weeks of his month long trip, he e-mailed every couple of hours. The boat has left the harbor, he was miserable, the vacation is hell, he couldn't stand to be near her because "all she does is bitch and complain." All he could do was think of me. He took his son out on the beach where he and I had been stranded on our earlier trip to the island and photographed his son holding a sign that said *Sacred Ground*. He emailed me the photo as a sentimental way of showing he had spent the day with this son thinking about me. These gifts and expressions were his way of "dialing me in" as I sat through another lonely holiday. I expressed my feelings one evening in an e-mail to him:

> *I feel very distant from you. It's almost like you are becoming a stranger in my life. You have been gone for a month, Blake. You have to admit that one gets used to not having the other in their life. We barely had our rapprochement before you left with your wife and family. Your emails and phone calls have slowed down, and my feelings are that you and Beth are working on repairing your marriage, and all that I am going to deal with on your return is more excuses of why you cannot leave.*
>
> *I don't have any reason to hang out for that. I am not attempting to accomplish anything but tell you how I feel. I don't understand why you cannot understand how I am supposed to believe that it is me you want to be with. If you were in my shoes, would you believe it? Everyone who knows about us thinks I am an idiot. I think that I am an idiot.*
>
> *I miss you and I love you, but I dread some things about your coming home. I am afraid of a big disappointment, that things will be worse between us than before you left. I am no longer in the mood to think of anyone but myself. I feel I have sacrificed myself for everyone else's sake long enough. I want what is best for me and my children. I want what I deserve in my life. I am no longer willing to take the back seat. I hope that you understand that.*
>
> *I hope that you enjoy your last day there and have a smooth departure. I'll leave the front door unlocked. I can't wait to see you. Maybe when I do, you won't feel like a stranger anymore.*

The e-mail I received back from him devastated me.

WOW. This was a pretty shocking letter. You constantly surprise me with how you are thinking. It's kind of scary!! I did a stellar job the whole time we were apart. I have phone bills to prove it. Not to mention the Internet. If you didn't like my communication while I was gone, then there just must be more to it than you are leading onto. You should tell your chitty-chatty sewing-group friends how well you were dialed in. I'm sure they won't think you're a friggin' idiot then.

Your mindset is so defensive with such a lack of faith and confidence. I understand that you have concerns, but what do you give a shit about what others think? I'm listening to myself. I don't care what others think anymore. Who is everyone that you have made sacrifices for?

Did you ever think for a minute that we are in this together because I want what's best for me and my children and I don't want to take a back seat anymore? I'm hoping that you are just freaking out because I have not been around. I have been uncomfortable, too, dear. You don't seem to care about me at all in this letter. You even question why I can't understand why you can't understand why you would think that I would want to be with you.

After reading this, I can tell you that there has not been any reuniting with Beth, so stop that immediately. I can tell you that I will not be coming back home a single man. I can tell you that this disturbingly scary email you sent definitely delayed my unmarried status by at least a day, so stop being selfish, stop being unsmart, and maybe if we are lucky we will get what WE deserve. You are self destructive. You just need to chill, even just for a little while. Relax. I love you and miss you. We have work to do, its crunch time indeed and I am ready to pleasure you, so don't shoot yourself in a moment of glory.

Chapter 10

The Separation

To Blake, someone else was always responsible for my emotions. People's opinions were always working their way about, creating chaos in my head. They were never truly my own feelings or thoughts and, therefore, they were minimized. I planned to end the relationship as a result of that email but when they returned from Aruba, he finally left Beth.

Initially, I was overwhelmed. He'd finally done it! It was what we had always wanted. We were able to spend every evening together without feeling sneaky. We were able to have fun together freely. We were very active. We went on snowmobile excursions and other regular outings. We flew to San Diego with his son and took him to Sea World, the zoo, and other tourist destinations. We drove to Mexico and ate dinner beside the sea. The three of us had a wonderful time.

We also visited his attorney again to get the divorce under way, but as time neared to serve Beth, Blake became detached from everyone and most certainly from me. He started to take off without telling anyone, flying to California to spend time with his mother or to other destinations with other friends. He would leave the house and tell me that he was meeting a friend for lunch or say he had business to attend to. Later, I would be on the phone with him as he would arrange to meet me in an hour and hear a boarding call in the background. I could not count on him for anything, could not trust a single promise that he made. From one day to the next, I never knew what I was getting from him. One moment, we would be laughing, cuddling, loving each other, discussing our interests, planning our future, and the next moment he would ruin it with his bizarre behavior. He became moody, withdrawn, closed, irritable, and hypercritical. He stopped telling me what was going on in his thoughts. I tried my best to back off and not pressure him for answers or commitments. I understood that it was impossible for him not to experience a grieving process and figured he was dealing with internal guilt. I needed to allow him this time to heal from all that had happened during the last two years and the pain of ending his marriage. But each time things began to look up, he changed again, leaving me feeling shut out and lied to about what he was feeling. I was soon depressed and exhausted.

Almost three months went by with his behavior being unpredictable. One day I noticed that he was exceptionally withdrawn and asked about it. He assured me that nothing was wrong. He was just dealing with business stress. He added that he was heading back into town that afternoon to pick up his kids and bring them back out to the lake and suggested that I go retrieve my own children from my mother so that we could all play on the water. I felt a true peace inside of me. Things were going to work, we were meant to be together, so it was all going to be all right. Then he drove off and I waited for him to come back with his children. Soon I felt that same sensation that he was no longer in the state. "He's gone again," I cried on the phone to my girlfriend, "I can feel it." She didn't believe me; she thought I was letting my thoughts get carried away. I began calling him. I received an automated message, "All circuits are busy," which confirmed my suspicion that he had left.

I reached him the next day—in Maui. He said it was about the kids. He was missing them and didn't feel like their spring break should be affected. He didn't know how to tell me that he was flying away with his family. Even though I had asked him weeks before if there were any discussions between them regarding their annual trip to Hawaii. There had been, he told me, and promised that no, he would not be going.

He assured me that he and Beth had separate hotel rooms and that they had been up the night before doing the paperwork for a quick and easy dissolution of their marriage. They were dividing assets in a friendly manner instead of an ugly divorce. This would make things happen more quickly. Dissolution was what we wanted he said. It was all a strategic move.

But this time, his excuses weren't enough for me. I phoned Beth for the truth. She gave it to me. "That's not true," she said to me when I told her he claimed they were sleeping in separate hotel rooms and not having sex. She didn't answer me about the dissolution.

Blake was able to turn my upset emotions around by blaming me for reigniting the war. I stalled Beth's willingness to sign the divorce papers and as a result of my phone call, he said, Beth had come on to him that evening as a last-ditch effort to save the marriage. She had lied to me and told me they were sharing a room because she wanted me to feel the same pain she was feeling. I was, he told me, causing more harm than good by being upset at his vanishing act. He blamed me for seeking the truth and slowing the process of the divorce.

I had been pretty friggin' stupid for a pretty long time, but even a total jackass has more sense than to buy what he was saying now. As I considered all the bullshit I had tolerated, my self-worth plummeted again. I became physically ill. I lost fifteen pounds in less than two weeks. I was so depressed I was almost catatonic. If anyone had told me a story like the one I am telling now, I would have called her an imbecile.

As the events rolled on and on and I continued to excuse Blake and give him chance after chance, I was creating my own living hell. Meanwhile, he lived by the adage, "it's easier to ask for forgiveness than permission," and I tolerated it by believing that I understood things out of love for him. Now I had two humiliating choices. I could go back to the society I had cast myself out of, where I was sure to be completely alone and hated. Or I could give it one more shot and hope he really meant what he was saying this time. Maybe, if he was telling the truth, I would be able to say, "I told you so," to those who saw my fate from the beginning.

Our relationship began to center on my having something to prove to all the people who laughed at my stupidity for believing in a positive outcome. We had been so close to things turning in our direction before he left. I knew in my heart that once he took the chance away from fear and left his marriage, we would be happy. Could I trust that his current flight was only a minor setback? I wanted to believe it. I wanted to sell my home, pack my things, and start a new life under a new name somewhere else, even more so.

I needed relief from my depression. I poured my time into researching retreat spas to escape to. I was desperate trying to get my mind back, to find balance again. I longed to put space and time between us so I could explore inside myself and find out what was real. I could not understand why there was still this battle when Blake told me he knew that I was everything he had always wanted. He kept assuring me of that. For two years, I had been listening to him say he knew for certain that his marriage was dead and that he had found all he was searching for in me. I believed that he really loved me. Why was this still going on? He was still condemning my insecurities and searching through my faults to find excuses for his behavior, but his behavior was creating my insecurities. I couldn't get him to realize that. Every time he filled me with hope, he abruptly abandoned me. If it was his marriage he wanted, then why did he hold on to me? Why did he keep me in the fight? Beth and I were both in hell. Did he care so little for either of us that he could not put us out of our misery by sticking to a choice? I longed to know what it was like to live in a relationship where there were comfort and trust present. I wanted to know what it was like to live my life without having to be on guard, without having to watch for every sign and listen extra close to every word. I wanted to not have to rethink or second guess every word spoken from someone I loved.

I remember a daydream I had while boating one afternoon almost two years into our affair. As I was looking at the homes lining the shore, we came upon a ratty cabin. I suddenly saw myself standing on the dock of that dilapidated shack, on the arm of a man who loved me without question and surrounded by friends who were happy for us. No controversy, just freedom to be ourselves. In that moment, I knew I would rather be visiting the dump with a man who wanted me as his one and only than shacking up in Blake's castle, posing as princess, with a man who was never sure what he wanted. Thoughts like this continued to develop in my mind as I listened to apology after apology and excuse after excuse. I realized that it must be the same for Beth. He was doing the same thing to her.

I would never be sure who he really wanted or what he really felt. I was begging for the truth from a liar. I had poured myself out to this man, but I wasn't getting anything back from him anymore. I wondered if he could even handle a normal life. So often, I had ignored the needs of others because they came at the same time of Blake's urgency.

Knowing that one of his biggest complaints was that Beth gave her free time to their children's school and gave him insufficient attention, I had been afraid that if I did not put him first at all times I, too, would disappoint him. How would I live a normal life with this man? Living with him, I wouldn't be able to commit myself to community, friends or family. I always knew he would be dissatisfied if I didn't give him all my attention, but at the same time I could never count on him giving me his complete. What had begun as two people enveloping one another, had turned into a one-sided relationship. He became a sponge that sucked me dry emotionally.

From the beginning, I told Blake that I would never tolerate an affair like the one that had developed for my friend Sasha. Sasha's lover Wes, dropped a bomb on her a year into their affair, saying that he would never leave his wife. When Sasha began to complain about the neglect she was feeling and her loneliness, Wes bought her a cat.

I still remember sitting in her living room silent and dumbfounded as we stared at the little grey, out of control fur ball that was climbing and scratching Sasha's new designer couch. "Well, what the hell should we name her?" she finally said in surrender. I looked up at her equally bewildered and said flatly "Jezebel" and that was that, it stuck. From that day forward the Biblically named whore evoked the feeling of an evil presence every time she crept into the room. One night, Sasha and I were baking cookies in her kitchen. Right in the middle of a humorous story and while in hysterical laughter, Jezebel suddenly jumped up on the counter. We stopped cold and just stared at her wide eyed and on guard as she prowled about. The cat seemed to smirk at our notice of her bringing a demonic presence into the room as if to say "That's right girl's, you're destined to become The Cat Lady." Sasha and I looked at each other trying to pretend that neither of us felt the hair stand up on our arms and cookie baking became a very serious and fixated task. It was down right freaky the way that cat could sober us.

Sasha's lover had been divorced before and refused to fail at marriage again. He had a child he refused to share in joint custody, and as a successful businessman, he would not give up half of his assets, which had taken him a great portion of his life to accumulate. Thus I showed my cards by telling Blake about all of these things with Wes and Sasha. Blake knew that he could always promise a "future" for us until I was at the bottom of the rabbit hole, searching for the magic door, and so lost that nothing was as it seemed. Only then, did he begin to make comments like, "I don't know if I can do it." The division of assets would ruin him, he started saying, in ways that I would not understand. Now the pile of excuses grew into mountains. Every time the "clutch was pushed," it was my fault that he could not shift gears properly. More and more, he was finding fault with my words or actions or my failure to "roll" with things as he implemented "the plan." Time and again, I had to prove myself worthy of all the trouble he would endure if he divorced her for me.

Vacations seemed to always save our relationship, so after each dramatic or traumatic occurrence, Blake would plan a trip away for us. The scales made a substantial tip, however, when he booked a trip for us to Las Vegas and I declined to go. I had spent far too much time away from home, away from my children and (worse) away from my business. My finances were beginning to suffer greatly from my inability to consistently be available for clients and to market my business. My friends began to say, "He expects you to jaunt off at the drop of a dime, but he's not supporting you and your children." Or, "Beth can do whatever she wants because she has him to pay for everything. You don't have that luxury." And, "If things don't work out for the two of you, they will be financially OK, but you will be ruined. You have to take better care of yourself."

They were right. Reality smacked me upside the head. I was going broke while attempting to keep up with him, to meet all of his needs, and never failing to be there for him while neglecting my own responsibilities. I was exhausted. I was stretched to the limits in my struggle to make ends meet, balance my children and obligations, but still drive hours at a time to meet him and comfort him, as he always seemed to need me. When I had scheduling conflicts, Blake would win. If not, I'd be like Beth, who made everything else more important than he was. I had spent so much time and energy fighting to keep everyone else happy that I no longer was capable of determining what it was that made me happy, or if I was even happy at all. Further, when I expressed my financial fears, Blake always assured me that I had nothing to worry about. He said I was fretting over little things. He added that if I wanted to remain active in business, then we would build a powerful team and I wouldn't really have to work after his divorce. My need to support myself and his inability to help me financially was only temporary. What I really wanted, however, was to be encouraged to grow and succeed myself before we built the fabled partnership. In the meantime, I was fighting to make my car payments and buy groceries, even as the public perception was that I was a gold digger and with him only because he was successful. I had less financial security than I had ever before even as I was being assured that my sacrifices would pay off later. Except for the trips (which were quite grand, I will say), I received less from Blake, by way of gifts, than I had from any man I had ever previously dated. What I did receive for a greater part of the relationship, was more emotional attention and connection then I had ever experienced before. The memory of that connection is what aided me in living the life of a willing prisoner.

A prisoner I was. Blake had become so distrusting of me in fear of his own behavior being mirrored that I was unable to feel comfortable with anything I did. He had the password to my e-mail account and often snooped on me. I was being treated as if I were the cheat and liar. He checked my voicemail and drove by any location where I was supposed to be. Once, when I was having lunch with a client and his daughter, I looked out the window to see Blake sitting in his truck and watching us. When I accused him of being suspicious because he was a liar, he handed me all of his passwords. This began a sick and unhealthy cycle, with both of us constantly checking up on the other. I longed to breathe free again. I yearned to be trusted and to trust in return.

I promised myself to be honest with Blake at every turn, even about things that might upset or anger him, I wouldn't lie. I would always be a supportive partner and act as a sounding board for all his emotions. I would listen to things that wounded my heart when he spoke about his marriage, and do so with the understanding that I would never close the doors to communication between us. I was sure that truth and honesty would always prevail. But we weren't living our lives that way.

Our relationship had become very unbalanced, to say the least. I had been his only friend for a very long time, but I could see that he was no longer behaving as a friend to me. When I needed him, when I was hurt or suffering, he ran away. I bottled up my emotions until they burst. Things that could have been resolved through simple communication became catastrophes. Instead of healing, we both became more deeply wounded. He claimed to feel insecure that I would stick life out with him. No matter what I did, I couldn't do enough to convince him that I would always be there. He feared leaving his life with Beth only to find that I didn't really love him, so he brought me to my knees to prove my love.

Things had dramatically changed. At the beginning, I could never have predicted where we would be now. But as I was gaining strength to cut the tie between us, Blake offered another temptation.

His lies were killing him. His lifestyle was driving him to an early grave. He didn't want to be the man he was any more. He wanted to "remove all of the evil." He was, he assured me, going to be open and honest at all cost now. He held to his word. No longer did he make phone calls to me from other phones (Beth examined his phone records every day still). No longer did he hide me in any way. There were no more joint vacations with Beth, no more staying in the same home with her.

He and I began to spend quality time together as a normal couple without the tension. We threw a party at his home on the lake that became so large that a radio crew filming a Jet Ski competition came over and broadcast our event. In our quiet time, we began gardening at his lake home. His children and I planted flowers in the front that we had picked out together because he wanted me to feel like this was my home and have a part of myself there. We took a trip through the interior of Alaska and visited other old mining towns. We flew in a small plane to a remote village and visited a town called Coldfoot, where he jokingly decided we should have our wedding and started talking about our marriage more often. We drove along trucking roads to Prudhoe Bay, losing so many tires that we were stranded in the oil town for an extra day waiting for new tires to be flown in to us. But as adventurous as that sounds and regardless of how much fun we had on the trip, I didn't want to go and cried the whole way to my mother's to drop off my younger daughter. I passed up an opportunity to spend time with her alone while my oldest daughter was in Costa Rica with her Spanish class. Being gone with Blake brought me to so many cell phone dead zones that I couldn't be reached in an emergency, but if I had tried to explain my panic to Blake, he would have only said that I was being stupid, nothing would happen to my daughter and that I was ruining everything when he was "trying." I was stuck again in the position of ignoring my own desires. It was a silent torture.

Our togetherness became so accepted that friends, family, and business associates began to call one of us when they could not reach the other. During our two years, Blake had attended almost every formal and informal event in my family. I don't recall him ever missing a birthday for my children, my parents, my siblings or their children. He was my date at my sister's wedding. Even though he was present, the ability to enjoy those moments were often stifled by the drama of our circumstance. At the wedding we had to excuse ourselves from the reception every time Beth called and held the phone to her screaming children to make him aware that he was leaving her alone with them in order to attend my family's function. He was present at the hospital for two of my sisters' child deliveries. My large family makes every effort to share family time and dine on Sunday together at my mother's house. Blake was often there. In the summers, when we held family barbeques and volleyball games, Blake was almost always there. Our industry holds several annual events, fundraisers and holiday parties, which Blake and I attended, arm in arm. I was even receiving Christmas cards from business associates made out to both of us at my office. People expected us to be together more than not.

A trip we took to Boulder, Colorado, is one of my favorite memories. We went there so he could show me the town where he attended college; kind of show me his roots. We visited his friend Rocco, who had vacationed in Aruba with us. Rocco introduced us to his new girlfriend, Julie, whom he later married. It was a great few days, touring the area with another couple. I bonded with Julie, who kept slipping and calling Blake my husband. This helped me feel what it would be like for us to be "normal." We had many fun nights that included dining atop a mountain in a wonderful restaurant with a fabulous view, enjoying the spirits in a dueling piano bar, and hiking to the top of a small mountain with a bottle of wine to watch the sunset. Those moments brought peace to my heart. Blake always had a plan—Something to do and some way to make things romantic or cool.

One evening, we walked around the town until we came to Blake's old fraternity house. A party was kicking off. Julie and I found an abandoned shopping cart and convinced the young freshmen to let us push them in it down the cement steps in front in honor of the newly released *Jackass* movie and our passing youth. By the end of the evening, the fraternity boys had renamed me their frat mom and vowed to keep in touch and send us invites to their events. It was a goofy child-like vacation.

Blake and I also drove alone to spend a night in Aspen, where we stayed in a fabulous bed and breakfast that displayed photos of the owner with famous actors and politicians. Each room was decorated thematically, with collections from other countries. We wandered around sampling the night life of the incredibly rich, which made the merely "comfortable" feel extremely out of place. Then we headed back to our African-themed room.

There were some heart wounds and healings that evening, as Blake confessed some of the lies he told me in the past. Blake and I had toyed with the idea of someday having a child of our own throughout our relationship and on that night he told me that while we had been broken up, Beth had convinced him to get a vasectomy. She neutered the dog. He confessed to past relationships with other women he'd had during his marriage before me and divulged that he had been with Beth sexually a few times during our relationship. He was hoping that we move forward with deep honesty from that day on. It was a difficult night for me. I cried many tears, but in the end I felt we were more bonded than ever before. We woke the next morning to the sounds of preparation for the Aspen Fourth of July parade. During check out, the owner of the B&B introduced us to her significant other, an actor in the movie Easy Rider. We went out to enjoy the parade. As we drove back to the Denver airport, Blake fell asleep in the passenger seat. I was astonished by all that had transpired. Never before had I believed so deeply that finally the day had come when all of my dreams had come true. We were going to be together. The divorce was definite and we were going to marry immediately after it was final. I remember every corner of that highway, every bit of the landscape, and the mountain range I was seeing. My breath was taken away as I drove in silence, watching him sleep. For the first time in a long while, I felt happy again. I was at ease and confident that our life ahead would be filled with joy. I knew that the rest of our lives would be spent sharing love, adventure and deep companionship. I would have the relationship that most only fantasize about. I felt content. We had decided that as soon as we arrived back home, we were going to load up our children in the motor home together and travel by ferry to an island off the Aleutians. He had already arranged this with Beth. She had agreed. She accepted the end of their marriage and was allowing him to move on with his life while still enjoying his children. The marriage was over.

Chapter 11

The Brutal End

I expected Blake at my house the day before we departed on our family adventure along the Aleutians, but he did not arrive. Instead, he phoned me the next day from the lake house where he had spent the night with Beth and their kids. When he called, I was running around town, picking up the things we'd need for our trip and was standing in a sporting goods store. When he revealed the truth of where he had been all night I began crying. I tried to hide behind the clothing racks and as I cried, I felt my heart began to harden. I was no longer pleading with him—"But you promised"—and no longer enraged by yet another betrayal. The last tear that slid down my cheek turned to ice before it fell off my chin.

He showed up later that day with only one of his children and when, after much prodding, his daughter stepped onto my front porch, she hid her face against the rail so she wouldn't have to look at me and screamed, "I want to call my mom!" Her tantrum made her father angry, but I saw instantly that she had been told by Beth that seeing me was not a good thing. I begged Blake to allow her to call her mother so that she would feel secure. The result was that he had to drive her home, an hour back, and delay our departure. When he returned he told me that, yes, Beth had told her daughter that I was evil, that my children were wicked, and that we wanted to take her daddy away from her. Beth had told her daughter specifically that my younger daughter, with whom she had previously gotten along so well, was a bad kid. That's why she wouldn't speak to her when my daughter tried to comfort her. I understood Beth not wanting me to be around her children and not wanting anything that had anything to do with me (that is, my daughters) around her children. But my girls are good girls. They had never done anything bad to Beth or anyone in her family. They were just kids. Beth had told Blake that my children deserved to die. Remembering that now, I think I hated her at that moment too.

We were already off to a bad start. When the ferry was pulling away from the dock, I received a call from my friend Tony, one of the friends I was not "allowed" to associate with. Blake's possessiveness kicked in immediately. Tony had always been forthcoming with his opinion of our relationship and belief that it was wrong. He had always voiced his mistrust of Blake to me and tried to help me get my head out of my ass and see what was in front of my face. Blake had once confronted him and tried to intimidate Tony, but Tony held his ground. This made Blake fight even more for me to end my friendship with him. I took his call on the ferry, therefore Blake announced that my friendship with Tony was one reason he was hesitating to divorce Beth. The clouds parted for me yet again and I saw his attempt to isolate me. He was afraid that my friends would shine the light on my delusion. He had blamed all of our issues on each and every person I was close to and because of this the dawn began on its own without the help of my friends.

Arriving on the island, we found a historical camp site at which to park our motor home for the duration of our stay. We left the site often to tour the town or remote parts of the area. But most of the trip was hell for me. Every time Blake walked away from the camp site or took too long in the bank or spent too much time in a department store, I accused him of sneaking off to call Beth. I am still sure that's what he was doing. I had the ever-present feeling that I was being duped. Perhaps he had lied to me again about being forthcoming with Beth and he was again trying to hide the fact that I was with him. Beth's and my roles seemed to be reversed now. She had become the woman he was hiding from me. One evening, Blake had fallen asleep while we watched a movie. I heard his phone vibrating and looked at it. Beth was calling. I snooped his voicemail filled with suspicion and listened to her message. She was crying about how she was feeling knowing that he was on the trip with me. I deleted it out of fear that it would make him feel sad for her and allow her to seep into our time together.

For most of that trip, he drank like a fish and was rude and agitated. One morning I woke to find him missing. I stepped out into the camp ground and began to search for him, following trails and calling his name for what felt like an hour until I gave up and headed back to camp. On my way back I met him on the trail and inquired why he had been gone for so long and where he had been. I received a hostile and defensive reply. But by now my days of frantic searching for him had passed. Now I only looked for him to catch him trying to make a fool of me.

Even in our worst of times together, there was always still much good. One day on the trip we golfed with the kids and laughed at the difficulty we were having in the pouring rain. Another day we attended a music festival filled with reminiscent hippies. When the plumbing system broke down in the motor home, we found a high school swimming pool to laugh and bathe ourselves in. We took a fishing charter with my children, filled with chuckles at both of my girls. One wouldn't stop sucking a stick into the tentacles of an octopus pulled aboard and the other cried for every fish caught. One afternoon we walked along the edge of the ocean playing and another afternoon we ventured off into a forest stumbling onto bear bait. "What is that thing hanging from that tree?" I asked. Then we heard a roar and broke all known running records. There were moments we cherished and found another exciting story to tell, but we also fought constantly. He treated me in a manner I was not comfortable with and yelled at me in front of my children. He was unpredictable. I was growing very bitter with Blake on that trip and this time, so were my children.

Time to board the ferry for home did not come soon enough for me. Blake stayed down in the car bay while the girls and I got ourselves situated on board. He was still absent while the crew began to announce that all passengers were to go above deck. I went down to the loaded motor home to look for him and discovered an empty vodka bottle in the trash and an open woman's magazine on the table, with a layout of Mary Kate and Ashley hugging each other. As the ferry took off, he befriended another (male) passenger and they filled themselves with more alcohol. It was a twelve hour ride back home through the night, and the ferry was overcrowded so we were forced to pitch a tent on the starboard deck, right near the fog horn. It was pouring freezing rain, the wind was horrendous, and the tent would not stay grounded. While I fought the elements and tried to use duct tape to stake the tent, Blake just stood there and watched. He did nothing but tip his drink to his mouth. I looked at him like he was a bona fide loser, because he failed to be a man and help me while I prepared our bed in ferryboat hell. I was furious with him. Visions of what a future with him would be like were flashing before my eyes.

When we finally reached the dock, we were in a small town about four hours from home. My father was at the dock, preparing to depart for his own trip to a different island. We ate breakfast together, and I shared with him the highlights of our trip. This gave Blake and me a break from each other. I also received some positive emotion from my father. The drive back home was mostly quiet, but I continued to test for vital signs in our relationship. I felt certain its death was imminent.

That night, Blake left my house saying that he was going to Taco Bell. I now lovingly call it his run for the border because he never did return with my *Gordita*. I was suspicious of everything that he did now and asked if he was coming back. He promised me emphatically that, yes, he would be back in a few minutes. Hours went by. Eventually, I drove to the house he shared with Beth. Sure enough, his car was in the driveway. I called the house, and when Beth answered, I went ballistic. I was tired of all the shit. I'd had it! I was done with the lies. Done with the sneaking around. Done with his worthless ass. Done with the games. I was filled with rage.

Then a strange thing happened. Beth began to calm *me* down. She assured me that he was downstairs working in the office. "You just spent two weeks with him," she said. "He needs to see his kids. What is wrong with you? Why are you so upset? He's already told me that he loves you. He's in love with YOU." She reassured me. Again, I was the fool and the asshole, to boot. It really was about his kids. He really had been honest with her. He had even told her that he was in love with me, and she had come to a place where she was able to say that to me without hate. She even sounded at peace with it. I was floored. I was wrong.

I was insane.

But then he stayed another weekend with her. I started receiving phone calls from my friends inquiring about what was going on with Blake and me because they were seeing him at a bar on the lake with Beth. At this point, I didn't even care. Every concerned phone call was helping me stamp the death certificate of our relationship.

Then my phone rang at 5 a.m., and when I finally got up and checked my voicemails, I found several drunken messages from Blake accusing me of having had sex sometime in the past with a man he had spoken to at the bar that night. He accused me of letting the guy "fuck [me] in the ass" years before I had met Blake. I had never so much as touched that man, let alone ever been in a position to do what Blake was accusing me of. He had also left several messages on Beth's behalf, saying "Beth's concerned about this." Is it just me, or was that the craziest thing of all?

My brain was Jell-O. I phoned him back and Beth answered the phone. She woke Blake up—he was sleeping on the couch—to hand him the phone. I could not get a word in edgewise past the accusations before his battery went dead.

I took the bait. Furious, I drove all of the way out to the lake and was let into the alleged "ass fucker's" abode and woke him up with a slap to his face. I was promptly hoisted back out the door with many choice words certainly being shoved up my ass. Then I drove back into town. Back home, I snooped Blake's e-mail and found flirtatious and incriminating notes between him and another girl pertaining to the night before. This was it. I was truly over it all. The man I had loved was officially driving me out of my mind. Look at how I was living! Look at how I was behaving! What had my life become?

Later that afternoon, Blake drove into town urging me to go for a drive with him so we could talk. I didn't care what I said to him anymore. I didn't care how ugly I looked while I yelled. I didn't care if he never wanted to see me again. I screamed into his ear for the entire thirty-minute drive. I let everything out, not keeping back one word. By the time we returned to my house I had calmed down, but only for the sake of my vocal cords. When he asked me if we could have dinner together the next evening after I was feeling cooler, I did not respond, but stepped out of the car and refused contact with him for the rest of the day. The next evening arrived and he showed up, assuming we were going out together to talk.

I had developed an unwavering resolve to end the relationship. I no longer felt for him as I had for the last two years. Too much had happened. There had been too much mind-screwing and I knew I would never be able to live a life of trust with him. I knew that I needed to get out before I lost my sanity forever. I was growing to hate him bitterly—and myself even more.

I went to dinner with him. We drove to the restaurant in silence and dined almost in silence, too, but for a group of acquaintances seated nearby invited us to join them at another after-dinner spot. We walked downtown together with the other couple, and when we entered the next establishment I found a few other friends of my own. I ordered a glass of wine and began venting my frustrations of the last two years to the gals beside me, not realizing that Blake had seated himself next to me too. I was oozing my verbal hatred and as my anger peaked, I turned and saw him and made a snide comment about the e-mail exchange I had found the day before between him and another woman. "Be careful where you put your little dick," I told him.

I instantly alerted to him taking the remark as an insult to his manly member. I saw the hurt look in his eyes, but before I could recant my comment he picked up his glass, and threw it at me. The glass broke across my face. Soaking wet with what I thought was his drink, I cupped my face in shock. When I pulled my hands away, however, they were covered with blood and I fainted. When I awoke, patrons of the bar were laying white dishcloths on my face and I could hear men yelling, "Get that guy, he just hurt this girl." Before I could speak, I saw my blood staining the dishcloth and down the front of my shirt and passed out again. When I came to, paramedics were all around me and police officers were taking photographs.

After they took me to an emergency vehicle parked at the curb, and while I was trying to come to grips with what was happening and answering the police officers' questions, my cell phone rang. It was from Blake's house number so I answered it, but it was Beth. She was kind to me and asked in a tone that seemed to be full of genuine concern, "Are you all right? What happened?" While I was speaking to her, I also told the police officers that I didn't know what had happened. I told them to ask the crowd of patrons that had now gathered outside the bar. When the officer asked me who was on the phone, I replied that it was Blake's *wife*. Just as she was frantically asking if I intended to press charges, the policeman asked me for clarification about who was on the phone. I fell silent. What could I say? All I felt was defeat. I wanted to sink into the seat. When the officer left the vehicle to ask the others for their statements, I slipped away, feeling nothing but pure embarrassment and shame. As I walked to the parking garage where Blake had parked, I continued my phone conversation with Beth. Fortunately, he had put his car keys in my purse.

As I drove home alone, she finally spoke to me as we should have spoken two years before. She told me things that made my mind race, things that devastated me. I cannot remember everything she said, but nonetheless, the "bitch" sweetly comforted me for hours. In the morning, I woke to find her ringing my door bell to retrieve the keys to Blake's truck. She spoke to me kindly again in my driveway, saying a friend of hers was watching her children so that she could pick up the truck. No one knew were Blake was, she told me.

Beth hugged me and apologized for what I had been through at the same time that I apologized for everything I had put her through. She seemed exhausted, as if she, too, were over it. There had been too much nonsense during the last few years.

I later learned that Blake had been arrested the night before and that Beth had hired an attorney before she had ever arrived at my house to pick up his truck. Some time after that, I was told that her kindness was in order to persuade me not to press charges and to keep the drama from creeping out into the public. I still don't know what was real. In fact, I don't know if anything I was ever told about Beth was real. But I believe that I saw a genuine person that day in my driveway.

My eyes were black and I had nasty cuts across my cheek and nose, and glass imbedded in my lip. I could not bear to see my children look at me. They couldn't stop staring with sympathy and heartbreak. I felt like I was now weak to them. I felt like my life was a complete disgrace. I didn't know what to say to my children, or how to explain myself. Now, not only did the entire business community know that I had spent two years in a foolish affair, but now I also looked like a battered and weak woman. I was mortified.

The following afternoon, I received a call from an attorney who represented Blake. He informed me that Blake had been detained the night before and that he was attempting to have him released. He hoped I would state to the judge that I did not fear for my life so that he would be let out of jail without much penalty. I was sick inside and believed that Blake, too, was in the pit of despair. I was certain that now, sitting in a jail cell all night, he was feeling the ultimate grief. I imagined him overcome with shame for hurting me and sick with concern about me and anger at himself.

I participated in a teleconference for Blake's arraignment hearing. The judge spoke to Blake in a stern tone, instructing him that under no uncertain circumstances was he to contact me. Then in a sarcastic tone, he added, "Do you think you can handle that?" Blake replied with an arrogant and angry, "You bet, your Honor!" At that moment I realized that he blamed *me*. I felt a dagger in my heart. The teleconference ended, and within thirty minutes his attorney called me back and asked if I would come by his office with makeup on to take new photographs because, he said, "the photos from last night look so bad with all of the blood and I was hoping to get some better ones with you all cleaned up." I was still digesting the blow of hearing no caring for me in Blake's voice, and now I felt backed into a corner. All of these years, I had been used and I had allowed it by playing along, and now these people thought I was downright stupid!

I asked the attorney if I could call him back in a few minutes, then called an attorney I knew personally. After our conversation, I phoned Blake's attorney back and told him what my friend had advised me. "Oh, shit," was all I heard before he hung up. My attorney had advised against appearing in makeup to make the look all better, of course. He had also said, "Blake should be careful because you could sue him for a lot of money," and my friend also followed up with me regularly to check on how I was doing.

My friend Tony, against whom Blake was so set, was one of the few people who knew not only about what had happened but also the extent of my despair. He was persistent in trying to pull me through my depression. He brought me books to read and dragged me out of the house to be sure I got some fresh air. He took me on hikes and listened as I ran my thoughts over and over out loud. He also weathered curious looks from passers-by who would see my bruised face and then dart their eyes towards him. Tony is now and always has been a true and wonderful friend. I'm not sure if I have ever expressed how deeply I appreciate his friendship. I am fortunate that he did not give up on me. Like other friends who stuck by me, he did not allow me to push him out my life.

Right away, rumors began to circulate that were said to have started with Blake. There were tales of me waving a bottle at him over dinner at the restaurant we had dined at hours before our fight. I began hearing that he had struck me in self-defense. Many of these tales placed me in the position of attacker and him as defending himself. I was being made to look as a crazy person to my community to save his reputation. In my desperation to set the story straight and spare what little reputation I had left, I contacted my attorney again and filed a formal civil suit. I thought that by doing that, everyone would know the "crazy" tales weren't true.

I also knew, of course, that what I was doing would surely lead to the end of my relationship with Blake for good. My coming against him in legal proceedings was sure to make him see me as the enemy. I believed by doing so he would never contact me again and I would never fall vulnerable to another promise in a moment of weakness. I stamped the death certificate. *Deceased.*

Chapter 12

A Not So New Beginning

In time I began to heal. In time I was able to try to open my heart again. In time I began dating Shane, a man with whom I had developed a caring friendship. This was a seemingly nonjudgmental man who supported my happiness.

During our developing friendship, I was speaking to Shane one day about my stress over the public conception of who I was after the affair with Blake. He said "Those people who say those things don't know you, and if they believe them, they don't deserve to know you." This sentence touched my heart and opened me to chancing a start at a new relationship, one in hindsight I must have been desperate for.

For the first three months that Shane and I were together, I felt release. I was falling in love again and happy. I believed that I was with a soft, gentle and genuine person. He, too, seemed to be mesmerized by me the way Blake was in our beginnings. I was excited to introduce him to my family and friends and I booked a vacation for us to Florida. He would be the first man I'd ever taken to my best friend Janet's home. I had visions of the two of us having a great time with my favorite couple. I jumped head first into my new life, wanting to risk love and not allow myself to turn bitter and scarred by my past. I was anxious to live this new life with the man who could stand on the dock of that dilapidated shack I had daydreamed about.

Our departure date was the day after Christmas. Christmas morning came and we shared our gifts with each other. Afterwards, Shane left to celebrate the holiday with his family. That Christmas night, he phoned me and abruptly canceled leaving with me. He said that he wasn't coming because he had decided to get back together with his ex-girlfriend. He decided this, he said, because he believed that I would never love him as I had loved Blake.

That night I was a zombie while I packed random items into my luggage. Here I am again, I thought. Someone else was more valuable than me. I am not enough and losing me means nothing. Crushed is the only word I can think of to describe my emotional state, but using that word minimizes what I was truly feeling. Before departure, Shane showed up on my doorstep with a friend of his to help plead his case. He had made an error, he still wanted to go and in a whirlwind, we left.

When Shane and I started dating, I believed that he was honest and trustworthy. I remember thinking one night, if this guy turns out to be a cheat and a liar, I will never trust myself again. I was afraid that if he let me down in such a magnitude, I would turn into a bitter woman, never capable of trusting a man again. I felt there was no way that I could survive another painful experience. Shane seemed so innocent and grateful to be with me, I couldn't imagine him turning out to be another bad guy. Instead of letting him go after his decision to return to his ex-girlfriend and then coming back again, I decided much of his insecurity was a Blake factor. I was fighting myself, wanting to believe that I wasn't *really* this horrible of a judge of character. So I hung out, searching for ways to convince myself those good things I thought I saw in Shane were real.

I spoke to Shane often about my feelings about the lawsuit against Blake and my wish to not pursue it. Lawsuits take a considerable amount of time before they ever get to court. By now, so much time had passed since I'd seen Blake that I wanted to just move on with my new life and leave the past behind me. But Shane, my attorney and my friends all encouraged me to stick with the suit, saying that the only way for the kind of person Blake was to learn from his behavior was through his wallet. Shane was adamant that I had been done wrong and letting Blake off the hook would be a disservice to other women who had been abused. When I argued that if Blake worked for 7-Eleven, then I would not be suing him, and therefore it did not make sense just to sue for money because he had some, everyone insisted that what he had done was not right and I needed to serve justice. I had intended to donate whatever I won to a local shelter, but there was no honorable thing I could do. When I filed the lawsuit, it only caused "they" to start gossiping that my whole purpose for being with Blake in the first place was tied to his money.

Things suddenly changed when during a disagreement with Shane, he snidely remarked to me that he wasn't sure he wanted to date me anymore. He couldn't handle the things that others were saying about me. Shane was new to the business community and wanted to be accepted by the cliquing folks of higher society. So he became chameleon-like—clinging and contributing to gossip about me. He was starting to question himself as to who I *really* was. In hindsight, I see now that I was neither strong enough nor equipped emotionally to move on in a new relationship at that time. I was still too vulnerable. I wasn't healed enough to be centered and clear. My mind set was that there was something wrong with me and I needed to fix whatever it was. So I stayed with him adding four more years of struggle to my life.

I clung to the belief that through our time together, he would feel secure about the person I am and defend me.

But Shane was also filled with insecurity and mistrust caused by what I was dealing with socially. This perpetuated the cycle I was trying to remove myself from, and much of it was tied to the fact that I was involved with a lawsuit against my former lover, which Shane eventually concluded was my way of keeping me tied to Blake. In reality, it was the opposite. Had I not filed the suit, Blake and I would have eventually spoken again. I would not have been able to rid him from my life. Filing the suit, I was well aware, would cause Blake such anger he would never trust or speak to me again. In a sense, therefore, the lawsuit was the most solid way I could assure myself I would never fall back into the pattern with him again. I was putting my foot down. I was saying, loudly and firmly, "It's over! I mean it this time."

During our disagreement, Shane's sudden harshness about the matter devastated me. No matter which way I went, I couldn't win. I felt like, great, here I am trying to be happy in something new and honest and Blake was constantly screwing it up. If I sued Blake, it was because I was money-hungry and wanted to stay connected to my past. If I dropped the suit, it was because I was stupid, too forgiving, letting him off the hook again and wanting to keep the door open for him.

I sustained another emotional blow from Shane with regard to the lawsuit and his sudden, shocking feelings toward me because of it. This blow came right after I attended the funeral of a friend of my ex-husband's and mine. The funeral was one of four I attended within a few months. My thirty-four-year-old cousin died quickly after being diagnosed with cancer, my friend Sasha's nephew, who was only twenty one, was killed in a tragic accident, an extended family member in his mid twenties was killed after being in the wrong place at the wrong time and now this friend died tragically, too. On top of it all, I was alerted to my own health scare.

I kept quietly falling apart in my office after Shane screamed harsh things to me about being a money grubbing bitch, evident by my lawsuit and he laughed off my health concerns by telling me that Blake and Beth could dance over my grave.

It was more than I could take at that time in my life. My attempt to masquerade as someone who really had their act together wasn't working. I was dealing with too many things and tottered on the edge of a nervous breakdown. Looking back, I don't know how it was that I managed not to pull a Thelma and Louise.

I sat for hours, staring at the walls and sobbing. I felt lost. There were no right answers. There was no one who truly knew me in my soul. I needed the world to stop and let me rest for just a moment.

My hands dialed Blake's number. I needed a real friend. I missed his kindness, his ability to comfort me and the kind of emotional support he'd offered. He would have never seen me as Shane had expressed so coldly. I was feeling so alone, so attacked, so mind fucked. I thought Blake was the only one who might really care for me. When he answered the phone, I could barely speak. All I said was, "Can you talk?" In shock, he said, "Is it you?" He held his breath and I started to cry and hyperventilate. "I just miss my friend," I whispered. We got eight hours' worth of closure, and in the end I told him that I had never wanted to sue him and agreed to drop the suit. He offered to pay my attorney bill, and three days later we signed the release with prejudice that concluded the war.

In celebration, with our sickened minds, we toasted the end at the very location where we had last seen each other before the war began. Sitting together as two old friends, we asked our server about a story we'd heard about a couple who had once had a big fight there. The bartender proceeded to tell us about that night. "Yeah, man," he said, "it was brutal. This dude like busted his mug over this girl's face and started carving into her. The whole top of the bar was filled with blood. She was laying in it, I dunno, like she was drinking red dye or something."

"Man, that sounds intense," Blake said. "Were you there?" (We both knew full well he had not been there.)

"Yeah, man," he replied, "I was like trying to resuscitate her."

We closed the chapter in our typical comic fashion. We were able to laugh at the extreme spin our story had taken and felt united in nostalgia as the ones who knew they just didn't get us.

With nothing legal to keep us apart, Blake began to call me when I just happened to be with Shane, who soon came to believe that our communication happened more often and was about much more than it really was. Knowing that Shane felt insecure about our relationship,

Blake started doing little things to torment him. Such as sending Shane anonymous text messages, emails and voicemails. This put me on another roller coaster ride that I was afraid to get off. I was sure everyone would think badly of me because Blake was again the issue. I had enjoyed my developing relationship with Shane in the beginning and the initial affection he had offered. Shane seemed to offer the gentleness that had been missing from my life for so long. I thought that he was an innocent and caring person. Like Blake, in the beginning, he seemed to be enamored and in love with me, like I was unique and special. I felt fortunate to have finally found a situation where I thought real love and kindness had found me and this time, I was allowed to have it. Maybe by that time, I was so desperate for approval and affection, that I didn't see everything else that surrounded who Shane really was either. What is evident to me about those days, I needed everyone to know that I had gone on with my life. I wanted Beth to know that I wasn't going back there, that I had moved on. But the process seemed always stifled no matter how great my desire was to let go of the past and focus on the future.

Through the years Blake and I have remained friends. I don't hate him. How could I? Despite the bad, we also shared much good. I have never seen any reason to hate someone you once loved. Occasionally we speak or write an e-mail or two back and forth, and on a rare occasion I meet him for lunch. But I have never been tempted to return to the relationship the way it was, even though there were times when things were not going well in my new life and Blake's failure to choose me was rubbed in my face, I would then hope out of pride that he would finish things as he had promised and tell me it all was a bad dream so that I could show those who insulted me "I told you so." We stay fairly caught up with one another, and I still care for him and with genuine sincerity wish him happiness. Blake has asked me to go with him on many trips, but I have always since declined. He will still comment on occasion, his hope that someday we will have everything we wanted in each other. But each time we speak, it's the same story I have listened to for almost six years now. He is always closer than ever to getting his divorce. He is always more miserable than he ever was in his marriage. He still remains an overall wimp, claiming to be helpless with regard to his ability to control what he wants for his own life, which is never an attractive quality.

As part of our new found friendship there was the recognition that we mix well in business. Using that connection, he once dangled the carrot in front of my nose by offering me a business contract that would typically sign allowing six months for performance. If I performed, the deal held the potential of earning me a large commission. He gave me one month to do it and I did. The problem was I don't think he expected me to succeed, and he was away on Aruba at the time, which left me to conduct business with Beth. To her astounding credit, she was both kind and professional toward me, but when Blake returned, he canceled half the transaction, saying his reasons for cancelation was due to Beth's inability to have to deal with hearing my name on a regular basis. Then he used what I had procured to close out the last half, cutting me out of fifty percent the proceeds I had secured. I was later told that he informed mutual business acquaintances that he was forced to sign that contract with me as part of the law suit and that my business phone calls to his office were me stalking him. I don't know if I believe he said that . . . frankly, I never know what to believe anymore. There were so many people fighting to save face, or create gossip, I could write a book about it!

Though he constantly takes vacations and is rarely in the state, which further detaches him from his marriage and its perpetual state of dissatisfaction, I feel sympathy for him. He says he is "just living." Like Peter Pan, he is searching for Neverland. He has had several new lovers since our parting, and he still doesn't get it when I try to explain how my life has been traumatized as a result of our relationship. He speaks of himself saying, "My life was altered, too." He "just wants to be wanted" he says, lamenting his own loneliness while he leaves Beth alone to handle their life responsibilities.

Two years after our end, I visited with Blake and he said (again), "Maybe now we can finally be together."—No, my dear, we cannot. I looked him square in the eye and explained that it was far too late. It had never occurred to me that after all of these years I would need to expound upon my reasons, but I dredged them up for him anyway. One reason, I said, was that I would never be certain that I was his *first* choice or that I would remain his *only* choice. Too much time, I said, and too much heartache; it was beyond too late. The man was truly floored. He seemed to believe that he had all of the time in the world. He could not fathom that I would adjust well to living without him, that I wouldn't return for yet another empty promise. Tears welled up in his eyes and he quickly excused himself and ran to the restroom. When he returned, it was as if the words had never been spoken to him. He was oblivious to "no."

A few months later, he ran into my mother. When he asked about me, she shared some of my business plans that I had with my friend Sasha. "Huh!" he replied. "If it weren't for Sasha, we would be married by now."

Obviously even unto this day he lives another reality.

As I look back, I see that if I had stayed in the relationship with Blake, I probably would *still* be waiting for his promise of a divorce to be kept. I wonder if he had divorced Beth, would I have spent my life catering to his needs without ever having mine met. Would I have felt in debt to him for the sacrifice he made to be with me? Would I have used up my energy in pouring myself into him, and later grown bitter feeling that he selfishly took my energy and never refueled me? Toward the end of our relationship, my desire to share intimate moments with Blake had began to wane. I was feeling used and unimportant. Why would I want to share intimate moments with a man who neglected my feelings, thoughts, hurts, and obstacles in my daily life that affected my mental or emotional state? He had to have been of the belief that my love and desire for him were so great that I would sacrifice almost anything to be near him because that is what I had proven for so long. If he had gotten his divorce, I would have worried constantly that if I fell from perfection and stopped meeting his every desire, then he would have sought another woman, and I would have suffered everything that Beth suffered . . . . and still does. I once said to her, "Beth, sometimes when you win, you lose." I wonder if she gets that now.

I learned after the ultimate end of Blake and me, that he simply moved on to the next woman . . . and then another . . . and then another . . . and on and on. He now flies new and younger girls to new and perhaps more fabulous destinations. Even if I had stayed with him, it probably would not have changed him. Some of the other women have been smarter than I was and left more quickly. Some have hung around for what they receive. (I'm told that Beth no longer controls his funds and so he is now able to give monetary gifts.) One other woman feigned friendship with Beth to forestall her suspicion. Blake remains married and holds me partially responsible, as he accuses me of leaving him for someone else.

I did leave him for someone else. Myself!

Blake has also admitted to me that he cheated on me during our relationship. The irony of this is that I had stumbled onto some pretty clear evidence of it, but because of his passionate display of undying love for me, I could not believe that he would do that or could do that to ME. When I confronted him, he told me all the things that I wanted to hear. When I heard them, I accepted them. I accepted what I wanted to believe, just as his wife had done for so many years.

I believed for so long that Blake always loved me. I believed that our affair was different from any other. Even years after our affair ended, I believed that he always had loved me, but that circumstances had proved to be too difficult. I came to accept that it was his fear that had cost us everything that we longed for. The screwy situation cost all of us a greater portion of our sanity, and it was his inability to gain control of his freedom of choice and forge ahead with what was in his heart that had caused all of the crazy craziness. Maybe, I wonder now, I romanticized what existed between us. I thought we were soul mates, but did I really know what existed between us, verses the fantasy vision that I bought into? A vision perhaps quite perfected by an artist long before it ever reached me?

Blake and I once spoke at great length about the choices he had made in his life, and I listened to all of his same complaints about Beth and all of his same justifications for staying married and having affairs. My heart broke for Beth at a level it never had before. In some crazy way, I have developed affection for Blake's wife. It is strange to have a love of sorts for a person who rightfully hates you and to fully understand her pain and have no expectation of her forgiveness. I began to reason with Blake about her hostility, hatefulness, and bitterness toward him. I was trying to be a voice he heard when speaking her defense. A voice I was certain fell on deaf ears when she spoke them to him herself. I begged him to go back and give her a hundred percent or let her go so she could be loved, like she deserved, by someone willing to share his life with her. I asked him either to love her enough to give her what she needs, or love her enough to let her go. He has done neither.

I learned much from my experience with Blake and had many adventures that I had only dreamed of, for which I am grateful. Because

Blake has also had a positive impact on my life I'm not sure that I would ever trade the experience if given the chance. That is a tough thing for me to admit, given that much of the positive came despite a torturous time in my life. Through him I have grown tremendously as a person. He helped me to expand my knowledge and confidence in business. He encouraged me to explore my intellectual interests and fed my hunger for travel. He also freed me of my fear of commitment. I am now very clear on what type of relationship I want and deserve in my life. Through this time, I have become stronger and more connected to myself than I ever thought I could be. But although the only dime I paid was for a subway ticket in London, I paid abundantly for my lessons in the deepest parts of my soul. Finding personal value through this kind of struggle is a much more difficult way to discover self, then setting out to discover self alone. I hope any other other woman who reads this will avoid the hurt and shame that comes when every skeptical person is proved to be right, that their love affair is not so unique and different, after all.

It wasn't until after the affair was history that I realized how much of a mess I had made of my life on so many levels. Never once during my relationship with Blake did I think about how poorly my future would be affected. If I thought my life was difficult enough during the affair, I dare say the aftermath was worse.

When we figure out that the forest we're lost in is unsafe, we need an incredible amount of strength to find our way out. Then we reach a clearing, only to discover that real life is on the other side of a canyon. We are weak, withered, and dehydrated. We're only able to muster up enough fuel to go on because we can see the other side. We use up our last bit of strength to run, pole in hand, and plant it for a hearty vault across. However, the habitants of the other side are likely to protest that we're bringing disease to their valley. Other women are unwanted guests everywhere they go, and should we reach the other side, we now must face another fight; one against those who would seek to throw us off the cliff.

A heartfelt caution to those who are involved in an affair

Looking back, I wonder how I would have read a story like mine in the beginning or in the heat of my affair. I know I would have still convinced myself that *we were different*. The story didn't apply to me. If this were your story, I could have told you that you were a damn idiot several pages ago, probably right after the start of the first chapter. I would have said I was smarter than you, I would never let things get that out of control, I would have ended the relationship at the first major ordeal. I would never have put up with that kind of crap.

But it's not that easy. Things happen very slowly and very fast at the same time. The beginning of an affair feels beautiful, the development can be full of rough patches, and the end is hell, no matter what kind of married guy you've got. If I were reading this book, I would have quickly searched my thoughts for ways to validate what I wanted to believe. I would have sold myself on the belief that my situation was different, better, and more hopeful. I'm certain that as you read about the physical arguments in my relationship it will offer much balance to the belief that your relationship is far from the same of what I experienced. I am quite sure that most affairs do not end so extremely, though I will say I am uncertain which ends really hurt worst. A softer ending where I was simply told goodbye might not have made things as easy on me as the anger of having a glass busted over my face did. I wasn't left to long for him much, after that. The thing is, it didn't have to go that far to cause all of the emotional destruction to my life.

It has taken years of struggling to learn one very valuable lesson that may be universally applicable to a woman who feels helplessly in love with a bad situation: *The easiest way to fall out of love with someone who is bad for you, is to fall in love with yourself.*

Part 2

The Players, the Stages and the Aftermath of an Affair

Nothing is as easy as deceiving yourself,
for what you wish you readily believe

~ Demosthenes

Chapter 13

Who is The Other Woman?

It took a great deal of emotional healing and soul searching for me to find my way back to who I was before I met Blake. As I have become older and wiser, I look back in wonderment at how I ever got so caught up, let alone how I even entered into the whole ordeal. Although I learned much about myself, being a mistress was certainly never someone I believed I could be. Being part of an extra-marital affair was something so against my belief system that I felt compelled to retrace my steps and discover where I lost my way.

My first step was to ask myself, and other women who became involved in similar affairs at some point in their lives, if we were so different from other women. What let us get involved with a married man? What makes us different from women who refuse to cross the line? I asked the other women if they had the same feelings and thoughts I'd had. What were the similarities (or differences) in our characters? In our relationships? Was I a good person gone bad? Were we all inherently good and had we somehow cast ourselves into the pit? Why did we self-destruct so blindly? Did I, or did they, unknowingly suffer from low self-esteem, which is commonly associated with women who allow themselves to become the other woman? (Nope, I learned. The low self-esteem came as a result of the affair.)

I forced myself to painfully and honestly find the most obvious factors that would allow a woman to become involved with an unavailable man. Had I been so desperately lonely? Maybe, though I don't think so. I knew plenty of available men who were interested in me. I think that I was experiencing some regret for not giving another man with a previous similar circumstance an honest shot, but my life was very full of other things that kept me occupied and content. I can even say, I had no time to slow down enough to notice any void in my life. Was I struggling with other things that were happening in my life? Perhaps.

I lost a friend who died abruptly a year before my involvement with Blake. This had a great impact on my life. It cratered my spiritual belief system and left me emotionally drained. I could no longer find meaning or purpose. The reality that someday we all will pass was in my thoughts, and the glorious afterlife suddenly seemed like something I might be selling myself to comfort me through the inevitable. Maybe I was angry at the fate of human life. Maybe I didn't care anymore. Maybe moral foundation became "what's the point?"

It's human nature for us to look outside ourselves and find someone to blame, and so the thought crossed my mind that perhaps Sasha was an influence on me. I mean, I had just recently started to spend more time with her, and she was involved in an affair with a married man. But no, I couldn't make her my scapegoat. I am an adult woman, and even in my youth, I was hardly a follower. And the way Sasha spoke about her situation didn't make it sound appealing to me.

Then I had another thought. Blake was very wealthy. I had to boldly back myself into a corner and look for the truth. Was I desperately seeking marriage or a committed relationship with someone who would take care of me and ease my life's burdens? Blake's lifestyle certainly was tempting. It seemed to me that being his wife required nothing but the will to have fun, travel, and hold power and control in any business dealing I might choose to engage in—IF I chose to work at all. I'm not going to lie, the option of a luxurious life was enormously tempting. His having money did not hurt my feelings.

On the other hand, I think that most people would like a companion and lover. If he happened to be well off, all the better. Like a large percentage of women with a shoe fetish, money equals shoes to me and so I always view wealth from that perspective. How many pairs is this worth? It actually really helps me to place a value on just about everything in life because in the overall grand scheme of things—I'll speak the curse words—shoes just aren't that important. I was not looking for just anyone, and no number of shoes are worth the loss of love to me. In reality, the best looking shoes (and most expensive) always hurt the most to walk in, and regardless of my closet full of pretty pairs, I find myself always gravitating to the comfortable ones the most. No—it was not his money that made me love him. I would have rather he gave it all up so that we could be together.

Next, I asked myself, was Blake a safe partner for someone who was commitment-phobic? Did I harbor negative feelings about life partnering? Was I afraid of future disappointment within the confines of marriage that allowed me to secretly move into a situation that would offer an easy out? Perhaps this IS a good answer.

Maybe there are good answers to all my questions. But I still hadn't come to the heart of the matter.

I learned a lot from the women who confided in me with their stories. We were all lost souls enmeshed in affairs with married men.

While each story was different in its particulars, they were all the same. These women were not lower-class whores so hungry for the affection of a man they were willing to take on anything. They were not so empty of self-respect and pride they would bed down any man or do anything it took to steal the upstanding husband and father of a righteous family. The women who spoke to me were not vicious, heartless tramps who lured some vulnerable husband away from the clutches of his loving wife for the simple pleasure of laughing at a wretched, crumbled woman. Far from worthless sluts, these women weren't ones to spread their legs for anyone.

Women are much more complicated than men. No matter how strong we are, our lives are often ruled by our emotions. Our choices are often based on what we feel, not what we think, and our brain chemistry often outweighs our logic. We only choose logic if it *feels* better, and often times, as our emotions overpower our thinking, we choose something illogical. Take, for example, stories about women who give up their children or tank their finances and surrender their entire lives all for the love of a man. I have personally known women who have sacrificed their business and all their possessions, women who have turned custody of their children over to their former spouse, women who turned their backs on their family and friends as if hypnotized—all to be with the man they fell in love with. These women were people most of us would see as intelligent, self-confident, and successful. As we watch their lives deteriorate, we say, "What the hell are you doing?" And they give us what sound like reasonable explanations. They forsake all for the glory of love. They believe they will find happiness with the man they have chosen.

In her book *The Female Brain*, author Louann Brizendine goes into great depth when explaining the chemical make up of the mind of a woman. "Once a person is in love," she says, "the cautious, critical-thinking pathways in the brain shut down." Brizendine goes on to say "Hormones then activate the brain circuits for loving, nurturing behavior while switching off the caution and aversion circuits. In other words, if high levels of oxytocin and dopamine are circulating, your judgment is toast."[1] Oxytocin is a neurohormone that is triggered by

---

[1] Louann Brizendine, MD, *The Female Brain*, Broadway Books, 2006 p65,68

intimacy. Brizendine cites several studies which conclude that the female mind is wired to build relationships and sustain them.

How many of us have experienced infatuation that was not reciprocated? Or tried a little too hard to impress a crush? Have any of us not made a fool of ourselves at least once stemming from nerves of being smitten? I suggest that even the best of us are vulnerable to foolish decision when we have relinquished our hearts to love.

The other woman is not sub human. What she is and who she is isn't different than any other woman. She simply wants to be happy and hopes to someday share her life with a loving companion, someone who will brighten her day and on a bad one, offer support and comfort. She wants a man who will love her through life, and who she'll never have to fear will someday be absent. Most any woman needs to feel appreciated and unique. She needs to feel supported and to feel a deep, intimate emotional connection exclusively with her partner. She wants to feel feminine, sexy, and beautiful to a man she shares everything with. She needs a successful, satisfying, fulfilling love relationship.

As I listened to the women I interviewed, I noticed that most of them had been through some serious difficulties before getting involved in their affair relationship. I also found several studies supporting the theory that women who involve themselves in impossible relationships typically do so because they have difficulty with the intimacy that a real partner represents. These women live with the fantasy that they are able to control the circumstances in which they meet their lover, what will happen when they do and how connected she will allow the relationship to become despite the limitations to the relationship. Historically, many of the women drawn toward limited relationships have experienced abuse or trauma in their lives. If she believes that she is able to control the relationship, she is unable to see its shortcomings. It is intimacy she is avoiding, and a relationship with a married man helps avoid it well or at least demands for its compromise under what she feels is in her own control. She can cut her time with him if she subconsciously feels that he is getting too close, or convince herself that what she is experiencing is a greater closeness than ever before because subconsciously she is free to open herself without feeling trapped. His marriage gives her a way out.

Of the numerous women I listened to, Sasha was approaching the end of a long term relationship that had destroyed her feelings of self-worth when she became involved in an extra-marital affair. Amy, too, had ended a long term relationship filled with feelings of rejection and heartache, which was followed by a series of additional bad relationships. In both cases, these women lived with their companion for eight years and were victims of infidelity by men unwilling to commit to marriage. Lisa had recently divorced, as had Angela, Vickie, Crystal and Jennifer. They had been married to men they described as not being their "partners." They had not shared their lives with their husbands doing things together that were fun or connective. Their former husbands were rigid, controlling, possessive, not present, and either physically or verbally abusive. Trisha's husband died of a drug overdose long after he had abandoned her and their children for the party scene. Wendy's three-year-old daughter had been killed in an auto accident just two years before.

In fact, almost every "other" woman I interviewed had suffered a monumental change to her life, spanning from a frightening career change to traumatic loss, within a significant time of their becoming involved in their affair. I noticed that many of the women had also had difficult and extremely hurtful relationships in their past. Their childhoods had been filled with dysfunction, rejection, abandonment, or abuse. Their histories were a major factor in their romantic relationships.

I have been acquainted with numerous women who are needy and desperate for love and attention. I am sure they, too, are susceptible to the lure of an affair. However, the women that I interviewed were those who had single-handedly pulled themselves up from the ground and created astounding lives for themselves. They are strong, self-sufficient, intelligent, financially secure, and wise. They also have extroverted personalities in a crowd but are warm and comforting in intimate settings. These women do not display characteristics of low self-esteem that so many people assume other women have. They are women who are very well put together, women who seem to have no trouble putting their foot down about what they will and will not tolerate. They hold very high standards for themselves. I chose to interview these women because I think they offer the most insight as to how even the strongest of women can find themselves trapped in an affair.

Most of these single women who have affairs have had plenty of opportunities to date, but they hope to find someone unique who will become their best friend. They're looking for a man with whom they can live out their years, either starting a family or sharing the children they already have. Married women who have affairs with married men felt starved for attention, change, excitement, and zest, but still found themselves wanting the same things from their affair partner that non-married other women did—a sacred bond. Interestingly enough, married women who have affairs are more likely to leave their spouses for their affair partner than married men. Women love to sell themselves romance; that is, we love to be under the control of love, possessed—swept away. As if love is out of our hands.

I found several common denominators in women who became other women. Like most of us, they want to feel loved and appreciated. However, there seems to be a deep-seated fear in them, too: "I am not enough." This belief is not obvious. The woman has learned to hide it very well, perhaps even from herself. As we reviewed their history, these women revealed abandonment or a tremendous amount of rejection. It has been said that those who give the most are really those who need the most; appropriately, the other woman is almost always very selfless and giving. She is often a problem fixer, never believing that she might be part of the problem herself. She is an encourager and uplifts those around her, an ego feeder, if you will. Wanting to make others "feel good," she is most likely projecting her need to feel good. There is something in the other woman that needs to feel extra-special and adequate. The married man fulfills her need to be extraordinary and have a profound impact on someone's life—*she is his solution.* He makes her feel craved and needed, and this is powerfully tempting. It is as if he sees something other-worldly inside her, something she has perhaps not seen inside herself. Because she is his savior, her craving to feel special and exemplary is abundantly fulfilled for a time.

What is central in creating the affair is not necessarily sex but the attention that developed during his being primed to have an affair. He needs to feel affection from someone who craves him. He needs to feel the excitement of being sexually desired. He needs to feel appreciated and adored. His ego is in need of support and he wants to be lifted up. A steady flow of intriguing conversation exists between the married man and his mistress. She feels connected with someone who has genuine curiosity. She explores things with her lover. She has a companion who enjoys similar interests or wants to expose her to new things. There is a stream of honesty and openness, causing her to admire him. His interest is not confined to topics that will not upset her, as it often is with his wife; the other woman "understands" his needs and desires.

The other woman's needs are met by someone who has shown a strong attraction to her entire person, by someone who listens to her with a sincere interest. He enjoys her companionship. He fills her conversational needs and brings adventure and excitement into her life. Even though she is sharing him with his wife, the relationship feels much more exclusive than the beginning of dating a single man. She feels that his focus is entirely on her and that she is not competing with a handful of other prospects. Bear with me here. This may not make sense, but the married man is the man who is not afraid to commit to a woman, and this makes it easier to open to him emotionally.

Most people spend a minimum of eight hours per day at their place of employment. This leaves less than four or five hours to handle other daily tasks and juggle time with family. We return from work tired and lacking the desire to engage in energetic conversation. Our peak hours of awareness are during our typical work hours, and so it's at the office that we tend to develop relationships that impact our daily lives. Therefore, the other woman is, more often than not, a professional woman. She is often educated, independent, and financially secure, or at least capable of managing on her own. She does not represent a burden the man must take on and care for. As he sees her, this woman takes care of herself and does not make demands on him. She is not another obligation. She offers freedom, at least for a while. Their relationship is centered on what they share, not on domestic responsibilities. There are no to-do lists, no bills to pay, no children to manage, and no expectations to meet. Bitterness and selfishness have yet to arise. In fact, the man and the other woman idolize each other. They're probably experiencing the same euphoria that existed at the beginning of the married couple's relationship. If the wife has lost interest in sex, perhaps the added element of starvation makes the meal taste better. Butterflies and falling in love . . . live again.

Though the other woman never intends to hurt anyone, all the women I spoke to admitted that even though the beginning of their affair had nothing to do with challenging the man's wife, it was an ego boost when he was drawn away from the wife because of her. It was as if the other woman offered the man something exceptionally different from anything any other woman could offer. He had to have met many women during the course of his marriage. "Why me?" the other woman asks. "Why now? I must be REALLY great!"

Again, because a woman is hardwired to build connection, a man's openness to communication and connection with her sends the message to her that he approves of her—something she chemically needs to feel. It is in her nature to try everything to continue to elicit emotional expression from him. According to Brizendine, "It's the same kind of instinct that keeps a grown woman going after a narcissistic or otherwise emotionally unavailable man—'if I just do it right, he'll love me'." [2]

Loren, another woman I interviewed, explained her reasons for falling into the trap this way. "He boosted my self-esteem and feelings of self-worth at first. He was so attentive and it was all about me. I was flattered that he was willing to take such great risks to contact me when his wife was around. It made me believe that I was all of those things that he told me." But a little later, she added, "Anyone who allows herself to get into a relationship with someone who is not available is acting on something she is not receiving. Some need. She is using the affair to feed her own ego, though she may not realize it."

Felicia said, "He was spontaneous. I wanted excitement, and that's what Ron offered me. He always wanted to do things with me, and they were never half assed." He made her feel that she was his top priority. Eventually, however, as the man's vacillation between wife and mistress began, Felicia's belief that she was not enough was reinforced.

Most other women did not go into the relationship thinking about hurting someone else. The usual thought is *what she doesn't know won't hurt her*, and when the wife does learn of the affair, the typical other woman is quite uncomfortable with herself. Many times, the other woman chooses not to know anything about the wife, believing that this ignorance is in some way noble. I myself went through this one. I somehow thought that if I didn't know Beth's heart, it would make me less "bad." I think I considered her to be a character in a story, not a real person. I spent a great part of the beginning of our affair pretending Beth did not exist.

---

[2] Louann Brizendine, MD, *The Female Brain*, Broadway Books, 2006 p15

The other woman eventually perceives the wife as having the life she wants with no appreciation for it. Thus a challenge is created, and she wants to be the man's exclusive partner. She believes she is more capable than his wife of cherishing him. But every time the man goes home to his wife, the other woman loses this challenge. She has to keep fighting to win him back.

"The female brain has a far more negative alert reaction to relationship conflict and rejection then does the male brain," Brizendine writes. "In women, conflict is more likely to set in motion a cascade of negative chemical reactions, creating feelings of stress, upset, and fear. Just the thought that there might be a conflict will be read by the female brain as threatening the relationship, and bring with it the real concern that the next conversation she has with her friend will be their last. When a relationship is threatened or lost, the bottom drops out of the level of some of the female brains neurochemicals—such as serotonin, dopamine and oxytocin (the bonding hormone)—and the stress hormone cortisol takes over."[3]

The women I spoke to all made comments similar to Rebecca, "You are fooling yourself if you think you are special and different. He may say all the right stuff, but you are not special to him in the right way. Special is when it's real." When a woman thinks of her perfect mate, never do the words married man enter the equation. When asked to describe their ideal partners, all the other women I interviewed used these words (though not necessarily in this order): Communicative. Compassionate. Giving. Expressive. Honorable. Respectful. Supportive. They described their ideal partner as one who would cherish their companionship as their true best friend. And, without fail, the number one quality that fell from every lip was TRUSTWORTHY. It seems the other woman is just a woman, after all.

---

[3]   Louann Brizendine, MD, *The Female Brain*, Broadway Books, 2006 p40

Chapter 14

The Behavior of a Cheater

Much of what I have to say here is pretty obvious, but it's amazing how not obvious something suddenly becomes when we are looking for signs that reinforce what we want to believe, for example, that the person we love has not betrayed us.

A man who is having an affair usually becomes more concerned with his appearance. He begins to purchase new clothing, better cologne, and the latest, trendiest things. This is a red flag, especially if in the past he didn't care how he looked or what he wore that no one else could see and now he suddenly does.

A man who is having an affair finds a sudden new found fascination with diet and fitness. He may be realizing that he is not as young as he used to be. He may be focusing on his health for the sake of health, but fitness also is something a man having an affair usually starts paying more attention to.

A good dose of mid-life crisis can lead a man to do some soul searching. He may explore subjects that were once foreign to him. But his interest in new things may also be a sign that he is connecting with someone else. For example, my ex-fiancé was always a lover of The Top 40s pop music, but when Ann came along, he suddenly developed a taste for country music.

A demanding job or the feeling of being overwhelmed and pulled in many directions can often make a man turn his cell phone ring tone off or turn on its vibrate feature when he comes home. But he may also be inspired by his fear that his mistress might call at a very inconvenient time. When he leaves his cell phone in inconspicuous places or suddenly begins to forget the phone when he's with his wife, chances are he doesn't want to get calls from someone she won't approve of.

It's neither abnormal nor unhealthy when he wants to spice up the sex life. When he's suddenly pulling new moves, however, you might want to wonder where, or from whom, he learned them.

The big tell-all is when all of the above are happening right alongside other changes in a husband's behavior. His spending habits change. His coworkers and friends seem awkward or uncomfortable in his wife's presence. He seems less comfortable around his wife. He shows signs of stress or agitation or seems withdrawn or touchy.

Another clue may be when his spouse answers the phone, the caller hangs up, and the call is usually coming from a blocked line. She finds erased caller IDs on their home phone or his cell phone. He speaks in whispers when he's on the phone and suddenly hangs up when she enters the room. He seems to always have a mysterious errand to run, and it takes him four times longer to finish than it should. He works late more often or leaves to work earlier than he used to. He suddenly becomes very selfish in his requirement for "guy time" or hobbies that do not involve his spouse. He picks ridiculous fights over nothing and then storms out of the house for hours afterwards. He says he is unhappy in the marriage, but he cannot specify exactly why and he's reluctant to work through the issues. He is disconnected.

Men who are insecure, controlling, and accusatory often are having a reaction to stress caused by their own behavior. If you are dealing with constant jealousy and accusations and being snooped on, when you otherwise see no reason for him to behave that way, toss your feelings of flattery away. He's probably projecting his own dishonest behavior on you.

Insecure men respond to feelings of rejection by giving back rejection, and they are quick to act on these feelings. So if, say, his wife is behaving in ways that allow him to misinterpret the behavior as rejection, then as he feels rejected, he may move to get back at her, even if she is innocent of any wrong doing. Men with a low self esteem look for women to build them back up. His insecurities will probably drive him to another woman, the "back up" he turns to when his wife refuses him, the one who massages his ego and is open to his advances. She doesn't see his character flaws as his wife does; she hasn't had to deal with him long enough.

Men who are prone to affairs are often those who rise quickly to success. Women want someone to take care of them, so rising stars start to receive a lot of attention. While they are big headed and feeling magnanimous, their egos are already out of control, they think they *can* have it all and *should*. When his wife is complaining about the things he's doing that are wrong, he's not listening. It seems to him that the rest of the world thinks he is awesome. That means the problem is his wife. This belief will make another woman look spectacular, no matter if her true attraction is to the powerful person he appears to be. I call this the Closet Full of Shoes effect. Successful men are most attractive to single women, especially women who desire prestige and want their friends to envy them, something all too common in today's consumption driven society. Men embrace their new found desirability instead of seeing that they are really only as good as the things they can buy her and the social status they offer. If these men formerly doubted their worth and are surprised by their growth, they are stuck on the praise they receive from outside sources and lean on this praise to validate their self worth. They themselves are confused, however, because they do not trust themselves; in other words, they are hiding their insecurity and continue to seek out those who will reaffirm their entitlement and worth. They forget that their wives have stuck by them through rich and poor. They're on a giddy ego trip, lapping up the attention they get from other women. They think it's themselves, not the success and power they represent. Yes, and then, (simply because they have the means to buy the latest Prada,) these pea-brained men show how infantile they are by destroying a family that has stood by their side in sickness and in health.

Evolutionary psychologist David Buss has traveled the world studying over thirty seven cultures and in every one of them, women are more interested in a man's social status and resources than how he looks. It is a primitive truth that these are the qualities we unconsciously search for in a long-term mate.

One woman who confided in me, Kathy, told me about how her husband, Joe, suddenly shot up the corporate ladder. He made a name for himself and basked in the limelight, which made him less interested in the mundane issues at home. Home became insignificant. His behavior toward his wife showed his belief that he was superior and that she was a mere housewife who had nothing to do all day. The "nothing to do" consisted, of course, of caring for his five children, ranging from infancy to high school. Kathy's need for his participation in their family activities made him feel that she was whining about things that he didn't have time for. He preferred to spend his time on meeting all of his corporate responsibilities and entertaining clients. When he did have the time for Kathy, he expected her to take what he could give and be grateful. One evening he didn't show up to their daughter's dance recital. She phoned him repeatedly and received no answer. Upon arriving home, it was evident that he had not come home after work. Concerned, she drove to every location she could imagine him being. Exhausted from frantic searching and worry, she went home. He arrived late that evening with an arrogant attitude. He excused his disappearance as punishment for her failure to be available to him earlier in the week. She was sad and defensive. She later discovered that he had been off with another woman.

Mark also climbed the success ladder fast. Ego-driven, he soon began to see himself more important than his wife, Jenny. He had an affair with a woman who pampered him and stroked his ego. It made him feel powerful to be in a position to juggle women who would fight over him. Movies present powerful men as always having a family in one home and a mistress in the swank apartment. I think many boys who suddenly find themselves in a position of power have a little of this fantasy in them.

Also prone to having affairs are the party boys who think they're still living in the college dorm or frat house. They live for time with the guys and never want to drag their wives along. These guys have an insatiable need to have fun. This includes the quest to conquer women.

It's pretty normal for men to want a little time with the guys, but I am talking about the guys who put themselves in risky circumstances night after night. These men are fair game for the women who bump into them. They're vulnerable to a constant flirtation that just might go too far on a night the husband is not feeling so happily married.

A guy who is hungry for adventure, a thrill seeker, will cheat for the thrill of the chase. A man who was very sexually active before he married is also likely to cheat. Don't expect a leopard to change his spots. If he has a lot of female friends, these friendships are a common starting point to having an affair. If he has cheated in the past or in past relationships, you know the saying: once a cheater always a cheater. And don't underestimate the power of peer pressure. If he has friends who cheat, he likely will too. Men who travel frequently are left to roam freely and often do. I have a saying I made up when I was younger; absence makes the heart grow fonder, but it makes the weak ones wander. Men who are in an unhappy home feel emotionally starved for something else. Guys with a fear of intimacy seek "fun love" where they are not forced to connect so deeply.

For much of my adult life, I have been intrigued by the science of people. This interest has lead me to explore topics like the chemistry of the brain, human movement, and the overall art of reading people used in professions ranging from sales to jury selecting. I have become quite talented at unmasking liars.

Unfortunately, no matter how confident I have become in my skills, throw emotional attachment, adrenalin, anxiety, and the want to be wrong about my suspicions into the mix, and all of the energy I have put into avoiding deceit is to no avail.

As women, we have become quite skilled in filling our heads with self doubt so that we can create a world we want to believe in, but sometimes our self deception leads to psychological injury. How many times have you listened to someone insist they were telling the truth, but somewhere in the back of your mind, you knew they were trying to deceive you? When the lie is discovered, you find yourself saying "I knew it all along."

Because I have had the misfortune of telling myself "I knew it all along" I got pretty tired of being an idiot and putting my intelligence on the backburner. I started to pay more attention to my *want* vs. *real* and began to not accept self deception but instead worked my way through confusion by digging for the truth. Once I became conscious of what I *wanted the truth to be* and recognized that I am capable of self deception easily, it became much easier for me to step outside of myself a little bit and recognize my intuition. I started to spot the lies.

One evening Shane and I agreed to sit down and really work through some of the issues that were appearing in our relationship. I wanted to know what was really going on with him. I had a constant sense of insecurity, the feeling that I was being duped. Something wasn't right. I couldn't understand why he was always acting irritated. We usually spoke to each other many times throughout the day but suddenly I was the only one who was calling to check in and see how his day was going. I would call in high spirits and greet him with a cheerful "Hi Honey." I noticed that his mood soured immediately. On the other end of the line, hatred was spewing about every person in his office and every petty difficulty he faced. The conversations were short and when he spoke about what he had been doing for much of the morning his voice would trail off omitting words that got to the point. He would abruptly stop with no end to his point or divert the conversation. This was all a change in protocol and also traits I learned to watch for. I also noticed that several times when we spoke he would mention a person randomly that had no part in our conversation and he seemed to have his mind engaged in another direction.

That night as we sat on his couch while I listened to him convince me that he was just really stressed about things going on at work, his home phone rang. I saw panic cross his face. His shoulders drew in and his eyes focused on the phone while I watched the up and down movement of his chest indicating his heart rate had increased. When the answering machine kicked on, he made a rash decision and flew up to answer the phone so that the caller's voice and intentions were not broadcasted. The moment he answered, I saw relief. His body began to relax and color returned to his face. But he walked into a different room to speak to his caller. I could still hear his voice but I could not see his face any longer. I heard discomfort in his voice and he was speaking to his caller with short abrupt answers. "No." "Ya." "Can I call you back later?" When he hung up, he went to use the restroom. According to interrogator Gregory Hartley, author of *How To Spot a Liar*, when someone has successfully lied his rush of relief will cause his system to regain function and as his blood returns his bladder also becomes filled. While he was in the bathroom, I looked at his caller ID. It was a male friend of his that I didn't get along with much. My mind began to rationalize his reaction.

He returned to the couch and we began our conversation again. "Who called?" I asked him. "Oh, it was Chris." He and Chris had been friends since childhood but had a disagreement many months prior and hadn't been speaking to each other. "I didn't realize that you two had patched things up, what's going on?" I inquired. "Nothing, he just wanted to know if I went out this weekend," and then began to trail his sentence again. This seemed like an odd line of questioning from Chris since Shane was much of a home body. But as I started to vocally quiz and rationalize the question Chris had asked him, I watched his shoulders drop and his eyes fall down to the left—usually an indication of calculated thought. He was guilty of something, I just wasn't sure what yet.

Things continued on with his disconnected behavior but when I would ask about it, this would only cause his irritation to be increased and his anger at me for making him develop a "guilt complex" when he shouldn't have one. He didn't do anything wrong he would say, overly defensive. So in effort to keep things light and not create more issues, I stuffed my feelings of something being *off*. It wasn't just his disconnected emotions that made me uneasy. He had been complaining about his lower back hurting him and kept asking me to apply ointment. After I had finished, we snuggled up to watch T.V and he placed an ice pack between his legs—right on his sack. I hadn't stayed with him for a few days. We had just gotten through the holidays and I had been spending time with my family. He claimed that he must have pulled a few muscles by twisting wrong during a golf swing. That night I spent the evening at his house and when I went to use the bathroom to wash my make up off for the evening, I noticed a blue brush sitting on the vanity matted with a tremendous amount of blond hair. I'm a brunette but his mother has short blond hair and had recently visited a month before—could this be her brush? I thought to ask him who the brush belonged to but stopped myself because I knew that regardless of who the brush belonged to, his answer would be "it's my moms" and my asking would only cause an argument.

I used the restroom one more time before we climbed into bed and noticed that the brush was still there but a wash cloth had been placed over the top of it. After we turned out the lights he got up to use the bathroom and I watched him in the dark as he walked out of the bathroom and went upstairs for a minute. The next morning, the brush was gone. "Where is that blue brush that was sitting in here?" I asked him and he became instantly angry "What brush? I don't have a brush." But I was adamant that I had seen the brush the night before sitting on the counter. His irritation persisted until I dropped the matter. Had I dreamed it? I kept asking myself. The matter would not rest with me and I became depressed throughout much of the day.

That night as we were getting ready for dinner he said sweetly (he was suddenly and abnormally catering to my emotions) "What's wrong honey? You don't have that lovey look in your eyes, you have that questioning look." I decided that honesty was best and told him that I could not get the matter of the brush out of my mind. His reaction was anger and defensiveness. If I couldn't trust him, then how could we be together, he wanted to know, as tears welled in his eyes. I felt guilty for being suspicious and causing a problem when we were set to have a good evening. If he had been cheating, he wouldn't have been that stupid he claimed, and therefore, it was all me—more of my "crazy thinking." I apologized and groveled for hinting at an accusation.

As much as I wanted to believe him, I knew that I had not lost my mind—but I *was* losing it while I continued to try and convince myself that I had dreamed up the blue brush. I had to get to the bottom of this matter; I HAD to find that brush or figure out where it came from. I had to prove to myself that the brush existed because convincing myself that it did not was convincing me that I was going insane. A clue to the matter was that he did not harass me (as would have been in character) about the accusation. The matter was dropped all together and not discussed. This set me on an investigative mission. I searched every part of his house when I had the opportunity, even emptying out his garbage. He had been smarter than that. I think he knew that I was unsettled and probably tossed the brush out of his car window on his way to work.

Not finding the brush was not good enough. I began to check his voicemail regularly for about a week until a woman left him a very strange sounding message. She was "checking in on him" and asking him to "don't be a stranger." I jotted the number down that she called from but dismissed any importance to the call and continued to listen to the voicemail system for a few more days. Another message arrived from the same girl, "Hi this is (pause) Paula. No, I'm not a no show, I was with (she stutters) *other friends.*" I went back to my notes where I had written her number down and Googled it—her very descriptive call girl service ads appeared on my computer screen. To be certain there was no mistake, I forced my brother to call her and plan a "hook up" which she agreed to for $300 per hour. My ex-boyfriend still denies the brush. And of the call girl—he has "many questionable characters as friends." I forwarded her advertisements to his email but he had no interest in looking at them. I speculate that was because he was fully aware of what they had to say.

I'm a runner when faced with emotional duress . . . this was an emotional breakdown that I did not have a mental mailbox to draw from in order to deal with this experience. Nothing in my past had taught me how to handle this kind of discovery. This wasn't just cheating, this was a health risk! A health risk, mind you, that I had nurtured his injuries from! I had to run away. The thoughts I had been dwelling on with regard to what I'd NOW like to do with that ice pack and sports crème, and a gas can, and a book of matches . . . . anyway, leaving town was probably the right thing for both of us—and his house.

I booked a flight to Hawaii by myself and told my friends I was going to "Ohm on a rock." While I was away, I received countless phone calls and text messages from Shane saying that I always point the finger and that I had no "proof" and he even went as far as to have the call girl call me. She did him in more than helped him. She acknowledged that she was in the entertainment business but "I'm not a prostitute." (That's not what one of her customers said online when he rated her services and told descriptive detail about the way she likes her sex) She claimed to be a long lost friend of Shane's through other friends of his that he'd never spoke of before. As for the advertisements and my brother's phone call—she couldn't explain these. Shane had just purchased a new home and she told me that she had never been *up* to his house before. When I asked her how she knew he lived *up* on the hillside, she danced. All the while Shane begged for "our love" and was relentless in trying to save our relationship despite *my* serious trust issues.

In the spirit of emotional attachment and for the sake of thwarting psychological trauma, if I were still so capable of selling myself what I wanted to believe—that he was not bedding hookers and that the man I had given four years of my life to would never be capable of such despicable betrayal—would I have been convinced after all of his effort to make me believe him that I had really gone off the deep end? Probably.

If I ever had a moment's doubt about this type of man's ability to change, there is always something that will solidify my belief that they cannot.

So, there I am, minding my own business, filling myself up with a third cup of fuel at Starbucks and a muffin to get me through the remainder of the day. As I race back to my car, sipping my pumpkin spice latté and digging into the bag of broken bread, I catch a familiar sight out of the corner of my eye. Oh shit, I think, and I slam the door and put my car in reverse. Before I can back up, Blake is rapping at my passenger window. He opens the door, climbs in, and decides that his first words to me should be, "Man, you look really tired and worn out." (I had been up for twenty-four hours writing this manuscript.) Before I can give a witty reply, I see he's wearing a new wedding ring. "Huh, did you guys renew your vows or something?" I ask him. "That's a new wedding ring I see." I said nonchalantly chewing my muffin. I'll be damned if the man does not look me square in the eye and say, "No, it's not. This is the same ring I've always had. Who cares, anyway? My marriage is the same it's always been."

Most people would say I'm fairly perspicacious. But this did not require a keen eye. Blake's wedding ring before was a simple gold band that was worn and tarnished. The ring that sat on his finger that day was brushed and etched silver.

My sister met a guy who fell in love with her at first sight. She is divorced with two small (and very perfect) boys. Despite her cautionary feelings, he convinced her to move in with him just shy of a year later and insisted that the boys call him Daddy. He integrated himself into our family well and seemed to connect with my other brother in law like he was his new best friend. He and my sister did everything together; she couldn't even attend a baby shower without him wanting to be with her. Pretty nifty guy, huh? A man who actually WANTS to attend a baby shower—whoda thunk? He bought a home for them to renovate and she spent a substantial amount of time pouring herself into designing the house. He also had convinced her to quit her job so that she could be home with her children and tried to talk her into becoming pregnant right away. She decided (thankfully) that after marriage, she would plan to have another baby. She fell head over heels for the man and made him a top priority. It was beautiful to see my sister so happy. Every time we went shopping, her thoughts were on him, buying him little thoughtful gifts rather than a new coat for herself, it was almost sickening how mushy they were about each other.

Then suddenly he started to act strange. He seemed to be sleeping a lot and acting like "a dick" all of the time. One morning, they were in the shower together and she mentioned to him that she noticed it had been a while since they had "done it." He became angry at her telling her that he was in a stand off, because he had already told her he was frustrated that it was he who initiated sex and not her most of the time. She thought it was a silly little tiff and after they got out of the shower, he took the boys outside to play waving at her from the window, throwing snowballs and laughing with much silliness.

When he and the boys came inside, he sat on the couch appearing to be sad while she got the kids prepared to leave to a super bowel party they were all supposed to be at that afternoon. "Are you going to get ready?" she asked him. He responded with not only was he not going to attend, but that she needed to pack her things and move out. She thought that he was joking at first but quickly realized he was speaking to her very matter-of-factly.

He left the house until she moved and refused her phone calls. She was left high and dry with no home for her children, no money in her wallet, and a broken heart. She drove herself insane questioning everything that she could have possibly done wrong. She was angry at herself for wrecking the life that she had grown to love. She was left with not having any answers—for awhile.

I thought it was pretty easy to figure out what happened, as one of my male friends once said to me "you don't shit the bed overnight for nothing." But I couldn't hurt her by suggesting what I believed. Eventually, one of his friends felt for her devastated emotions and confessed the truth to her. Jacob had found another woman around the time my sister was noticing his "dick" behavior.

Life offers various stresses and men can certainly be "dicks" from time to time. But in my experience, nine times out of ten, if erratic attitude is present along with strange unexplainable behavior—an affair is, at the very least, in the works. "You have a reason to be curious, and even suspicious, if your spouse deviates from a long standing routine for no apparent reason," write authors Gregory Hartley and Maryann Karinch in their book *How to Spot a Liar*. [4]

Like me, if you suspect something is wrong in your relationship, you are probably right. If you feel that you are being betrayed or deceived and you want the truth, stop asking the liar for answers.

When I was in my early to mid-twenties, I was engaged to a man named Brock, whom I loved very much. He was a raised right family guy from the Midwest who often and strongly expressed his feelings about fidelity. But something just didn't feel right. If I went by what he said, he seemed like the perfect man, but what wasn't right about him? I began to notice that when I came into the room while he was on the phone, his tone would change. I finally got wise. I planted a Dictaphone under the couch and took the dog for a walk. I later listened to the recording and heard a few things that sounded suspicious. I began questioning him and, like a fool, showed my hand by revealing the tape. (Bad move,

---

[4] Gregory Hartley and Maryann Karinch, How to Spot a Liar, Why people don't tell the truth and how you can catch them, Career Press, 2005 p158

this only forced me to have to become more crafty.) When I found a cell phone in his car and told him that someone had left it, he quickly claimed that it belonged to a friend and bolted off with it. I could see the panic in his eyes. He became increasingly controlling of me and suspicious of what I was doing in my free time. Given that nothing had changed with me, this seemed odd. As I continued to question and accuse him, our relationship quickly turned sour, and eventually he moved out. He said I was losing my mind. He blamed me for the end of our relationship.

I took a vacation alone to unwind. Brock promised that on my return we would start fresh. I asked a friend to check the parking lot of his apartment from time to time while I was gone. She did. She told me about a car that was often parked next to his space. I asked her to take down the plates, and when I returned I went to the DMV to find out who owned the car. The woman at the counter informed me, however, that she could not disclose the owner of the vehicle because the driver had placed a block on the plate. Nearing absolute frustration (I thought he'd caught on to my creative spying), I began to cry. The DMV clerk asked me if the person had hit my car or something, and I blurted out, "Yes!" In her sympathy, she quickly scribbled the woman's name and address on a sticky note and passed it to me. Gold! I even saved the $10 payment required for the report. I found the woman's phone number in the phone book and called her. A man answered. I asked if Becky was there, and he replied no. "Oh," I said, "is she with Brock?" He stuttered, "Who is this?" I hung up.

After a moment's thought, I called back and asked the man if he was her husband. He said yes. I told him why I was calling. He said he, too, had been suspicious of his wife's behavior of late. I told him that I believed that she was with my fiancé right then. He said she had told him she was going to a soccer game. (There was a soccer field near Brock's apartment.) "She isn't at a soccer game," I said, and I gave him Brock's address. Not thinking twice, I sped toward Brock's building to catch the fireworks. I arrived in time to see a rather small man knocking on Brock's door. (Oops—Brock was tall and well built and had a wee bit of a temper. I had not thought of this potential outcome.) When Brock opened the door, I heard the man swearing that he could hear his wife's voice inside. Brock angrily swung the door wide open and asked, "Is this your wife?" The woman with Brock wasn't the man's wife. She was screwing around with the man who lived above Brock. But there was a girl there, and that was the end of that. For both relationships, I suspect.

When you live with a man, it would seem that finding things would be fairly simple. It is when you are not living together that discovering things becomes more complicated. Women snoop. It's a fact that I (and most of my honest girlfriends) admit freely. If you don't snoop, you have been conditioned. However, a man can learn to be careful to never allow the opportunity for snooping. For example, Shane never left me alone in his office or at home much, and he always kept his cell phone close to his body on vibrate or silent. Unfortunately for him, I learned the password to his voicemail. If a man seems to be guarding everything in his life, then he probably has something to hide. It's that simple. I never felt suspicious or needed to snoop on a man when his body language was honest and he showed no signs of hiding important things from me.

If you really want to know if something is going on, it's easy to get the evidence. But don't bother looking if you are going to talk yourself out of believing what you find in front of your face. You'll only drive yourself insane. Beth stumbled across Blake's online phone bill and was able to see not only who and when he was calling, but from what town inside of the state or elsewhere. My number had to be on that bill two hundred times with calls of long duration. When she confronted him, he just started calling my office's main line and asking them to transfer his call to wherever I was. He also started calling from other business phones. Finally, we just broke down and got him his own phone so I could reach him whenever I wanted to. Beth was later informed of our "love line." She also became aware of our communication via his private Hotmail account, and she continued to check his cell phone and Yahoo! account for evidence. When she found nothing in the places she knew she wouldn't, she convinced herself that the affair had ended. But nothing had changed. We continued to spend nights together regularly at his lake home, but never once did she show up to find out why he wouldn't answer her calls. The lesson here? If you really don't want to know, don't look.

I am *not* advocating snooping through a good guy's stuff. That's mistrustful behavior where it is not warranted. It's a huge waste of valuable energy and the difference between being smart or crazy.

Everyone deserves to have their privacy, but when something's going on and you know it, the rules change. When he's feeding you bald-faced lies that affect your life in an extreme way, sometimes the only way to find out what's going on is by digging. Call me nuts! You may be appalled at my admitting to snooping, but I will say this: *Every time I've felt the overwhelming need to get to the bottom of things, I was right*. Most of us can spot a cheat a mile away. It's when he's so close that he's in our bed that we miss it.

Chapter 15

The Convincing Stage

In the beginning, the relationship between the married man and the other woman is most commonly admiration or an innocent, light flirtation. If they are coworkers, a friendship develops in the pressure-free atmosphere of fun or teamwork. Soon he discloses his marriage problems, and voices his complaints and weaknesses. His starvation for emotional and physical contact is exposed as he vents. He needs someone to confide in. Once he realizes his confidant has admiration for him or he feels a connection with her, things begin to develop quickly and seemingly out of either of their control. The other woman starts to feel the sensations of a schoolgirl crush. His wife is the weight. The other woman is the hot air balloon. It was e-mails like the following that I received from Blake as he and I began.

I feel absolutely comfortable with our relationship. I think that it is wonderful and I want you to feel comfortable with it too. I trust you 100% and want you to expect the same from me. I want to spend as much time with you as possible. I enjoy every moment with you and I adore your children. I just want you to know that I support you. I am dedicated to you. You obviously don't know how into you I am. I cherish our relationship and would not jeopardize it for anything. I want us to develop some business together. I know we could and it would be fun. I want you to make the choice on what you want to do. If you and I team up, we would do well. I want what is best for you and your girls. That is your decision. You should always be all that you can be. I have been most impressed with all that you have been.

According to an article written by Stephany Alexander (see www.womensavers.com), the reasons men cheat are:

Because he had the option. Citing the old saying "men are only as faithful as their options."

It boosts his ego. There is nothing like the thrill of the chase for men on the hunt. When they are rewarded for their efforts, their ego swells even larger.

He and his wife have grown apart. Maybe they do not have the connection or as much in common as he thought.

He and his wife argue a lot. He wants to get away from someone who is overly critical or argumentative.

He's falling out of love. Sometimes men become so comfortable in a relationship they don't know how to get out.

The sex life between husband and wife sucks. He has an uninterested partner or isn't getting enough to fulfill him.

To get revenge. If he feels he has been cheated, he uses the same to get back.

A relationship with a new woman is different and exciting.

To see if they can get away with it. "What she doesn't know won't hurt her."

Because his wife has allowed it in the past. If she has forgiven a cheating man a couple of times, they are more than likely to cheat again because they know if they plead enough she will forgive him.

We other women are usually only given four of these reasons. The man tells us that a connection no longer exists between him and his wife. Something is missing in their marriage. She is either too busy for him, having interests that seem selfish and exclude him, or she never wants to participate in anything with him, having no energy or drive to do things he is interested in. She is too wrapped up in their children, her career, her hobbies, her friends, her family to give him the attention he feels he needs. So he feels emotionally neglected and rejected. He feels that his needs are not worth her effort. He has been starved for time that involves just the two of them in an atmosphere of lighthearted fun, but he has given up by now because he has been neglected for such a long time. He is over it, he says, and is just existing.

When I interviewed Julie, I learned that Jim complained to her about his wife, saying she kept a dirty home, never made dinner, and was always off socializing. He suggested that his wife was having an affair and described her as a selfish person. Julie told me that he often appeared dejected when speaking of his home life and said he had awakened from the dead when he met her. To her, he looked like a lonely man on his way to divorce court. One day she asked him if he would ever leave his wife. He said no. They had young children, and his finances would be affected. But then Jim kept recanting by thinking out loud, speaking about how he would divide assets. One day he asked Julie how she felt about step-parenting. He talked about places he hoped they would travel to with his children. He told her how she was like his mother, suggesting how well they would get along, and he also compared notes on each others taste in decorating, creating the image in her mind of them having a home together.

He tells you that his wife constantly nags at him, which makes him hypercritical of her and of the smallest things in their marriage. He describes their home life as "miserable" and filled with constant bickering that drags him down. Or their marriage has fallen away to nothing; he and his wife are roommates or strangers with nothing to share. He makes her sound completely petty like, a whining bitch or a lazy bore with no interest in her husband. Although he "loves her"—after all, they have spent so many years together, have history together, and (of course) there are the children—he is no longer "in love with her." But he doesn't know how to leave. There are so many complications involved, so many fears (and so many excuses), but in the deepest parts of his heart, he seems to want to free himself from the trap of his marriage. He just doesn't know how.

When I interviewed Brandy, she told me that Jason shared much of the dissatisfaction in his marriage with her, but also said that he had no intention of leaving his wife. Brandy thought that, had she met him at a different time when he was available, they would have really had something. He wanted to be able to play the field and have a good time without losing the security he found in his wife. He told Brandy that he had deep feelings for her and that she was special to his heart. He wanted them to commit to meet someplace on the globe every year for the rest of their lives to ensure they always maintained their romantic love for one another. At the same time, however, he would then mention the idea of permanently relocating to her area and always financially supporting his wife to make up for the years she had given him while he shared the rest of his life with Brandy.

Last but not least, the wife doesn't like to have sex. Many men claim that they sleep in separate rooms or long ago got tired of her rejecting his advances. He's tired of begging for it. She acts like love making is a chore, and when he does get that blue moon piece, it's as if she wants to hurry up and get it over with. She doesn't seem "into it," he says; "there's no passion." Therefore he has no physical attraction to her anymore, either, because the fun of doing it with her has long since ended. In *The Female Brain*, Brizendine says, "If she doesn't want to have sex, it can signal a waning of attraction or perhaps another man. In other words, the fading of love." Brizendine explains, "It's just like what happens with a woman and verbal communication. If her partner stops talking to her or responding emotionally, she thinks that he disapproves of her, that she's done something wrong, or that he doesn't love her anymore." [5]

Jennifer's married man told her that his wife didn't want to have sex. He told her that he was going to leave his wife, but wanted to keep their relationship a secret until then because he didn't want it "to be about another woman." He asked her to be patient while he determined the "right way to leave" and helped his wife accept that their marriage was in shambles.

I once had a young neighbor who visited me one Sunday after she returned home from church. She was really frustrated. Knowing of my fascination with the study of religion, she wanted to know if there was a place in the Bible that said that she HAD to have sex with her husband. (There is.) "He bugs me and bugs me," she complained, "and I don't like to! Sometimes I just go ahead so he'll leave me alone for a little while. I just roll over and lay there until he's done." She had better keep his ass glued to the pew, I thought. But this is the story I always hear in my mind when I listen to men complaining about their wives not wanting to have sex with them.

> Let the husband render to his wife the affection due to her, and likewise also the wife to her husband. The wife does not have authority over her own body, but the husband does. And likewise the husband does not have authority over his own body, but the wife does. Do not deprive one another except with consent for a time, that you may give yourselves to fasting and prayer and come together again so that Satan does not tempt you because of your lack of self control.
>
> ~ 1 Corinthians 7:3-5

---

[5]   Louann Brizendine, MD, *The Female Brain*, Broadway Books, p92,93

Sometimes the wife is a woman he married in his youth. He grew, he tells us; he matured and came to be in touch with who he really is, whereas she did not develop alongside him. They are no longer compatible. She is no longer his equal. They have different needs, wants, and desires. She is no longer capable of stimulating him emotionally, physically, or intellectually. But, he asks plaintively, how can he just walk away from a girl he shares so much history with? One who depends on him? What would all their friends say? How would their families react? They would not understand, he continues, because they do not know what it is like to live in his home. They would think that he was scum. And what about the kids? He would ruin them, destroy their innocence, disrupt their lives completely.

Todd did not even mention his marriage to Christine. After he had courted her for several months, she woke the morning after their first night together alone in his house. He had left her to sleep in and jaunted off to work. As she pulled back the sheets and sat up and rubbed her eyes, she found herself staring right smack at his wedding portrait. In dismay, she phoned him for an explanation, but before she could get dressed and out the front door, he had arrived back at the house that belonged to him and his wife. He swore that he did not love his wife he only stayed because of the children and (you'll never guess) the money. He had gotten so caught up in Christine as their friendship and attraction was developing that by the time he had to tell her, he was afraid he should have done it long before and didn't know how to say it now. He gave a passionate story about falling in love with her and so, Christine reluctantly continued to see him for over a year. When she learned that Todd's wife was expecting another child, he excused this as a "devious ploy" by his "sly spouse," to whom he had said he wanted a divorce. Apparently the wife was so clever she was able to narrow down the exact moment of fertility, successfully seduce him, and thus trick him into another reason for staying. For the sake of millions of women who spend thousands of dollars at fertility clinics, I hope she shares her secret!

Because he is now mature enough to decide what really suits him, this poor man has *finally* found his dream woman, the other woman who meets his every desire. But he is trapped. Because he is such a kind and loving man, he is tormented by the hurt he would inflict on everyone connected to his marriage, especially his wife, whom he will always love in some way. But at the same time, he cannot stand a moment away from his lover! Whatever will he do? Oh, the grief, the torture of having so many complications in one life and everything he ever dreamed of in the other life. The other woman feels overcome with understanding. She pets and comforts this wounded puppy. It hurts her to see him suffer like this, and soon she is bound to him by her sympathy.

One the other hand, maybe he claims the wife is a selfish spoiled bitch who has no appreciation for her husband, who has given and given and treated her superbly. He has offered her the good life, but that good life is in ruins because she abuses him in every way with her sense of entitlement. She is such a hateful woman, so spiteful and mean, that if he leaves her, she will take his children from him or, worse, make them hate him. She is likewise sure to relieve him of any property, retirement account, or other assets they have accumulated together. And if that's not enough, she will make everyone he cares for, friends and family alike, despise him. He will have nothing.

Another story a man will tell is that he was "trapped" into marrying her. She got pregnant, or they dated for so long she blackmailed him while he was still unsure of his feelings for her, or he was pressured to marry her by family or friends, who thought she was the right one for him. The world ganged up on him and made him doubt to his reasons for not committing to her. He thought he had to marry her.

What the man tells us is usually some variation of the above, or all of it. Either way, his life is just a mess that he is in the process of resolving . . . or he seems to be willing and wanting to resolve everything. What he really is, is (we believe) open to finding and experiencing *real love*. In fact, he's longing for it! When we other women meet this married man, it's like meeting a man who has been lost in the woods for days without food or water. He had been wandering through the wilderness, almost passively accepting his fate, until he stumbles onto a picnic table piled high with his favorite dish. Wow, this guy really likes the macaroni salad!

To summarize, we are led to believe that the wife is either a raving, controlling bitch or a weak, wimpy, needy woman who wouldn't be able to handle life without him. He is imprisoned by either her hostility or her dependence. If he left her, she would either destroy him at the very heart of his being and do everything possible to make his life a living hell thereafter, or she is so delicate that the mere act of putting gas in her car without his aid is a task too overwhelming, and so if he left her, he would be leaving her for dead. In either situation, we are sad to see the cross he bares.

What he tells us about the relationship he has with his wife not only builds up our belief that we are not *really* sharing him with his wife but also creates the vision that our beloved is the true victim. What he tells us about his awful marriage makes us feel sorry for him. We yearn to comfort him. What he tells us about his feelings for us makes us believe we should endure every difficulty to come because he promises a better tomorrow. Men know how to feed women emotionally, and they do so with great skill in order to get what they need.

Blake flew me to Europe within two months of the beginning of our affair. Give a girl a break if she deduced that his marriage was dead! What woman do you know who would think nothing of her husband leaving for Rome for three weeks? By himself? Obviously, her husband lacked importance and wasn't an overall big factor in her life. This was my logic. Every other woman I interviewed had her own justification for "logically" seeing the marriage of her lover as "dead." I could not argue with their reasoning. None of us, or course, knew the other side of the story.

It is the forbidden element and lack of commitment that adds excitement to an affair. Add the fact that our culture feeds us fairytales that sell us on the belief that if we just find that one magical person, we will be happy forever. A woman involved with a married man typically comes to believe he is this magical soul mate. What the other woman can't accept, is that he not only long ago promised his wife that she was his soul mate, but that he most likely still believes she is.

The other woman comes to believe that the man who has charmed and intrigued her is headed for certain divorce. His marriage is over and just a technicality. Nervous excitement takes over, just like it did the day the captain of the football team asked us to high school prom. There is something about this guy that makes him different from all of the others. He's our "soul mate," the kind of guy a girl wants to settle down with. He has all of the makings to become "the one." He hones in on what he wants and he goes after it, with purpose and seemingly without games. He is relentless in his pursuit. He begins with flattery and showing a constant interest. His unusual amounts of attention are followed by pretty words that beat the heart. Blake emailed, *I just want you to know that I am so into you right now. I think about only you 24-7. We all have our pasts, but I see you in my future and the present is only good now because you are in it.*

It is very common for a mistress to hear from her lover that his wife is an Ice Maiden. Of course she doesn't know the other side of the story. She has not lived in the wife's shoes for a great number of years to understand how bitterness has possibly developed for her as a result of her husband's neglect. She has probably been hurting for some time due to her husband not giving the marriage the energy it deserves. As she begins to display these bitter characteristics, he uses her behavior to excuse his affair. He is not innocent in the matter and in fact, is just as guilty as the wife.

When a man has an affair, he disrespects the other woman. No matter how he makes her feel, she is second best. He hasn't left his wife because he loves his wife. He is living his life based on the moment, surrounded by selfish feelings and not commitment. Lasting relationships take work and commitment, which he isn't able to give. He lacks the skills to create a happy relationship.

I am (as most mistresses are) one of those "understanding" types, so when Blake told me how dissatisfied he was with his marriage and how he wanted to get out but was afraid to leave, I quickly searched my memory banks and found a place where I could relate to him. Not to have an affair, but to be a friend and offer understanding and suspended judgment.

I married young. We had a daughter and I adopted my husband's two-year-old son, from a previous relationship after his biological mother had abandoned him. My husband was not a good spouse but, being so inexperienced, I had nothing to compare him to. He never participated in family events and was always gone, involved in his own various interests. He had bowling leagues, skeet-shooting teams, golf, fishing, and hunting, and they filled up almost every evening. I didn't mind his activities much, except that I was always alone and never felt that I had enough help managing our responsibilities. I never had a real life partner. Men's leagues are famous for their after hours beer sessions. This would not have been a problem, except that my husband was an alcoholic who relapsed all the time. Sometimes he exhibited aggressive behavior. Each relapse was followed by tremendous remorse, and he would go out of his way for a while to show exceeding acts of love.

With each occurrence, however, his apologies were having less affect, and because the unpredictability of his behavior hardened my heart, our marriage lasted only a few years. I struggled with leaving him because I wanted my daughter to have the luxury of being raised by *two real parents*. Nor did I want to abandon my son. I would not be able to retain custody of him because there were no legal adoption papers signed by his biological mother. Finally, I knew that leaving my husband would devastate him, and I did not want to see him suffer the consequence of his actions in such a large and irreparable way. I felt that my desire to leave was extremely selfish. I felt that I should sacrifice my own happiness for theirs.

When I realized that I really wanted to divorce my husband, I went back to church, not because I wanted to learn to bow my head and obey God, but because I was raised with religion being a major influence and wanted to find the freaking loop holes. I wanted permission to get out! Not one of the religious personnel I counseled with gave me permission, so I felt trapped and tormented all the more. The Clash song, "Should I Stay or Should I Go," played over and over in my head. I even caught myself singing it out loud while washing dishes from time to time.

It was with much fear that I finally did leave. I was afraid that I would regret my decision. I was afraid I would be punished for it. Every hiccup I had during the next few years led me to worry. "Here it comes," I told myself. "My penance for vacating." I was sure that my life would suffer, that I would be defeated and impoverished as a result of my "bad" decision. Caught in an upheaval, I was not equipped with the foresight to see that I was making the right choice for myself and my daughter, and maybe some way (I hope) for my son. The sin of leaving brought no repercussions, and I have never regretted my choice to leave my husband. That was more than sixteen years ago.

So, having left a failed marriage, I was able to relate to Blake's plight. I just figured he hadn't gotten past the part where we fear failure and regret and open our heart to what lies ahead.

Initially, I thought I had Blake pegged as the "exit affair" described in some of the books I had found on affairs. In the exit affair, the husband subconsciously wants to get caught. Though he may go to great lengths to hide the affair, he also leaves small, mindless clues. He uses the other woman as a catapult to get out. In theory, the man does not want to be the bad guy by sitting across from his wife and having to look her in the eye while she is being devastated when he says, "I don't love you anymore." He wants her to discover his affair and force him to leave.

When I was pissed to the ninth degree with my husband, I made a point to always attempt to look my best while I was screaming my face off (if I had time to think about it) because I had noticed at a very young age how ugly and unappealing a person becomes when they are enraged. Spit flies, noses crinkle, and hollering mouths contort to hideous deformities. When I was young I could tell the shit was about to hit the fan just by looking at my father. A monstrous vein in his temple would bulge to almost the size of a pencil. How much easier it is to be caught cheating and watch the wife turn hideous and display all of her "bitch" qualities. It would be much more difficult to watch her sob.

I came to believe Blake was an exit affair when I noticed that he was not careful about clearing out the evidence at the beginning of our affair. I sure as hell did not want to be exposed, so it was me who picked the long hair strands off of the bed and wiped my lipstick off the glasses. An exit affair seemed like a plausible assessment. I foolishly thought he would leave the marriage out of his own unhappiness and she would be none the wiser.

I was working from that plan!

Chapter 16

The Tumultuous Stage

As time went on, I decided Blake was the "fence sitter," as also described in affair books. This guy lives in a constant state of anxiety and comparison. He cannot make up his mind. He cannot bear the thought of losing either his wife or his mistress. I could see Blake's fear of losing his safety net. With Beth, he knew what he had, and when he considered a drastic measure like divorce, he could easily convince himself that the marriage wasn't that bad, that she was a good mother and took care of her family. Staying with her meant he would not have to grieve after letting go or face a difficult life. He had a choice. He could continue in the marriage, knowing what to expect, or he could move away and into an intimate relationship with a woman who might be his "soul mate." But there was no guarantee that his life would get better. What if he gave up everything to be with me and things did not work out? He would be alone! He would have nothing!

"I don't expect you to sit around forever." He wrote "my worry is to be left with nothing when the dust settles. It's a friggin dust bowl right now. I'm hanging on to you for life support."

Because we believe that our beloved is living in torment, we confuse his feelings of torment as a sign of him being goodhearted. We see a man backed into the corner, wretched with confusion, and we search for ways to relate to their troubles. My heart softened when I imagined my brother or step-son (my "good guy" references), both of whom are innately upright. As arrogant and cocky as they are at times, deep down (I know) they truly care when they have wounded a woman's heart, and they are wounded, too. Through the years, both my brother and my step-son have brought girls into our family. We adored some of them, but with others we held our breath until the day they skooched her from our forced niceties. Many times, I watched my brother or step-son hold on to girls they had come to care for but knew she was not what they were looking for to share their life with. In essence, they knew deep inside that their current girlfriend was not "the one," but they still held on because she was "nice enough" and they didn't want to hurt her. My brother is a secretly sensitive soul. I can see the potential for him to unwittingly trap himself by not wanting to hurt a girl who loves him and will fall apart at the mere hint of his withdrawal.

My step-son loves his wife with innocence only the young can have. While I'm writing this, she is pregnant with their first child. One night, she and I were having a catty chat about a woman we knew who had let herself go. Every time we saw this woman, she was wearing dirty sweat pants, a T-shirt, no makeup, and ratty hair pulled into in a ponytail. Before her marriage, she had been a bubble headed cheerleader who dolled herself up regularly. She visited a group of young girls one evening and showed photos of her former self to them. "That's what marriage will do to you," she told them.

"That is what will get her divorced," I said to my daughter in law. My son did not understand, and his wife tried to explain it to him. What, she asked him, if she were to gain 300 pounds and never put herself together? He was visibly confused, but with beautiful innocence said, "Well, I wouldn't like it, but I wouldn't leave you!"

I know my son. He really believed what he was saying. He cannot imagine never loving his wife. For their sake and their child's, I hope he is right, but he is young and naïve and has yet to experience a lot of what life tends to hand us. I imagine what it would be like if my brother or son might come to me one day swallowed by the confusion that accompanies being torn between two loves. I'm sure pain, guilt, and fear would engulf them. Whatever choice they made, they would definitely experience grief at the end. It was with this image in mind that I was able to empathize with Blake's situation.

It is images such as these that are self-created by the other woman and abetted by the cosmetic storytelling of her lover. Once we become convinced to set aside the rather large fact of the existence of a marriage, we become even more susceptible to delusion as he fills our ears with words that we want to hear and does thoughtful things that show that he means the words. That's not to say that he doesn't believe what he's saying at the moment, but rather he is careless when he dumps his momentary thoughts. He does not understand the depth to which the other woman is clinging or reading into his words and how much hope she attaches to them. Blake once wrote to me,

> I am on your side, sweetie. We need to be together on this, we just need to be together, period. Please just keep being you. I am in love with YOU! You are so awesome. I knew I fell in love with you for all of the right reasons. This is just a chapter in the middle of your book. I think you should write it.

(He might think otherwise now.)

It was letters like these that I received during our affair, letters, e-mails, cards, and daily hour-long phone conversations filled with these sorts of sentiments that were powerful words to me. I had never met anyone who made me feel as if I made them so happy just by breathing.

> *I can just sense you right now. Maybe you are thinking of me. I have had an awareness of you that is very curious the last fifteen minutes or so. I can almost see you clearly on the horizon of my mind's eye.*

When I interviewed women who had been involved in an affair, each of them spoke of loving embraces and being told things like, "Why couldn't I have met you before I was in this situation?" Or, "You are everything that I have been looking for my whole life," or, "There is not one thing about you that I would want to change," or, "I am such a lucky man, so fortunate to have someone like you." They tell us we are their soul mates, we are everything that is missing from their lives. We not only bring them happiness, but we ARE happiness itself. Tom Cruise has just entered our living room saying "you complete me."

When Blake was soft and emotional with me, there was no one like him in the world. I had never been with anyone as open and intimate. He met my need for intimacy at its deepest level. I believed that weathering a storm as his marriage ended would be worth it. I knew that marriage and togetherness were not always a fairy tale, that there would always be times that as a couple we would walk the rocky road. I knew that beauty would fade and money might go away and that life should be spent with a true companion who is your best friend. But until I met Blake I did not *know* what that truly meant.

> *Meeting a girl for the first time*, he wrote to me, *who you instantly know is absolutely compatible from the second you meet her = FORTUNATE. Developing a relationship with said girl under storybook circumstances = A GIFT FROM GOD. Maintaining the precious relationship with this girl despite herculean obstacles = FATE. For everyone else, there is emptiness.*

Another woman I interviewed explained a lot to me:

He might tell her beautiful things that she wants to hear and maybe he treats her like a princess, but he's not thinking about the future. Women always want to find the one, so they generally look at every relationship as a potential future. Man's nature since the dawn of testosterone is to get a piece. They want to have a good time, get laid, and call it a good weekend. For him to get to the point of making a commitment is usually a big deal to him. The other woman is not about commitment . . . Maybe the marriage isn't everything that he thought it would be. It rarely is. Marriage takes work.

According to some anthropologist studies, natural selection in genetics favored men who were able to deceive women to have sex with them. And here is a big surprise: Studies show that young male college students admit to being deceptive and pretending to be kinder, trustworthy, and more sincere in order to talk women into doing the nasty. According to, *The Female Brain*, "Mothers often warn their daughters not to get to close too soon with a new boyfriend, and this advice may be wiser than they realize." Brizendine explains, "The act of hugging or cuddling releases oxytocin in the brain, especially in females, and likely produces a tendency to trust the hugger. It also increases the likelihood that you will believe everything and anything he tells you." [6]

We walk ourselves mentally down the aisle because we hear the things that we want to hear and omit the ambiguity in things that do not jive with that image. Blake wrote, *"You mean a great deal to me. I do not plan to just walk through your life, but perhaps to stay awhile."* What I read in this note was that he planned to stay in my life forever. That is, I read "awhile" in a very, very romanticized way, even though what he really meant was only "awhile." These things are said in such a way as to lead us to hear what we want to hear, just as I did. If the man decides he needs to end the affair, we cannot confront him and say he deceived us. He did not lie. He used ambiguity to speak to our hearts.

One of the items Blake and I purchased in Turkey was a piece of blue glass called the "evil eye." Superstition has it that the eye will ward off those who are envious or wish evil upon you. Blake had the piece cemented into the tile design on his bathroom wall in his new home on the lake, where we spent most of our time. To me, this was symbolic

---

[6] Louann Brizendine, MD, *The Female Brain*, Broadway Books, 2006 p67,68

of the life and memories we were building together. To him, I suppose, it was just a cool thing he picked up while traveling abroad. It would be interesting to learn how he explained it to Beth, who now has a constant reminder of our affair permanently affixed to her décor.

In every story I was told by the other women, the man promised or alluded to a future life with her. Even if he in fact said no when she asked him if he would ever leave his wife, he was quick to contradict himself with complaints against his wife and praise for his mistress. Every other woman I talked to came to believe that over time her lover would come to his senses and jump ship from the marriage. As Blake wrote to me,

> *"I love you and have loved you from the moment that I met you. I felt great today with you. I have felt great everywhere with you, as a matter of fact. I can make this work if you want it to. I have always believed that we have a future together. I only seem to laugh when I'm with you."*

A man having an affair is usually telling his affair partner how much he cares for her, and how unhappy his marriage is. If he is able to lie to his wife, he is able to lie to you. A dishonest person doesn't suddenly become honest when having an affair. He will tell the truth when it suits him and he will lie when it suits him, too. He isn't living by principals. If he marries his lover, there will be times when he is not happy. He isn't capable of working through a relationship and creating a successful one when things are not easy.

In the beginning, the married man will always find a way to phone or meet up with his mistress. He makes excuses to his wife about why he is late or has to leave early. He creates errands or picks fights so he can get away. A person having an affair is on such an emotional high that his behaviors become similar to a person who has some form of addiction. They become very difficult to reason with. It's as if half of their intelligence has evaporated.

When I interviewed other women, I found that it was almost always the married man who pursued the prospect of having an extra-curricular love-life. That is not to say that he wasn't given a few obvious cues by the woman or that mutual attraction did exist, for it most certainly did.

What I am saying is that once he was pretty sure his pursuit would reap the reward he wanted, he did take the major step of going after it.

The other woman dismisses her higher thoughts because she feels that she is in a paradise of sorts—that is, until she becomes too familiar and he comes to think that she is "not all that." A time will come for the other woman when she has a bad day. Something upsets her at work or there is conflict with a friend or family member, there is trauma or tragedy. Whatever it is, she is upset and she immediately thinks of him as the one who will give her comfort and support. She needs him. She can think of no one else to share her feelings with. She picks up the phone and calls him. "Can't talk now," she hears. Click. Already suffering, she is now filled with hurt and resentment. Where do I fit into the equation? She asks herself. If I'm so great, where is he? Why didn't he drop everything and come to me? She has always dropped everything to nurture and support him. She realizes that he can't reciprocate.

As in any partnership, the newness of an affair will fade. Eventually, he is just himself, he's not trying so hard to win her anymore, and she is no longer perfect in his eyes. As the relationship becomes more regular, the dynamics shift. She begins to feel the loneliness, rejection, and lack of self-esteem that accompany involvement with a married man, no matter how engrossed they are with each other. She begins to feel the pain of loving someone who is "owned" by someone else. Everything is his wife's and nothing belongs to her. She begins to feel she is not enough, because he isn't leaving his wife. Her focus turns inward and she seeks out all the things that are "wrong" with her. She tries to "fix herself," to be better. She wants to bring back the feelings she once had that she was extraordinary. But all she can find are her negative qualities. She becomes so fixated on her negative attributes that she loses sight of her lover's shortcomings and his selfishness.

Even if the other woman does not have hopes of marrying her lover (though most confessed their belief that the man would commit to them), she is still affected by being put in the back seat. She will always be put aside if he has family obligations. She knows that if an important event occurs in her life at the same time as one in his family, her needs will never be met. She will never be number one in his life. His family will always come first.

Social settings lose their appeal. She watches him from afar, being unable to share the event as a couple. If the partnership is "out" and they have become public, she is also aware that her peers believe that he has not completely chosen her. She begins to feel conspicuous, judged, and scrutinized. She's a public fool fighting an internal battle. Now she begins to complain, perhaps making demands on him while expressing her feelings of unfairness and hurt. He begins to feel pressure and either breaks off the relationship or offers promises or tokens meant to temporarily keep her happy. But soon his attempts to appease her become not enough. She is bitter, and another page in the story book turns.

They begin to fight. The relationship becomes tumultuous. She blames him for her high emotional state. She's angry at his lack of movement, his lack of consideration for her feelings, his ingratitude for what she has sacrificed for him. At some point, she either accepts her fate and chooses to remain in the relationship as it is, or she moves on. Rarely does she ever get what she wants: his divorce. If he does divorce, it's hardly ever satisfying for her. He uses her while he copes with the divorce. She is his comforter, ensuring that he is not alone. She's his security blanket. He begins to date other women. When he is no longer afraid of the unknown, he doesn't need her anymore. He leaves her. She is all the more broken and consumed with feelings of rejection and abandonment. She sees her foolish choices. And now, as a social outcast, she has no one to turn to. It is highly unlikely that the man will remain with his mistress, and even if he does stay with her, the relationship has become so fractured over time with hurt, bitterness, and mistrust that they are seldom able to survive together for a lifetime.

It is very common for a man to tell his wife, "She pursued me," when an affair is discovered. I think there are several reasons why. First, and most obviously, he doesn't want to jump from the pan into the fire by admitting to being the total dog. If he did, then he'd be admitting to searching out the woman and planning the deed of hurting his wife, he'd be admitting to being a lying, conniving sneak who could have been restrained and should have taken the time to ponder the consequence of his actions. If he says he was the pursued and not the pursuer, he receives a bit of grace for falling in a moment of weakness while the deviant woman broke him down. Second, saying he was pursued keeps his wife in the game by making him seem more attractive and wanted by others. Yes, this allows him to have an ego boost right in the middle of his wife's near-death breakdown. It's as if he is saying, "See? Other women want me. You do not appreciate me. You are not doing enough." As he's pointing to his wife's fault for failing to see what the other woman has, he can maintain his own innocence in the affair. He is the victim. It's an effective tactic. After her rage and despair have faded, she is left to beat herself up for all of the ways that she neglected him, took him for granted, and forgot to place his needs above all else. Since we women tend to be self-blamers who search for ways to make things our fault and ways to right where we feel we have wronged, she'll pamper him. She'll give him more of what he wants in effort to save the marriage.

More often than not, once the wife discovers the affair, the heavy wool is brutally pulled away from the eyes of the other woman. Sometimes the other woman actually precipitates the discovery. She believes the wife will get out of the way and allow her lover to run permanently into her arms. But to the other woman's dismay, she is herself thrown carelessly onto the pavement, with her heart destroyed and her mind a whirlwind. He returns to his wife in a fight to save his marriage. Then the other woman is left to replay over and over in her mind all he said and promised, everything they shared, the passion, the depth of the love he proclaimed. She is in shock that he has cut her so easily and quickly returned to the loveless wife who held him captive. More devastating, the other woman usually has no one to turn to for comfort and support as she would after a "normal" breakup. When she turns to friends for comfort, she is only further destroyed when they ask her, "So what did you expect?" or say, "He was married, for God's sake." The implication is that there was never a real relationship and the other woman should not hurt. None of it is real. She is thus reminded of her foolishness and her self-esteem plummets, even though it was already planted in the sub terrain.

A man faced with choosing between his mistress and his wife is faced with distinguishing between ego and emotional honesty. Our egos tend to lead us astray. We women are usually more capable of humbling our narcissistic selves, whereas men don't always recognize how much of their ego is really driving them. Thus he has a bit of a split personality when speaking to both the wife and the mistress. He means it when he says to his wife "I've made a mistake" and he also means it when he says, "I don't know what to do, I don't want to lose you" when speaking to the other woman. From the primitive perspective, his "attachment chemistry" and his testosterone drive to procreate are in direct conflict with one another. His long-term vs. Short-term mating desires produce two entirely different chemical reactions in his brain.

He puts himself in his own hell by refusing to take a time out from both women to examine his thoughts. Perhaps he should seek professional advice or come to grips with reality. Instead, he drags both women who love him into the pit alongside him. Both women, feeling they have something to lose, buy into any prospect of being able to retain him. He wants both women, so he starts juggling wife and mistress. In his guilt, he steps up his affection for his wife. He spends more time with her, opens his heart to her again, and makes the promises she needs to hear. He does special things for her, helps her around the house more, and reaffirms his commitment to her. He tells his wife his excuses for having the affair, but he uses the other woman as his scapegoat, saying that she tempted him and tricked him into continuing the affair long after he realized he wanted to break it off. For example, my friend Ian told his wife, Janet, that his mistress, Kelly, was threatening to tell her about the affair if he refused to spend more time with her. He realized what he had done, he lost control of the situation and was forced to continue giving in to Kelly for fear that Janet would find out and leave him. He turned Kelly into Glenn Close's character in *Fatal Attraction*.

The married man's wife sees that he feels deep remorse and agrees to try to piece the marriage together and fence her family away from the psycho-woman. To his mistress, he explains that he is worried that his wife has lost it, perhaps she's bordering on suicide or is hatching a plan to annihilate him socially or financially. He needs to watch over her a little more carefully. He asks his mistress to be patient while he figures out how to handle things. He also remembers to call her often, sends flowers, and buys her things during her period of saint-like forbearance.

I thank you for being supportive of me during these times of woe and want. The fat is indeed in the fire! My gut tells me to not let you go. I may be a somewhat sick and crazed individual, but you have brought sensibility to my individuality. I consider you my friend, my cohort, my colleague etc. I want to be with you because we are a perfect match. I want to talk about our daily things. This is our us. You need to know that I am up for drastic changes, but I need your support. I have been threatened with divorce. If I promise to take care of you and the kids, could you move to the beach? This might be too much for you to handle right now, and I understand that, it just happens to be on my mind right now. You are the best and I need to see you.

Loving words like these from Blake lasted only so long. Soon, like me, the other woman will feel neglected. She is in a state of anxiety, unsure of what the future holds. During this time that he is consoling his wife the other woman wonders if he will be convinced to change his mind and abandon their love. "Strangely enough," Brizendine says, "The state of romantic love can be reignited by the threat or fear of losing one's partner—of being dumped. Being dumped actually heightens the phenomenon of passionate love in the brain circuits of both men and women. Moments of feeling as if your very survival is threatened occur, and a state of fearful alert is triggered in the amygdale. The anterior cingulated cortex—the part of the brain that engages in worry and critical judgment—starts to generate negative thoughts about losing the beloved." In essence, the fear of losing love places the brain in a drug withdrawal state. "Rejection, it turns out, actually hurts like physical pain," Brizendine says, "because it triggers the same circuits in the brain." [7]

The mistress begins to feel that her lover is being manipulated. She starts fighting for the relationship.

I sent frustrated e-mails to Blake:

I have been miserable these last several days. I told you that I could not handle the drama, the angry wife, or you being led by your nose to hurt me, and I made it clear that I will not deal with that and have not altered, corrected, or changed this statement of fact in any way. My attitude has been that of a very confused and reserved individual who doesn't know what to do or think, what to expect. What is right?

---

[7] Brizendine p 75

I am emotionally exhausted with no one to comfort me in any way while you comfort her. This is a very sad and lonely feeling. You said that you knew that you could not make me happy in your current circumstance. This statement followed me telling you that I would be OK if there was a future together. Tell me where I am inaccurate here.

And he would reply, *I thought you thought we had a future together, I always thought we had, I wish I could hold you now."* This left me just as confused as I had been with no real answer.

Blake would find ways to argue with me or twist my thoughts, using blame tactics to justify his reluctance to separate, pointing to behaviors he felt *I* had shown that caused *him* to doubt that he should leave her and be with me. They were clever tactics. They made me fight to behave in ways that gained his approval. They kept me on the hook and exclusive to him while he was juggling Beth and me and buying himself more time. He put me on the defensive. He used my hurt as a reason to step back. We argued about things that didn't seem logical.

I once received flowers at my office while I was away on an appointment with a client. My secretary had called to let me know they had been delivered. A few moments later, Blake called, and I answered my cell phone with a sappy, "Thank you, lover." "For what?" he asked, and I said, "The office just called. I know you sent me flowers." But his tone of voice quickly revealed that I had mistaken the identity of my admirer. When I returned to my office and read the card, it turned out that the flowers had come from a man with whom I had just finished a business transaction. Noticing that I did not wear a wedding ring nor were there any personal affects or signs around my office of having a serious relationship, he was expressing his interest. The card said he hoped I would entertain the idea of dinner with him, but if not, he asked for my forgiveness in presuming and thanked me for my service. I thought the effort adorable and flattering and felt embarrassed for the thoughtful gentleman. From Blake, what I got was rage and an accusation that I had encouraged the man, plus an attempt to dictate who I could do business with. "You seem to have a constant stream of dudes," he said. "I'm just telling you what is unattractive to me. It's also a good thing for me and you to check some of these things and people as I see necessary." My argument was that I was a single woman who was not known to have a serious partner in my life. "You are top secret,"

I shot back. "Remember? This is just another stupid excuse for you to tell me why you cannot leave your wife . . . because other men find me attractive, intelligent and of interest? When I am your wife or your public girlfriend, we can discuss this further." It was circumstances like these that Blake used to excuse avoiding a divorce.

Struggling to keep two women happy, the husband tells both more of what they want to hear. He also uses them as a sounding board against each other. Blake expressed all of his negative thoughts about me to Beth, then he turned around and vented about Beth to me. He even told us the same things, using the same words. It made the lies easier to keep track of. Beth and I both felt we had an edge and a disadvantage. We were both wondering what was really happening. Blake was telling us both that the other was troublesome, that he was over the other.

The loss factor is ever constant in the other women's thoughts. So caught up in the disaster that they fail to see the obvious, they decline what is most healthy. Simply put, they cannot think clearly. If one decides to get out for the sake of herself, the man finds ways to use reverse psychology to bring her back around and still hanging on. Blake wrote to me:

> *I am in love with you, just like I was in the beginning until now through all of the bad. I can survive the breakup that you are insinuating, but I don't want to do it. I revolt the idea. I was then and am now, totally into you. I guess I can understand if you want to let go as you said. You have dwelled so much on the past and I guess I have dwelled on the future. I know that I am married. There have been so many days of bliss that most of the time I feel that you are my wife for lack of a better term. It is you who I express my emotions to, you who I plan things with. I guess that I don't fall in and out of love that easy. I have loved you through all of this and I have never talked about bailing ever. I don't want to fight with you honey. I love you too much. I can't do it. I wish we could run away together. I'm sorry. Will you please forgive me?*

Wife and mistress both hold out hope that she is the woman he truly loves. He gives each of them a glimmer of promise or a show of evidence that she can count on him, and then he drops her again.

As tumultuous as it has been, isn't there a sense of overwhelming calm when we are together? I'm going to stay until after Christmas, but I might be on the redeye that night. I am done. I have no energy. I don't want to be here. You tell me to take some time but that only makes me wonder that you don't want to be with me. I want to be with you. Can we go away somewhere?

But instead of leaving Beth after Christmas, he took her to San Francisco for a shopping spree after New Year's. When I could not handle being told one thing and then being harshly treated instead, I always explained away why I had to end the relationship. He used "reasonable" excuses to keep encouraging me to stick it out for just a bit longer.

He also did things to reassure Beth that he had no intention of divorcing her. At the same time, he used my discovery of some of those things as weapons. Remember the phone call I received from my friend Tony, who thought it was important to inform me that Beth had been visiting one of his co-workers and had displayed her new large wedding ring? My stomach dropped and I felt sick, but I knew it was impossible. Not the way he loved me! There could be no way! When I asked him for an explanation, Blake used every ounce of my inquiry against me. Tony was trying to sleep with me. He was making things up to destroy our relationship. My refusal to end my friendship with Tony was, Blake said, making him back off. That I would even ask or question him, he said, showed my insecurity and caused him to doubt our future together. He was afraid that I would never trust him, that I would never rid my life of these people that he wanted because they were causing so much trouble. He accused me of making things up and blowing them out of proportion. My "crazy" thinking was scaring him and making him wonder if I was really strong enough to be in a relationship with someone like him, who would be going through a shit storm to be with me.

One evening Blake and I were discussing our situation on my couch and I told him that I couldn't handle the mess much longer. "That means that you don't love me unconditionally," he said. I responded, "If the condition is that I lose my self-respect, no, I don't." He appeared to be profoundly struck by my assertion and then shared with me a conversation that he'd had with Beth's sister after the affair was out of the closet. He had asked her why Beth had stayed with him, and her sister had responded, "Well, Blake, some people love unconditionally." From Blake's perspective, I lost several points for dignity.

I kept trying to tell Blake about my suffering. I tried to explain how much it hurt me to be hidden away, to live behind the scene. I told him how my finances were being affected, how not taking clients to give him all of my time and be able to travel at the drop of a hat was costing me a great deal.

"It's not that I am keeping you top secret," he said. "The whole program knows what is going on, it's just not rubbed into everyone's face. It's more suave for both of us right now".

How foolish I felt when he would be seen with Beth out on the town and how ridiculous it made me look for believing that he was in love with me and planning on divorcing her. What a laughing stock he was making of me in the community. He was making us both laughing stocks. I tried to explain how my children's lives were at risk, how their hearts were in jeopardy when I brought him around them and they bonded with him, believing he was to be a great part of our future. I was beginning to believe he would not keep the promises he made to them, that he would not follow through.

"Why does everything have to be a friggin' issue?" He said "Can't we just relax and be? Just for a little while? What the hell is wrong with that plan? My God, I am exhausted. You just gave me a vote of no confidence. How the hell am I supposed to feel?"

He would not hear of my hurt at not being able to interact with his children, my need to just live a normal life. I wasn't asking him to divorce Beth. I was asking him to be honest with me. If he had no intention of doing so, then I could stop wrecking my own life. He replied,

I have no problem with my place or status with you. I am proud of it and love you and love being with you. There are just a lot of hits, that's all. I guess I am saddened that I make you feel so bad. It is obvious to me that you have not been yourself these last couple of days and I am devastated that I seem to be the cause of it. You have tried to explain yourself to me and I apologize that I don't seem to understand. It pains me to bring such sadness to someone that I love, for that I am sorry. It is not intentional.

We women allow our egos to control us, too. Set the heartbreak aside. We do not want to be humiliated. The wife believes she will appear to be unwanted, that others will see her as having something wrong with her. She is afraid that "they" will look at her knowing all that she didn't; a fool for all that has been going on under her nose. She thinks that the other woman will feel as if she's the proud victor at her (the wife's) expense, that she will be laughed at with a mean winner's sneer.

Peggy Vaughan, author of the book *The Monogamy Myth*, writes:

> *When people look for reasons to explain why their partner has an affair, they invariably start with themselves. Every weakness they ever worried about becomes a source of concern. They look for some personal inadequacy (either real or imagined) that might have caused the affair.*
>
> *The personal blaming often expands to include any area in which a person thinks they failed to be "the best." They see their partner's affair as a sign that they weren't smart enough, or successful enough, or attractive enough, or interesting enough. Since nobody's perfect, it's easy to find some personal shortcoming to blame as the cause of a partner's affair.*
>
> *For instance, a woman who was a full-time homemaker and mother was convinced that if only she'd been out in the world, she would have been a more interesting partner and her husband wouldn't have had an affair. At the same time, another woman who was career-oriented was convinced that her involvement with her career limited her time and attention to her husband and was the reason he had an affair.*
>
> *Accepting personal responsibility for determining the behavior of another person inevitably leads to failure.* [8]

The other woman rightly believes that she will be laughed at, too. "You stupid idiot," people will say to her. "You should have known that the relationship you swore was different will prove to be like every other extra-marital affair." In our fight for what we believe, we lose ourselves. Overall, I only see one winner here (if there can truly be one), and he doesn't have balls, either.

---

[8] Peggy Vaughan, *The Monogamy Myth*, New York; New Market Press p16-17

The wife and the other woman come to despise each other because of what they see the other taking from them. Both see the other as the obstacle to their happiness. "If she were gone," they both say, "everything would be fine." In reality, their hatred of each other is only the excuse they give themselves so they won't see the responsibility of the man in the middle. But the other woman doesn't owe the wife anything. It is not the other woman who made the promise to her. "Was I," the other woman asks, "The one who agreed to love, honor, and obey her until death?" That promise was made by that guy—finger pointed back. "What is my fault," the other woman continues, "is that I reinforced his hurtful method because I was stupidly thinking that I had anything to be taken from me to begin with." Neither woman realizes that the first step to making healthy decisions for themselves begins by declining to think about things as competition.

I learned that Ian once told his mistress Kelly that he was in love with her and Janet at the same time. Blake used to mime flipping a coin when his friends asked him what he was going to do about me and Beth. Maybe my preacher was right when he said, "He doesn't love you or her. Just himself. He only loves to have you both the way he wants you to fit to make himself happy."

When I complained to Blake that he had the best of both worlds and was considering only his own emotions and disregarding mine or Beth's, he seemed unhappy for a minute, but he still took no action to change things. Then he went on about how things weren't easy for him. Perhaps that was how he really felt. But no one can argue that Beth and I weren't suffering more. The funny thing is, he seemed to not let much faze him. To this day, he puts finding happiness for himself above all else. We women forget to do that.

What we don't forget is what happiness felt like, and so when we have tasted happiness and felt its high, we know where we found it. We believe we will continue to find it in the same place. Even when it seems to have evaded us or creeps beneath the sand, we just keep digging harder, and eventually we dig a hole so deep that our heads (and our hearts) are stuck below the surface. It is a slow progress. Our focus becomes fixed, and that is why when the man begins juggling wife and mistress, we are too deep to make sense of what he's doing, not only to ourselves but to anyone.

I remember a conversation I had with Blake. We were well into our affair, and he suddenly admitted to having a few "one night stands" some years before he and I had met. "I wanted to see if I could still do it," he told me. My friend Ian confessed that before his affair, he had reached an age where he felt he had lost some of his youthful charm. He felt a need to satisfy his ego and prove to himself that he "still had it." To a man, an affair has less to do with the other woman than with feeding his ego, fulfilling his sexual desires, or just curing his boredom.

What seems to be most significant that the other woman can't seem to realize is that the affair makes it *more* likely that he will stay in the marriage. If the other woman is willing to hang on, and the wife is unwilling to leave her philandering husband, then he has no reason to take any kind of action, like leave the marriage or stop the affair. Even though I lived though this circumstance myself, I still wonder why I didn't see it. It's been said that it's better to *be* alone than to *feel* alone in a relationship. I think I have always felt my loneliest *in* a relationship. So why was I so afraid to let it go? Why was Beth afraid? We both were alone already.

The brutal bottom line for the other woman is this: *he isn't going anywhere*. At least not right away. If he does leave the marriage, consider his reasons. Either he suddenly grows balls and walks out the door (which should alert you to a cold heart) or, more likely, his wife kicks him out. And if it's the wife who takes the action, then the other woman will never be confident that he truly wanted to be with her. Besides, he'll probably either beg his wife for another chance or continue the back and forth cycle.

Chapter 17

The Decision Stage

Sometimes as I write these words, I fear that I am coming across sounding like I hate men. Let me make it clear that I actually have more male friends than female because I find men to be straightforward, honest, and refreshing in a friendship. Men tend to take offense when women generalize them as "all guys" especially when they are courting her. But as their friend, men usually drop the guard of comparison and admit to being pretty much that—a guy. There are some men who live more in line with the good inside them, whereas others seem to be in touch with their more negative traits. Nonetheless, we are all capable of good and bad.

I have female friends who have cheated on their spouses and male friends who have done the same. I also know of acquaintances and business associates who have dabbled in the brook of infidelity. Some of these people, I believe, have fairly wicked hearts (not the ones I call "friends" of course). I can tell from their actions beyond just having affairs, there are other things they do that display their true character. Others are compassionate, if confused, individuals who have lost their grip on what is really important to them. I do not believe that a person involved in an affair makes a solid case for "bad person." When I say "most men," I mean most men who are having affairs. And most men are often incapable of self-accountability when it comes to accepting their part in the problems they have with their spouse. They tend to be very selfish thinkers.

Most men who have affairs seem to be running from something. I don't think they have faced their own responsibility for the dissatisfying state of their marriage. They do not take a deep and hard look at where things went wrong. His focus is on how she *changed*. She is irritable, moody, bitchy, she no longer seems happy. She lacks affection towards him or is too wrapped up in her etceteras to notice her husband's needs. He doesn't consider where he might have changed in ways that allowed his wife to detach. For example, a man stops courting his wife, sending her flowers, calling her just to let her know that she is on his mind. He forgets to do the little thoughtful things that let her know that her existence is vital to him. As he becomes comfortable in the marriage, he starts taking her for granted while her reality is that the reason for her existence is to make sure he has clean underwear in his drawer and breakfast is on the table. His inattention to her leaves her feeling she is there because *she takes care of things*. She handles the majority of the children's needs and other domestic responsibilities. Incidentally, many of my divorced male friends discovered that they developed a more connected relationship with their children after their marriage had ended and Mommy wasn't taking care of everything anymore.

What these men fail to realize is that they brought the same behaviors into the extra-marital affair that they displayed in the courtship of their wives. Once they stop courting their new girlfriend, she won't feel any different than his wife who cleans his urine from the bathroom floor. What I am saying is that in the end, the wandering husband is simply switching players, if he refuses responsibility and doesn't change at all.

My very close friend Janet shared with me her thoughts while healing from her husband's affair, "when Ian and I were first married, I got all hot and bothered every time he walked in the door. It made him feel good and boosted his ego. After some time, though, responsibility and familiarity became factors. I forgot to be as expressive. Kelly gave him that ego stroke he needed because she was new, and she gave him that stroke each time he met with her." I suspect that over time, however, Kelly (or any other woman) would have been no different from Janet.

After a couple has been together for some time, studies show that their brain chemicals shift from intense romantic love to a calmer, peaceful connection. Some scientists argue even, that there is a separate network in the brain system for attachment vs. the high effects of dopamine found in passionate love. What this basically explains, is how a couple goes from being unable to keep their hands off of each other to developing a deeper more attached relationship through the consistent production of oxytocin.

Often times, the married man's conflict lies between the woman who gives him ego-boosting attention and a high sex drive and the wife with whom he shares so much more—a home, children, family, friendships. What he doesn't realize is that the frequency of sex with his lover will diminish as time passes and fall away, just as it did in his marriage, when he treats his mistress the same as he did his wife.

Sex is, after all, a factor in the affair. Part of what is so alluring about the other woman is her ability to make him feel that she is overcome with passion for him, that his sexual prowess has possessed her. What he doesn't understand, ironically, is that one way we other women have learned to hold an ounce of control in an affair is through sex. When he begins to vacillate and question his reasons for remaining in a relationship with us, we fight to keep what we have invested our hearts into; we know where to kick things up a bit. Many times I thought to myself, "Oh, yeah, here's something you'll miss," while in the throes with Blake. Whether we really think he's an excellent lover or not, we let him believe we are in exultation. The egos of men are often simple and easy to please.

When he claims "she doesn't give me sex," the man either cannot see his own responsibility or he secretly harbors feelings of rejection that he's using the other woman to overcome. He concludes that his wife has dried up like the Sahara and no longer has any sexual needs. He seems not to understand or care what a turn-off it is to a woman when she is made to feel like all that matters is the hole between her legs. When a woman feels reduced to a worthless sack of flesh used to satisfy his urges, then it becomes very easy for her to lose her desire and really not care so much that he is taking care of business while "reading" on the toilet. By the time we girlfriends arrive, we feel terribly craved, which inspires our immense and fun sex drive. But when he forgets to make us feel special, we will inevitably lose it, too, just as his wife did.

Jacinda's ex-boyfriend, who she lived with for many years, complained that she didn't like sex. Jacinda admitted to me that during their last year of living together, she didn't recall having sex with him because it was all about him and did nothing for her. On the other hand, Jacinda and her married man had many wild sexual experiences. I believe this was because he made her feel like she was the fulfiller of his fantasies. He craved her and it made her feel like she was the oxygen he breathed.

While Blake and I were together, we used to sneak off during the day to unusual places to enjoy each other. The secretiveness and rush to connect added an element of excitement to our affair. His fascination with my willingness to "get down" at risky times, lead me to believe that he had a very domesticated sex life prior to our involvement. I'm also sure that Blake boosted my ego every time he said, "You're the best." I now know that Beth was quite untamed in her younger days, and I have to wonder if her slowing sex drive wasn't related to his inability to please her on other levels. Maybe after fifteen years of handling every responsibility they shared, she was exhausted. She just didn't have anything else to give him at the end of the day. Maybe her sex drive didn't really slow down at all. When lying becomes the norm, where is the truth? What I'm telling the other woman here is that just because he behaves like you are bringing something new and exciting to his sex life doesn't mean that is the case.

Blake and I found many odd and public places to have sex. Maybe he was just hungry for a little variety. Now a days THAT seems more likely than love, and most other women should think about that before they go compromising their reputations—and hearts.

Another woman I spoke to shared with me a revelation she had during her annual pap smear. The doctor had asked her if she would like him to run cultures, and at that moment it occurred to her that she had never considered that she might be at risk for any sort of sexually-transmitted disease. She had always assumed that because her partner was married, she was safe. Suddenly the thought flashed through her mind—If he's so willing to do it with me, why not with someone else? We imagine that since we are giving him so much sexual time, it will keep him from not only his wife but from other women too. When we discover that we are wrong, we're surprised. Ironically, many other women I spoke to were shocked to find out that, "He cheated on ME! His lover!"

If the main power card the other woman has is sex, then it is *highly* doubtful that he will give up his entire life to be with her. Are you kidding me? Give up everything for thirty seconds of pulsating? What he will do is continue getting what he can until she gets tired of being used and leaves him. He will, of course, use his powers of persuasion a few times, heartfelt words and acts of sadness. When she becomes too demanding, however, chances are he will move on to the next sorry victim.

If I said that affairs always end, I'd be wrong. Look at Audrey Hepburn and William Holden or other famous movie-star affairs. Look at billionaire Warren Buffet who stayed married to his wife until her death in 2004 then in 2006 married his mistress of thirty-five years. That made headlines, so I suspect this marriage was rare. The odds are much more in favor of the man, the other woman, the wife, or all of them tiring of the bullshit. In affairs where the men leave their wives, the others woman seldom makes the final cut to become mistress turned wife. In fact, according to statistics I have found, only three percent of married men leave their wives for their mistress. And of that three percent, only one third make it beyond the first year. Less than a third overall of marriages to the partner in an affair work out.

Let's hypothesize a perfect scenario for the other woman. Her lover has sat down with his wife, with whom he has shared history and a promised commitment. He has disclosed the truth and stated that he loves the other woman. He has been man enough to own his faults and speak his heartfelt apologies. He has attempted to make an amicable break and walk out the door into a new life.

But every time in the future that he says he's unhappy, how is his mistress/new wife going to feel? Will she feel secure? Will she feel afraid that he will reach for another woman the way that he reached for her? Does she not live with a higher risk of rejection than she would in a normal marriage? Right from the start, she is gambling with a lifetime on unstable ground. When your relationship is built on an extra-marital affair, when love begins as a secret, when you've watched him lie to his wife and reinforced those lies, there really is no possibility for you to trust the man completely. Regardless of how "honest" the mistress/new wife believes he is, the moment the smallest thing reminds her of the time he deceived his former wife, she will be alert for deception against herself, whether he is innocent or guilty.

Take Doug, for example. When he met Natasha, they were working together, so they were able to build up a friendship. But their friendship grew into something more when the crew headed out after work for evening toddies. "We'd all go out and have a good time," he said. "Dance, laugh, whatever." One night Natasha and I got to talking. "Wow," they both said, "we have a lot in common!" Doug admits to being no different from the other men I interviewed. He says that he had no designs for a future with Natasha. He was having a good time with her and enjoying his feelings of infatuation. He had several children with his wife and they were in the process of building a summer home. While his wife was focused on this project, he was left with time to spend freely with Natasha. "We were just having fun," he told me. "I wasn't thinking about tomorrow." Both he and Natasha were married, and he believes her being married took the pressure off him to be her everything. They both had lives outside of each other. They both knew the deal. But then Natasha surprised Doug with an attack of guilt. "I can't do this," she said. "I can't live this life. It's either in or out." So Doug went home that evening and spilled his guts to his wife. She told him to pack his things and he did. Doug and Natasha spent twelve years together in a suspicion-filled, untrusting relationship. It finally broke them. Doug never married Natasha. He said something always held him back. He was looking for freedom. He wanted to have a good time. Why would he ruin that with marriage to his good-time girl?

Another case: Adam left his wife and moved in with his girlfriend. He quickly realized that he was not ready for another marriage. He was, in fact, unsure of his belief in the whole institution of marriage. Their lives became tumultuous as his girlfriend regularly moves into and out of the house. When she is not residing in the home, she sits at the end of his driveway at all hours of the night, waiting for him to come home. When she is living in the home, she waits on the couch. Adam keeps the relationship going with his girlfriend, but he's also using his freedom to date and explore other options.

Jerry suffered a life-threatening disease. His wife stood by his side as he faced death, caring for him, preparing to grieve for him. But he turned a corner, and once he was in full remission, he began having affair after affair. He promised the world and his undying love to this series of other women, but could never leave his wife because of his sense of obligation and gratitude for her sacrifices during his illness. They also had children and assets. Eventually he left her for another woman, whom he immediately moved into his house. Then he began to complain about the new woman's dependence. He just couldn't seem to allow himself to be single for any length of time. His girlfriend, Haley, lived in a constant state of anxiety when she was unable to reach him. She became mistrustful and very accusatory. Though he was always able to calm her fears and assure her that all was well, she was right to be worried. He spoke to me of at least two women he had shared intimate outings with after Haley moved into his house. I am certain there are several more. But, even when she was warned, Haley refused to believe the truth. She wanted to trust him. She finally stumbled across an undeniable truth and could no longer deceive herself. Later I ran into Haley and she let me know that they were no longer together. He had been cheating on her and when she found out for sure, she left him. He had already moved the latest one into his house.

Pam's married man left his wife for her, and she stood beside him during all the brutal court battles, through the grief, anger, and hostility blasted at her by his wife, and through the difficulties of building a relationship with his children despite the influence of their mother. Knowing that he was enduring a tremendous amount of stress, she struggled to keep an element of happiness in her lover's life. She held onto her own sanity by a thread. Once things settled down and a steady flow of normality came into their lives, he no longer needed her as his crutch. He left her to try the single life he had missed for so long.

Tonya married Geoff five years after his repeated promises to leave his wife. She planned the large wedding she had dreamt of since she was a child. To her disappointment, only a small number of those invited, attended.

Tonya, a mother of two small children, was forced to begin a career after her first husband passed away. Geoff owned the company which hired her. Geoff offered sympathy and gave her more work in his office to help her financially. Their work together turned into hours upon hours of time spent alone with one another, and a deeply rooted friendship developed between them. Tonya's warm presence drew more consumers to Geoff's company and she became an intricate part of his success.

Tonya is half Geoff's age, intelligent and attractive. Not one year into their marriage, however, Tonya, sensitive to the signs of infidelity, became alert to subtle changes. Eventually, she discovered his attraction to prostitutes and caught him red handed.

Tonya was very open in sharing her story with me. Years of waiting for him to leave his wife as promised, had made her bitter and mistrustful. Her patient waiting for his promise to be fulfilled yielded a reality that was far from what she had dreamed. Geoff also agreed to speak with me about his marriage to Tonya, but when I asked him directly about his behavior, he denied any wrong doing. He then admitted to some of what Tonya said, but denied that actual cheating had happened. After our brief conversation ended, he dropped a wad of cash on my lap as contribution toward a charity I was involved in, and left.

Angela and James also married after a three-year affair. As real life set in, and James showed that he hadn't changed, Angela, too, became filled with mistrust. She regularly drank away her depression. In the end, she found AA, another man, and had her own affair. She left James with half of the half of the assets he had left from his previous divorce.

Tory and Jessica married after their two year affair. They had a child and continued to live the fast life they had shared from the beginning. Friends called them the "lovey dovey couple," as they seemed to always be so into one another and hopelessly in love. Until one evening, Jessica lost track of Tory during a Fourth of July party. She found him in the woods with one of her friends. They are now attempting an amicable separation and custody agreement while Tory secretly creeps out with a whole new girl.

Stephanie married Kyle after an eight-year affair. When she became pregnant two years later, Kyle tried to convince her to abort the child, saying that he already had two and "this was not the deal." Abortion was much against Stephanie's religious upbringing. She struggled with his heavy insistence, but in the end refused. Imagine her surprise when he informed her only a short time later that his ex-wife was pregnant with his child and keeping it, too. Stephanie now raises his child alone as Kyle continues to go back and forth between two women and still cannot make a choice.

I knew another woman, Arlene, who had spent years of her life feeling sad because her children were angry at her for abandoning their father and marrying Ted, his former business partner, who had also been married. "I know they're still angry," she said to me, "but what can I do? I've had twenty great years with Ted." It seemed to me that this was one case for a successful affair turned into a marriage. Ted seemed to pour his life into Arlene and her youngest son. I did notice, however, that Arlene drank a lot, and her son shared with me his belief that she was an alcoholic. But she was always smiling, and Ted seemed to not be bothered by a thing. Arlene died in her early sixties of cancer. What shocked her children more than her remarriage or death was that no sooner was her casket lowered than Ted immediately informed her children never to contact him again and went about the business of making amends to his former family.

Lisa has been married to her lover for almost fourteen years. They met while working together—she was his assistant. She kept her job as his assistant for the next ten years until they had a child. She did not stay at home with her child. Instead, she began to focus on growing their business endeavors, and then she went on to establish and run a separate business she and her husband created together while he maintained and ran the original company. Shortly after she went to run the second office, and was no longer up his ass all of the time, he began a new relationship.

Nick and Cindy were both married to others and left their spouses to be together. To the outside world, they appear to have it all. They own a successful business, have children in whose lives they are actively involved, and hold regular social shindigs at one or another of their various homes. But Nick fills his time with work and hobbies that keep him away from the home as much as possible. When he's absent too long, Cindy arrives at whatever location he is reported to be at, creates a scene, and leaves their crying and confused children with him. Cindy has confided in me that she has regular emotional breakdowns and has several prescriptions for anti-depressants. Nick confided that he has had several flings since they married.

Scott left his wife for Tammy a year into their affair, but Tammy was never able to enjoy being his partner. She was always seen as a bad person, and Scott's mother always referred to her as "the home wrecker" and kept her out of family gatherings. Scott's children were also coaxed by his ex-wife to say hurtful things to Tammy. She and Scott had a son together and she spent ten years in this painful relationship. He cheated on her numerous times, but she never left him. She didn't want people to think she had received what was due to her. Her close friends never understood why she stayed, or even why she had allowed herself to get involved with him to begin with. Shortly after their son was born, Scott moved in with a new girlfriend, LeAnn, who continuously engages in hostile arguments with Tammy during child drop-off and pick-up. LeAnn taunts her by saying she deserves whatever she gets because she was Scott's mistress who caused his former wife so much misery. Nine months after Scott's first wife died an early death of cancer, I received a letter from Tammy:

> I cried with disbelief when I read the article in the newspaper, then twenty minutes later it hit me! Oh my God! All of the years she and I fought, and for what? A man that screwed us both. He wasn't worth it, that's for sure. I think of this story and it's kind of funny because I was the other woman and got all of the shit, and now LeAnn harasses me and feels the same things. LeAnn feels the same way that I did about Kary. Now I am Scott's ex and going through the very same thing. I felt the same about Scott's wife. It's ridiculous in the end.

While researching the outcome of relationships where the husband has left his wife for the other woman I found consistently that each woman had similar emotions in the end.

In summary, all spoke of difficulties integrating themselves into his life with extended family. Most were not accepted by his parents or friends and all were left to bare the blame of his failed marriage. Many felt hurt and responsible for the pain their affair caused the husband, who suffered over children who refused to communicate with their father because of his new spouse. They talked about how heart wrenching it was to watch their lover experience torture in his decision to leave, and that it was brutal to watch the man you love suffer. They spoke of tension in the new marriage as a result of emotional problems directly linked to the first failed marriage. I found time and again comments made by the new spouse such as "I don't know that I will ever be able to forgive myself for the pain that I caused his first wife." They believe they will never be able to get over hurting other people. They spoke of ruined reputations and being treated as if it were she who chased him and ruined his marriage, as if he had no blame for the affair. Unrelenting ridicule and blame from society. Lying will always overshadow everything else as far as other people are concerned, no matter how long you are together, they say. And never in their wildest dreams would they have guessed the magnitude of misery they would be made to endure.

These other women-turned-wives seem to side with psychological warnings after they have married their affair partner. They say that they realize now that they had idealized the relationship and felt ecstasy in a love without the burdens of responsibility. They know now that they were living in a constant daydream because keeping their relationship a secret lead to further romanticizing it, because in the absence of being able to talk about it, all they could do was think about it. Originally, they believed their affair partner to encapsulate everything they ever wanted and then after marriage to their affair partner, their reasons for appreciating the relationship fizzled out. These new wives struggled with finding balance in maintaining a sense of self while trying to avoid feelings of being indebted to him for the rest of their lives for what he endured to be with them. They had adopted feelings that they unduly owed him and found no equality in the relationship.

In divorces where young children were involved, mistress/wives spoke of the contact they were forced to have with a woman (the former wife) who blames the new wife for ruining her life. Saying that the former wife now has a good part of the rest of their lives to affect the other woman. As one woman put it "there will be times when you feel like every hound in hell is nipping at your heels."

A point that I have often tried to make to men is that every woman is some father's little girl. What would they want their daughters to experience? What are the guys who stray teaching their children? It's no secret that girls often marry men who resemble Daddy, and so I asked Blake if our situation was what he wanted for his daughters. Women who tolerate serial affairs have daughters who learn to tolerate them. Daughters can learn to gravitate toward men who behave like their father. Cheating men teach their children to deceive. Their sons learn to devalue women. Blake agreed; he would never want someone like himself for his daughters.

Sadly enough, children are often stuck in the center of the tug of war of infidelity, especially when the husband leaves his wife for the other woman. The anger between the parties runs so deep that neither husband nor wife can see beyond red. They don't realize who is really getting hurt. Their hatred has long-term effects on their children.

After my father and mother divorced, my father would drive forty-five miles to pick me and my sister's up for our weekend with him. Before he arrived, my mother would rant as she packed our belongings into our weekend bag. As we drove for the next hour, my father would criticize my mother and all of her bitchy qualities. The only way to get his attention was not to share in our school projects of which we might have received accolades, but to report more of Mom's bizarre behavior. When we arrived back home on Sunday night, Mom asked how our weekend went, and we told her all about Dad's grouchiness. The only thing that was accomplished by all of this tattling was the immense feelings of guilt my sister's and I shared because we felt like we were betraying one parent or the other. As I grew up, of course, I learned how to manipulate this in my favor. If Mom disagreed with something or expected a behavior from me, I would run to Dad with her unreason. When my father placed restrictions on me, I ran to my mother who was more relaxed. They were still battling to be better than each other and more loved and approved of by their children. I could always win one over to my side.

DeAnna left her husband of twenty years after discovering that he was having a long term affair. She was so angry that her sons also began to hate their father for the tears they witnessed fall from the eyes of their mother. They hated him and refused to speak to him or visit with him. Later, when DeAnna remarried, she tried to bring some normality back into their lives. The boys resisted and eventually turned to their father, who was then able to tell them that her unreasonableness was why he had left her. This made DeAnna miserable. She thought her sons were going off to the dark side. She'd been deserted again, affirming her belief that she was unworthy of love. As the boys became teenagers, every time they were faced with a consequence for their misbehavior, they would run to Mom or Dad with stories that validated the hatred the parents felt for each other. The boys, who had been active in sports, received above average grades, and had promising futures, stepped off into the true dark side, which was rebellion and a storm of constant trouble. The boys have been arrested several times for possession and use of drugs. One was discharged from military boot camp after being charged with driving under the influence and the other moved out of his mother's house and into his own apartment before his eighteenth birthday, did not graduate from high school, and reportedly hates both parents.

When I was still involved with Blake, Beth told her children that I was a bad person and that my children were horrible and awful people and we were the reason that they were going to lose their dad. This could have backfired on her if Blake and I ever married. My children and I would have been a regular part of the lives of Beth's children. Wouldn't I have extended extra care to her children? Would I make a point in getting all the children together to try to bond them with fun activities? When we took Blake's children home to their mother, who was still angry, what conclusions would the children draw? Would they have begun to question her truth? Maybe not. Perhaps they would have aligned with their mother and always hated me. Maybe nothing would have ever been good enough and I would have been miserable. How would they use what they learned from the three adults in their lives as they became teenagers? What I do know is that it never would have been the fairytale I wanted for myself or our children.

Dr. Harley, author and a founder of Marriagebuilders.com, talks about how an extra-marital affair can affect the children:

There are two things that children learn from an affair. One is that it's alright to lie, because they see their parent not only lying about the affair, but also encouraging them to lie for them. And also develop an ethic that says under certain conditions, it's OK not to tell the truth. The other thing that they learn is that it's OK to be thoughtless. It's OK to do something that's good for you and bad for the people that love you most. It sets them up for a lifetime of failure because they don't learn two of life's most important principals: honesty and thoughtfulness. They learn that the opposite is OK. [9]

Though the chances of bliss are low for the mistress turned wife, the odds are not so bleak for the husband and wife who are rekindling their marriage and recovering from an affair. As husband and wife begin to heal the rupture in their marriage, the mistress becomes the scapegoat. The wife blames her. "We had such a sweet relationship," says Karen. "Even if it had its troubles, it wasn't so far gone that we were ready to let go of each other." Adding, "It would have been one thing if we were falling apart and she let the downward spiral take its course and the marriage end on its own, but she wanted him *now*." Obviously she holds the other woman more responsible for her husband's philandering than him. It has worked for them though.

My friend Janet says, "I will never get to a place where I could say that the affair was a good thing, but I can say that in the end we are much stronger now." After she first discovered Ian had been unfaithful, she was devastated. She called me at all hours of the night. But Ian immediately ended the affair and, with tremendous remorse, did everything possible to save his marriage. They phoned Kelly, his mistress, together, and he very abruptly told her it was over. He refused to take her phone calls and, when Kelly tried desperately to phone him at work, he had a third party answer and inform her not to contact him. He also informed Janet every time Kelly tried to contact him. He drove straight home from work every night, and his first words upon entering the door were "No contact" to ease her wondering. Janet and Ian sought

---

[9] Dr. Willard Harley JR, Surviving An Affair, http://www.cbn.com/family/marriage/affairproof.aspx
Interview by Terry Meeuwsen www.cbn.com Affair-proof your marriage
Accessed September 9, 2007

marriage counseling, but even then, she vacillated between accepting her role in neglecting him and taking him for granted and her bitterness for all the ways he had taken her for granted and deceived her. She also wondered if she was strong enough to make it through.

They survived his affair by working together with a great deal of love. They were able to come to a place of compassion where, through Ian's effort and remorse, Janet learned to let go. In many ways they are more united today then they were before. Although Ian's mistress told Janet that he had called her his soul mate, Ian told Janet, "Even if our marriage had ended, I wouldn't have been with Kelly, anyway." Many therapists report that, sadly enough for the other woman, most men tell their therapist the affair meant nothing to him.

"The woman I was seeing believed I was going to leave my wife and marry her." One man admitted. "I didn't set her straight because I didn't want her to stop seeing me. But I never planned to leave my wife. I knew I was leading her on."

Gordon and Melissa were also able to recover from his affair. He broke it off immediately when he was faced with losing his wife. To this day, I have never heard a man speak so beautifully about the love he has for his wife and the good fortune he feels because she stayed with him. He suddenly discovered all the beauty he had within the walls of his home. He has never forgotten the price that he almost paid and has become a better husband. I cannot recall a time that I ever saw them so happy.

There is no need for me to fill these pages with stories of successful recoveries from affairs. There are plenty of them in books that line the shelves of book stores. Essentially, they say it may not seem like it right now, but most people who recover from an affair find that their relationship is stronger because they have weathered the storm together. Recovered marriages are stronger. Husbands and wives grow closer. They are secure and don't worry about future infidelities if they work through things properly.

When a husband and wife choose to stay together after an affair, two outcomes are possible. Either they grow closer together in a more enriched and loving relationship where they discover better ways to communicate their needs to one another or he becomes a serial cheater. The marriage will be far better or much worse.

Seth, for example, married Bridget and they had children when they were both young. Over the course of fourteen years, he had many one-nighters and a couple of emotional affairs. Seth loved Bridget for their history together, for her sacrifices, and for their children. They shared some tough years, but Seth was never completely happy, never quite satisfied. But every time he strayed, Bridget took him back. She became less and less fun to deal with, however, and their home became filled with suspicion and arguing. He finally decided she was not pleasant to be around anymore. He couldn't stand her hatefulness, which did nothing to keep him home but in fact made him go out more often. Bridget was a sure thing. She would never leave him. She gave him unconditional love. Eventually, however, Seth did leave Bridget, and now he lives with a woman with whom he seems truly enamored. But they have only been together for a short time. He still hurts for Bridget and responds with jealousy whenever he hears that she is dating someone new. Seth says he knew that he wanted out years ago. The delays and back and forthing just gave him and Bridget miserable, wasted years. I'd be willing to bet money, though, that if things don't work out with the new gal, he'll be back on Bridget's doorstep, begging for another chance that she'll probably give him.

Lance sweeps women off of their feet in a whirlwind romance. They fall head-first into infatuation. He's always sure that this one is it. He has even gone so far as to purchase a few engagement rings. The moment "it" becomes real, however, Lance starts to withdraw. Many of his other women have given up a big part of their lives to be with him, and then they're emotionally trapped. His friends hate meeting his girlfriends because they find it difficult to look them in the eye while peering into the crystal ball set on the table. There is no sense in telling any of them what usually happens in their situation because each one believes that she is different. They are damaged souls. They just don't know it yet. His buddies refer to Lance as a Boot Camp Lancelot, because when a new recruit abandons the army immediately after boot camp, it's called "a failure to adapt." Lance can't adapt to marriage. I guess some people are just born without the ability to grasp the concept of commitments they sign up for. What can anyone say to a man who doesn't want to change?

We women have this funny knack for convincing ourselves that men will be different for us. That is, he will be better for me than he was toward you. It's a me thing, not a *he* thing. Because I am *me, he* will be different.

I know a dozen men who have remained married and continued to have affairs. Their wives refuse to leave them and forgive them time and again. Why should they change? They have the best of both worlds. They never have to care about how their behavior affects anyone else. As long as their wives refuse to walk out and their girlfriends think they love them, these guys will always get their cake and their Twinkie.

If he can save himself the hassle of divorce and still sleep with other women, why wouldn't he? If he does finally leave, he doesn't change and repeats the relationship with the next woman. Serial cheaters leave bitter women behind, women who hung in there time and again only to be repeatedly devastated. Heartbroken "girlfriends" who ignored every bit of common sense suffer damaging blows to their self-esteem and their reputations. They suffer rejection and hurt because they chose to love someone who did not honor or appreciate them. These men received love and returned only pain.

Chapter 18

Tragic Social Aftermath

A friend who is a therapist once said to me, "I want you to do something you have never done before. The next time you commit the large act of being human and say or do something stupid, hurt someone unintentionally, make a fool of yourself, or whatever it is that isn't perfect, I want you to say a word you have never uttered." With this, she leaned in close to my ear and whispered. ~ "*Oops!*"

Since then I have always attempted to handle my mistakes with a smiling "oopsy poopsy." People find humor in honesty, and a sort of bond is made in groups who feel released from the confines of perfection.

Being the other woman will never receive smiles, laughter or acceptance. Even if you've made the choice to walk away, rectify your error, and ask for forgiveness of any fashion, immediately or years later, you may as well carry a flag the size of a sail exclaiming "Town Slut."

I recall reading in one of those books on affairs that blanketed my bedroom floor during my relationship with Blake, that those who are engaged in an affair believe themselves to be in secret and invisible to the eyes of those around them. In reality, most are suspicious of the affairs occurrence almost immediately. Unfortunately, I read this only after discovering it to be true. Once stamped as The Other Woman, her entire social life changes. Rumors and gossip swarm, worse than any day experienced in high school. You find yourself in a world you never imagined existed, the only world you are truly welcome in.

Yes, in fact, the eyes do open upon eating the forbidden fruit. Other mistresses who knew I was once one of them began to confide their stories and experiences to me. They were seeking answers, direction, support and understanding. But, the stories I heard sickened me and nearly destroyed my ability to believe in love at all. I couldn't believe how ruthless and pathological some of these married men were. The stories they told their wives and lovers were whispered to them by the devil himself. I couldn't wrap my mind around the depth of their trickery, their blatant disregard to the emotional damage they were causing. I started to think that it was impossible to detect their deceit. I started to think deceit was part of every male's DNA. I came to believe that it was not a matter of *if* a man would stray but *when*. Having such a brutal experience of my own to relate to, I began to see all men as the same. Now I am wiser, I thought. The veil has been pulled from my eyes. I became skeptical and bitter. When you think that all men are cheaters, liars, and assholes, you don't bother screening for a good one.

Rather you focus on being alert to it happening, essentially attracting yourself to bad situations which only reaffirm the belief; all men are cheaters, liars and assholes.

While in the midst of my affair and after it ended, friends frequently reported to me rumors they'd hear about me from the lips of individuals whose names I did not even recognize. Going on a date only ensured that the man I was with would be approached with disparaging information as to the individual he had innocently stumbled upon. The desire others had to negatively penetrate my life was astounding.

Being the other woman thickens your skin. You make a conscious decision to choose love over public scrutiny. What is unexpected is that when we let our past go, others do not. Nosy gossips seek raw meat like vultures. Looking for something to make their life more interesting, they invade your entire world. You are a representative of the greatest evil married women fear, and fear activates their radar.

Women who are, or have been, the other woman will lack social comfort. If I shared a wonderful conversation with a woman on one occasion and in the future she seemed brief, I assumed she learned my history. It feels as though, because you loved one man who wore a gold band, you are perceived to want them all. Whether it was real or imagined, when I entered a room, I saw women make a point to cling to their significant other and give me looks as if to say, "That's right, bitch. He's mine and don't you dare touch him." When I was introduced to a man's wife or girlfriend, it seemed she would speak at ridiculous length about their perfect lives together, making sure that I was fully aware of their partnership. Husbands who knew me on a personal or business level and shared a comfortable relationship with me appeared to visibly sweat under the collars if I stopped to chat for a moment in public if their spouses were near. I felt I could see the hidden thoughts of those in my presence at all times. Feigning happiness was a very difficult task and many nights I cried myself to sleep in the abyss of rejected emotions.

Each and every woman I have encountered who has shared with me the truth of an affair in her life has also faced the "scandalous bitch" charge from those who knew she once was the other woman. Each one who moved on with a new partner suffered the hurt of being with a man who openly or privately questioned her character and sincerity because she could "do that."

Once, I attended a barbeque at the home of some new friends. I met a woman who had an affair more than eight years ago. When this woman entered the room, a man approached me just to tell me what a "conniving bitch" she was and how she "caused his buddy a ton of troubles" as a result of having an affair with the man, who "almost left his wife for her." I had to wonder what the buddy's part in all this was and why, eight years later, she was still the solitary conniving bitch of a two party saga? "I was an idiot," she shared with me. "I believed we'd be together. When it ended, though, I felt relief. I was free, no longer hiding an ugly secret. I could now love in public," she said. "But instead, I suffered extreme embarrassment and no freedom from the opinions of others. It has taken many years to heal from the after affects of my affair."

The other woman is always given the entire blame for the affair. I'm not saying the other woman is blameless by any stretch of the imagination. I'm simply saying the habit of being harder on any part a woman takes in cheating is quite peculiar, especially given the fact that it takes two to tango.

Ending my affair with Blake far from ended the suffering and drama. This was aided by the small town populated with 300,000 in which we live and the constant chance of Blake's presence. For many years following our break up, if I should see him in a public place and say hello, or even be within a mile of him on the same road, rumors resurfaced instantly that we were an item again. Our social network was suspicious of clandestine activity between us long after our affair ended.

Though time has caused much of the era to be forgotten, it still surfaces every now and again. On a small scale, others still associate me to him. In the last year, I received a call from an acquaintance who planned to bid in a charity auction on a donated week's stay in Blake's new home in Aruba. Assuming that I had spent a substantial amount of time in the home, this man wanted to know if the minimum bid was worth it. There are more frequent occasions where I receive phone calls from people who wish to do business with Blake and phone me to gain strategic advantage or get my advice on how to use his services. Others phone who are knee-deep in business with him and hope I'll serve as a buffer to save them from their poor decisions or indebtedness to him. These are the least of my worries, but the constant reminders that people have not forgotten my past connection with Blake.

On a much more grand scale, however, was the interference I received when I attempted to move on with my life the first few years after our affair ended. Especially when I hit the dating scene again. No sooner did I go on a date with a prospective interest and he was inevitably "warned" about me. Once I dated a man who was bombarded so heavily by a group of men warning him of my intent to harm him, that he became so paranoid and insecure for what I might do to break his heart. He began to see things that did not exist. One evening, while this man and I were enjoying a glass of wine together at a local restaurant, my attorney entered and greeted me with a hug and peck on the cheek. In the minute it took me to ask my associate how his life had been treating him, my date abandoned me. I had to take a cab back to his home to retrieve my car. When I arrived, he jumped in my passenger seat and, in a fit of hysteria, said I had kissed my attorney before his eyes and began to sock himself right in the face while making suicidal type comments.

Obviously, this was not a stable situation and so as level headed as possible, I demanded his exit of my vehicle and I left. I shared this occurrence only with my friend Sasha and my attorney whom I was accused of kissing, for the sake of venting. Then I went on with my life. It was later reported to me that my date had informed several mutual acquaintances that I had "gone crazy," and that was why he had stopped dating me. This story was largely believed because after all . . . . I am "that girl."

It seems that falling in love with the forbidden (that is, a married man) makes you a psychotic woman who wants to harm and break the heart of every man you dare have dinner with. As I quickly learned, once you have become the other woman, anyone can say anything about you and it is believed. Don't bother trying to set the record straight. If you were ever in your life the other woman, you are forever a conniving, manipulative liar.

I met another man at an event and shared a fabulous first connection. When he asked to see me again, I excitedly gave him my phone number. We had lunch soon after, plus some phone conversations in which we planned a date after his return from an out-of-town sporting event. But

I never heard from him again. Was it something I said? I wondered. I had not caught that. I thought that our lunch had gone fabulously. Or was it something he had heard about me? Eventually I ran into him and had a wind of gut. I asked him why I had not heard from him. He was very forward in letting me know that it was a result of rumors he heard, from "this incestuous little gossiping town." He had opted not to risk an involvement with me.

Soon enough, I got wise. The next time I met a new Prince Charming thinking of sweeping me off my feet, I began to disclose right up front what he was up against. They took it as a bit of a macho challenge. This worked to my favor (at least I thought so), and I entered into a long term relationship. Shane was quickly and dutifully warned, just like the others, as were his parents and several of his close and long time friends. They were told tales about my life. Some stories were true, but others were horribly twisted and most were outright bullshit.

Nonetheless, each of Shane's friends and acquaintances began to caution him so greatly that he himself began to question if I were who I seemed. He began to constantly berate me about having been involved with a married man in the past and constantly telling me how poorly I was thought of by others. Our dates soon turned into interrogation sessions. He wanted the "real facts" pertaining to this or that story he'd been told by someone. He doubted things I had honestly and privately shared with him. His constant and prompt disclosure of nasty things he was hearing about me nearly caused me a mental breakdown. I began to dread our daily lunches. Instead of devouring blackened halibut, I'd be swallowing tears and attempting to avoid public viewing of the black waterfall flowing from my eyes. I tired quickly of crying in defense and soon did the typical woman thing: I sought therapy to figure out how to fix *myself* of the negativity he was constantly dishing me about my character.

In my therapy, I did find epiphanies sprinkled in between a few of my $150 sessions. They are as follows:

1) Don't throw your pearls before swine. In other words, don't give the best of what you've got to pigs who roll around in mud.
2) Women don't always have relationships with men who resemble their father. They can also have them with those who resemble the parent they have the most unresolved issues with. Sorry, Mom, but

this now explains to me why the men I've always dated are so damn emotional and stubborn and also let me know apparently we have a few issues to resolve.

3) Finally—and this should be obvious—why would you want to spend your life with a man who does not uplift you? If someone makes you feel bad, it's your choice to keep letting them. The *only* reason to share a life with someone is to *share authentic love.* Love is about support when you haven't the strength to stand, encouragement when standing in the sea of self doubt, and sharing your life with someone who adds vitality. I handled my therapist's advice about my relationship. However, as most women do, I decided that I knew better than my therapist. It was my relationship, and she just didn't get it. I convinced myself that if I fixed myself, *he* would get better. Have you ever noticed that when there are relationship problems, it's usually women who seek therapy? This says a lot about the responsibility we women take for the state of our relationships.

The real problem was that I felt that I could not get away from being made to feel bad about myself. I was in a cycle of trying to prove that I was trustworthy and that everything inside me was not malicious and evil. Shane became "they" to me, and through him I tried to mend what I had destroyed in my life. Because personal defense was ineffective, I hoped that he would, out of love for me, defend the character he knew. Instead, he was drawn to the gossip and thought it was his duty to tell me about it—daily. His reaction both perpetuated my old problems of being made to feel I was unlovable and created new ones. It confirmed to my psyche that I wasn't worthy of being treated with sensitivity. When he claimed that he didn't believe that I cared for him (just as Blake had said) it made me think I must not be doing enough to express my love. Despite complements I had received in past relationships with regard to the way I express and show love, when Shane and Blake said this, it encouraged me to work harder at surrendering myself to them. I was led to believe that there *was* something wrong with me, since two men had now said this same thing. It was something wrong with *me*, which caused these men to feel insecure.

Shane didn't focus on all of the horrible things that I experienced with Blake that caused me to leave the relationship, instead he honed in on all I had tolerated. To Shane this said I must have really loved

Blake a lot. I must have loved Blake *more* than I loved him. He often asked me what power Blake had over me. He obsessed over my past. So rather than enjoy a developing relationship with each other, Shane became insecure of what must have existed between Blake and I and it began to tear at our relationship quickly. Shane kept bringing up the topic of my past, and he and I began to argue more and more. I kept fighting to keep us together. I couldn't bear to appear rejected again before the public who was so eager to judge me. Shane kept testing what I would put up with in order to prove to himself that I really cared. Essentially, causing me to endure an equal hell, if not greater, then I had with Blake. I had completely resolved that my relationship with Blake was a mistake, but there were times that I wondered in anger if it might not make sense to return to that relationship. After all, no one seemed to be releasing me from it and it was looking like there was a pretty good chance I'd be spending the rest of my life paying for the relationship with Blake anyway. His part in my life wouldn't die, even well after it was dead to me.

As time went on, Shane kept our relationship very low key, only seeing me at his home and rarely doing things with me in public. I believed this was largely due to the constant interference by the public. I figured he thought it seemed easier to stay out of their view. Again, I was a secret, prolonging all that I had felt and suffered in an affair. On his more forgiving days, Shane would say, "It's hard for me to understand because I don't see it in you. I just can't see you getting into that situation, so it sounds like a bunch of excuses to me. At the end of the day, you knew he was married going into it." Essentially, by being honest about my past, I had guaranteed the disrespect of future partners and led them to believe that I would always put up with bullshit because I had done so once before. It was one of those famous vicious circles.

I was afraid that if I left Shane, it would only solidify the public belief and also my private one, which was I didn't have what it took to create a long term relationship. I thought everyone would think I was one of those women who went from one bad thing to the next, but she herself was always the real problem. No one would believe my side of the story; I learned this from the face puncher. Since Shane was a pretty good story-teller himself, I knew he would blast me publicly, saying whatever fed his ego and he'd come out on top. After all, he already had a public ready to feed him examples he could use and gobble up anything he dished out.

That began a whole new set of issues. I'll be damned, I said to myself, if another asshole comes out smelling like roses at my expense. At the same time, I held onto the belief that once Shane became confident of my love, he would become all of the things that I had originally thought he could be. I was locked into a battle to prove something, to whom I don't know; maybe myself, Blake, Beth or the public in general. Whoever it was, I was fighting to the death. I could no longer remember what it was like to be shown love and affection, to have someone do thoughtful things for me, even to be an intimate friend. I went from one one-sided relationship right into another. Catering again to one man's needs more than my own. Perhaps this was my own self-inflicted punishment for having an affair. I went from being a confident woman who didn't care much about the opinions of others to being consumed by and hostage to them. I came to believe that unless I moved to another state to get away from my past that I would never survive. Remember the ratty cabin I'd hoped to find an idyllic existence in? I went from one "fixer upper" to an undeveloped prefab that came without the right instructions. Only it was missing the good guy who purely loved me for just being me and my bedfellow became my worst enemy.

Shane played soccer in a men's league in the summer. I loved to go to the games, but my feelings of not being welcome kept me sitting alone in the stands and not making new friends with the other girlfriends, as I would have done before my affair with Blake. I had always been one of the popular girls, the girl with the right friends in the right places, the girl who moved in and out of social networks with ease. Suddenly, instead of being the vivacious, youthful Chatty Cathy, I was feeling insecure, unattractive, reclusive, and both the proverbial and literal girl alone in the stands.

What never left me was the feeling of discomfort whenever I was out. When I entered a room, I couldn't help wonder who knows about my affair and who is talking about me behind my back. I had the ever-present feeling of being harshly judged and unwelcomed. When I met people, I no longer trusted them at face value as I had before. Before my affair, when others were kind to me, I always just assumed it was because they were nice people or that they liked me. I simply believed in and saw the best in people. I learned to believe that just because I had a delightful conversation with someone, it didn't mean the conversation meant as much to the other person as it did me. I've always loved people and back in the day became a loyal friend quite easily—fighting loyal! Thus I am sensitive when someone turns against me, so my circle of friends became small and very select. Recovering from the affects of an affair leaves the other woman with a constant sense of skepticism. She is cognizant of the shell around her.

As had happened in my affair with Blake, when I couldn't engage with my potential in-laws, Shane's parents refused to meet me or open themselves to our relationship. His whole family believed what they were hearing about "that woman" Shane had fallen for. Family has always been extremely important to me. As the oldest of eight children, with enough nieces and nephews to fill a classroom, I find no greater joy than connecting with family. I have never imagined a future without a mother-in-law who would drink coffee with me or a father-in-law who loved me like a daughter. In my affair with Blake, that fantasy had been destroyed. It was something I eagerly welcomed when I met Shane. Shane was very close to his family and leaned heavily on them for all of life's decisions. His dependence on them led to much tension between us, as he was caught in the middle with strong feelings for two parties who were opposed. He had to choose things such as which of us he would spend his birthday with. He had to keep secret the plans he had with either me or his family so no one would feel hurt or uninvited. They were constantly at him to depart from the trouble and baggage they perceived me to carry. I was constantly at him to talk them through things, to defend me and tell them who I really was against the ugly rumors. Instead, he used the discord to align with them when he was displeased with me, where he was sure to have an agreeing sounding board from those who were ill equipped to offer him good advice.

To everyone's credit, years later we dropped our blazing guns, met the challenge head on, built a relationship and grew to love and adore each other. Some of Shane's long-time friends never did come to accept me or open themselves to get to know me. Those friendships remained interference throughout the duration of our relationship. But other friends shared vacations with us, as well as other great experiences. They opened their hearts, for which I am grateful.

Though the past is understood and forgotten with Shane's family and friends, and we built memories of wonderful times together, we would have been saved a lot of emotional hurts, anxiety, and tumult if the affair with Blake had never existed. In fact, the affair itself ensured that Shane and I never stood a chance of survival.

I was not the only one who endured these after affair hardships; Sasha also endured more than she could bear when she ended her affair. Because hers was slightly less public than mine and more easily left to rumors, she was able to either evade or lie. She quickly entered into a relationship with a man completely opposite of everything she had previously looked for. This was a man who was entirely irresponsible and mooched off her for more than a year. Living with a man who was sweet but in no way right for her, Sasha went into another bad situation. I couldn't understand it, but my affair had not ended yet to be sure I would. I had no idea why she continued to put up with the guy. He had nothing to offer her. But as she struggled with the relationship and a whole new bag of issues, she was still perceived as a "gold digging whore" as a result of her affair with a successful man. Because the truth was never fully revealed, people made it a part-time job to seek discovery and fill in the missing pieces with their own tall tales. Sasha, who looked everywhere to find the right relationship for herself, one in which she could settle down and have a child, found herself in inescapable turmoil with each new partner. Everyone saw her as a woman she was not, and she was never able to open herself to complete honesty with her new lover. She was convinced he would reject her if she were to fess up the truth of her past. Eventually, she relocated to another state, where, I am happy to say, she did in fact find Mr. Wonderful and gave birth to a beautiful daughter. She can speak to me about her past with him sitting next to her, and I love him for loving her in spite of that past. Though this is a happy ending, Sasha does still feel sad that she had to leave her home town and large family in order to have peace. Sasha's daughter will not be blessed with aunties, uncles, and grandma doting upon her regularly the way they do her cousins.

Another woman, Maria, had an affair with a business associate who assured her that his love was endless. Even while she was tossing her reputation and self-esteem away, she began to notice changes in him that made her think he might be being untrue to her as well as his wife. She began investigating (basically, she tapped into his voicemail), and when she confirmed her intuition, she blew up in a fit of rage and broke it off. To date, she is still reclusive and presents a hard exterior to the public that considers her crazy because of her investigation. She does not have a love life, let alone much of a social life. Her former lover, John, has continued to have affair after affair with other "disgraces." While his peers call him a dirty dog, they continue to do business with him and invite him into their social clubs. He is still socially accepted.

Jackie, whose relationship with her family impressed me as being very close, became an outcaste as a result of her affair with Brian. She began dating him just after he separated from his wife after the wife informed him that she was leaving him for another man. Once Brian's wife left him, however, she learned that her lover did not want her anymore, so, wanting to repair the marriage, she went back to Brian. But Brian vacillated between his wife and Jackie. He thought it was right for his children that he put some effort into keeping the marriage together. He kept Jackie on the side as the one he "really loved." Brian's wife, of course, told everyone who would listen what a whore and awful person Jackie was, and once even entered Jackie's place of business to speak ill of her. This woman who had left her husband went as far as to befriend Jackie's family, casting herself as the victim of this tangle of affairs. Jackie's family rejected her because she didn't immediately step out of the way so Brian could repair his marriage. At the same time, Brian was giving her a completely different story. And lest we forget, Jackie wasn't the only one keeping him from working on his marriage. Eventually after the affair dragged her through hell, she ended it. But what she endured was no different from what any other woman endured in public judgment, abandonment by people she loved, and deep pain that she dealt with all by herself.

Barb, who had stuck things out with Troy until he finally left his wife and then, when she discovered him cheating on her, left him, rarely goes out in public. When I hear others speak of her, most people say she got what she deserved. She is an attractive woman, and so when she does go out, she is noticed, and people immediately fill the ears of any man who is attracted to her with rumored stories, and twisted gossip. They attack her from every angle, disparaging her mothering skills and speaking of her as if she doesn't even love her own child. Barb's life revolves around her son. She is an excellent mother. Since she ended her relationship with Troy, she has not exposed herself to the possibility of a new relationship. She is reclusive and spends her time working or being with her son, and nothing else. She is always alone.

It took years for Angela, but eventually she found herself with a new group of friends. She still hides from her old social groups, and she told me about her fears that her new group might hear the old rumors. She hopes she has created in her new life friends who will let her leave it all behind because they were not a part of that time in her life. She is as happy as she believes she can be, given the circumstances, but she still feels the ugliness when she runs into anyone who knew of her back then.

A great number of other women I've talked to have long since relocated to other states in hopes of starting over. One day I spoke to my friend Janet, whose husband had an affair. "Kelly is not welcome in our community," she told me. "I don't think that there is one single thing that she could do to change people's opinion of her. People will never let go of her past. They'll never forgive her. If she wants a clean slate, she needs to leave town." Janet believes that Kelly has paid a much greater price than her husband, Ian, did. Whereas Kelly was hurt and remains ostracized, Janet and Ian receive community support.

The women I spoke to all feel angry, hurt, and cheated of time. They believe it is only natural for men to try to deceive them. "No one is trustworthy," they say.

Today I am far more private and less of the socialite I used to be. A part of me misses the events, the parties, and the functions. I have always been one to say, "The more, the merrier." Socializing has always given me energy and uplifted me. I love to be around groups of conversing people floating about in laughter and fun.

My life is much more peaceful, now more than six years since the end of my affair. I have only recently come to a place where I no longer feel damned, discomfort, or insecurity when I attend an event. I have made many new and wonderful friends who have helped in bringing me back to life. I have an even deeper appreciation for those who are closest to me, now that I have emotionally endured the abyss of hell. My heart is soft and light again. It's almost as if a heavy black fog suddenly evaporated from my head and chest. Like the rain stopped, the hurricane settled and suddenly the clouds parted and there above, was the brightest Sun I've ever seen. Only now, after so many painful years, can I truly say I LOVE and feel it in the deepest parts of my heart. I love that.

I am far from being the first woman who has experienced the painful side affects of being the other woman. As I did research for material to support or refute my thoughts on the subject, I was overwhelmed to find the same cry in every story. Time and again, women hope to share their wisdom with others who may be beginning an affair with a married man. These women want their pain to be of use in sparing another woman agony. One woman wrote:

> He made me feel appreciated and worthwhile, something nobody I dated had ever done but found plenty of reasons to avoid leaving. People found out and we became the laughingstock at work. I left my job because the taunting drove me away. I realized finally that he was never going to leave, because he has everything that he needs right now! The mistress for sex and emotional attachment and his wife for security. I realized that the relationship that I thought was perfect was horribly dysfunctional. Did his wife deserve all of the pain I caused her? I thought she did, but I didn't put myself in her shoes, or imagine if my husband were having an affair. Leave while you still have some self esteem. Otherwise it's a long and slippers slope and it only leads down.

Women I've talked to are filled with regret over the wasted time and energy they poured into their lover, time and energy that could have been spent on being available to a man who could fully commit to them. It was time and energy they could never get back. The women experienced an overall loss of respect from friends, family, and community. They harbor a deep sense of shame and embarrassment. As much as we believe that our story is different, we still pay the same price in the end.

The other woman's life is the one most likely to be the biggest tragedy of any love triangle. Ironically, Sasha once said, "Regardless of everything that I went through as a mistress and knowing what I know, I still think that I would judge the other woman no different than before my affair." I searched my own mind when she said that statement. Sadly, I discovered that initially my conditioning was the same: My first instinct is to judge the other woman as a bitch.

As women, we risk abusing some of our most beautiful qualities; the ability to understand, comfort, nurture and care take. We hate to see those we love suffer consequence for their poor decisions. I'm the first to run down to my daughter's school when she receives the great injustice of being served an in-school suspension for chewing gum in class. Regardless of her "willful disobedience" and repeated offense that landed her there, I know of her other struggles and her regret for the outcome. I want them to give her *one more chance* to do right. We adopt this very same maternal love for the men in our lives and treat them very much like children when they make mistakes.

In cases where a man has committed adultery, the finger is pointed at the other woman for his actions, thus he never fully pays the price for his mistake. Authors Gregory Hartley and Maryann Karinch explain in there book *How to Spot a Liar* that when a person has suffered a traumatic situation, their thoughts begin to personalize everything that has happened and an internal dialogue centers on who is to blame. The person reduces blame to the person whose welfare is least important to them.

Each time any of us point the finger, we remove responsibility from having to focus and participate in solution. Men want to be in charge, the tough guy, the strong one, the man's man, the primary decision maker, the king and head of the household. If we're going to let him be that guy, then we have to hold him accountable to his belief in his divine right. Can society really let him off the hook for being a wimp about his commitment to being faithful, while holding the other woman to blame for his actions? The answer is yes, and they do.

Chapter 19

Tragic Personal Aftermath

I am now, and have always been, prepared to accept responsibility for the mistakes and poor choices I make. I am a firm believer in accountability. I accept what I have brought onto myself. What I was not and never will be prepared to accept, however, are my children being persecuted for my choices.

Two years after my affair ended, my older daughter was employed by an upscale department store. She had become quite good at spotting individuals affiliated with my industry. One day she began helping a customer, and as they chatted their talk turned to the woman's son, who attended high school with my daughter. Eventually my daughter complimented the woman on her perfume, stating it reminded her of a friend of her mother's. "Who is your mom's friend?" the woman asked, and my daughter gave a name. The woman said the name rang familiar, at which point my daughter asked if she was in the predicted industry. She was. My daughter then asked if she knew me, and gave my full name. "Oh, yes," the woman replied in outrage, "I know her VERY well!" She proceeded to say ugly things about me, my affair with Blake and the kind of person I am. My daughter responded, "Well, Blake told my Mom lots of lies." The woman, now slightly embarrassed by the realization that she was speaking to my child, made a weak attempt to recover. "Well," she said, "I'm Beth's best friend. If that tells you anything."

As soon as the woman left, my daughter phoned me upset. She gave me the woman's name, which she had retrieved from her credit card. I recognized the woman as the one-time traveling companion Beth had gone to Hawaii with. This gossip was from a woman Beth reportedly despised because of an embarrassment the woman had caused her at a society event after their trip. This woman and I would not recognize each other if we passed on the street, yet she stood firm in claiming to be the best friend of a woman who didn't even like her—all in effort to condemn me. A woman I've never met!

If that were all, then I could certainly apologize to my child for having to endure such a thing at my hands. My daughter is one of the most sensitive, loving, and genuine young women one could be blessed to encounter. She should never have endured such gossip or hatred, especially because I had made a mistake. I will accept responsibility for some of the attack that my daughter faced. But what followed was much worse. The woman ran home to her son and identified my child to him as the daughter of "THE Whore," effectively encouraging him to return to school the next day and taunt her in class. He publicly teased and humiliated her for days until school officials ordered him to cease his harassment. The woman thought it was funny.

While I am still quite baffled that an adult woman would behave this way, what this episode shows is that many lives are affected by affairs beyond what we initially imagine. Things happen that we can never foresee, things that will affect not only the life of the other woman herself, but will also punish those she loves most. Affairs draw forth hatred from more than just the family immediately affected. Those who fear or are already bitter about an affair in their own life or family will attack anything and everything that elicits any reminder of the affairs.

My children were also affected in other ways. Like me, they had grown to love Blake. But he lied to them, too, and promised them many things that never materialized. He promised them vacations and family outings in a future with him. He promised college to my older daughter and extravagant gifts that certainly excited her. My younger daughter, who wanted him to be her father, was always cheered by the "daddy love" Blake bestowed on her. She had private dreams of her own for our little family. The ugly ending of our affair crushed my children, and when their eyes opened to the deception, hurt, and brutality, it made them skeptical of any man who might enter their lives in the future.

My children have always been more of a blessing than I could ever ask for. I suppose most parents feel that way about their children, but despite our one-parent household, I find it amazing they have beaten the odds. My older daughter has always been the teacher's pet. Her bubbly personality and good-heartedness make everyone around her fall in love with her. As she has become a young adult, she has impressed me with her many accomplishments. She toured Costa Rica with her junior high Spanish class for a humanitarian outreach program, and in high school she landed jobs most high school students would find very difficult to handle. Despite my protest that she enjoy her youth while it lasted, she has juggled work and studies, with no time off. She began attending a prep school to prepare to enter the fashion and marketing industry, and after interviewing with executives, she applied for and received the position of vice president in her marketing class. Her school recently allowed students to compete before a panel of selected VIPs from around our city who were chosen to help judge students to fill eight positions for a trip to New York to explore the fashion and stock exchange. She made it.

Once in a while, of course, she has gotten pretty snooty, and I've wanted to lock her out of the house until my real child repossesses the body sitting before me, but for the most part, almost every thing she has done has been sound. She is a bright girl with the world at her fingertips.

This child of mine has seemingly allowed me to almost bypass the horrors of teen years. With one exception. Shortly after my affair with Blake ended, my daughter began her first relationship. She chose a boy who at first seemed very nice. He was highly involved in sports and seemed to be an overall good kid. Then he suddenly began a downward spiral. He dropped out of everything that was important to him and started drinking a lot, eventually using drugs and then getting into every sort of trouble imaginable. He started lying and cheating on her and using manipulative behavior to make her forgive him. This lasted for three years. I agonized over her always surrendering to him and tried in every way I knew to get her to see what she was doing. But time and again, she brought the boy back into our lives, only to endure the same disappointments again. Every time he called her, pleading for sympathy and crying his "I'm sorry," she felt sad for his pain. Not considering his disregard for her pain, she took him back. I wanted to beat her head against a wall, and then my own.

This is what she learned from her mother as she saw me beaten down, pick myself up, forgive him, and restart the affair. I did the same thing in my next relationship. This is the pattern I taught her. Though her forgiving heart is beautiful, it is unbalanced. She couldn't see the fine line between forgiveness and self-respect. How could she have learned to see it, when her own mother had set such a bad example?

My younger daughter is equally impressive, though in many ways opposite of her sister. She's an observer, not as extroverted as my older. She is the one you have to get close to in order to see what is inside, but once you see it, it only takes a quick glance to know where her thoughts are. She has an eye for detail that shocks me sometimes; the child may have a future in forensics. Since kindergarten, she has been bi-lingual and is so brilliant that sometimes she has to dumb herself down in order to fit in and feel normal among her peers. She is still experimenting with who she is and wants to become, which has kept me on my toes, never knowing what will come next. For awhile, she was on a cheerleading squad with whom we traveled throughout the U.S. for competitions. My introverted baby suddenly was center stage without an ounce of stage fright. After she won several competitions, she became bored and moved on to her next personality. It keeps things pretty interesting around here. She is very sensitive, but she has a tough shell, thought-provoking when speaking, her words are always impacting and her meaning is shown more than heard. Before my affair with Blake, she was a happy, secure child. She did not question who she was and she was far less serious.

I am certain that some of her personality changes have more to do with growing up than with Mommy's break up, but I will say that she outwardly was the worst affected at the time. She experienced what most children do when their parents divorce. Her behavior in school changed, her grades began to slide, she slipped in and out of a depression that lasted two years and caused me great fear and anxiety. Her feelings have been crushed on several occasions when she has run into Blake's oldest daughter, who now attends her school and glares at her and runs away from her for reasons my daughter cannot understand. Reasons I doubt his daughter understands, either.

At fourteen years of age, my younger daughter often declares that she will not make the same mistakes that her sister and I have made with the men in our lives. It breaks my heart. I worry that she will never open her heart to trust and love. Worse, what if she falls harder? I'm already noticing her gravitation towards those she feels have been dealt an unfair hand in life.

About a year ago, my father and I had dinner together and he said to me, "honey, what is it with you? You have all of these gifts to offer anyone who shares your life. You are beautiful, intelligent, and fun. You have a unique, witty personality. Why don't you date men who treat you like a lady? It's almost as if you seem to think that you don't deserve it, or something. I don't understand that. Why don't you know that you deserve so much more than you accept?" I sat there, forcing myself to really *listen* to him. I was conscious about looking him in the eye as he spoke. I could hear my inner voice screaming at me: "Soak that shit in, goddamn it!" But while he was talking to me, all that I could think was, "My God, this is the same conversation that I just had with my daughter. Only I was on his side of the table." I think if we made choices for ourselves the way that we want our children to make their choices, life would be exactly what we want.

I realize that not every woman who is involved with a married man is involved, as I was, with a loaded one. In the spirit of sarcasm, let me say this: If you're going to do yourself in like this, there's no point in wasting time with a poor guy. It all ends up the same, and if you're still willing to take the risk, then get a trip to Rome out of the deal!

The reality is though, I went broke trying to keep up with Blake. I did not perform well, career-wise, because I was always giving him my free time in order to compete with Beth who refused to travel with him or give up her tasks in order to spend time with him. I thus had hardly any income flowing in. I had racked up so much credit card debt by trying to look nice, contribute my portion to a tab once in a while, and flying him away from the guys and back to me when he was supposed to be on, say, a fishing trip, that I had nothing in the bank to pay my electric bill. When I say that there was no food in the house, I don't mean that a few of those mystery cans with the label peeled away were lurking in the cabinet. I mean Ol' Mother Hubbard's cupboard. Being lost in the delusion of love, I had taken so much time away from work and responsibility that when the affair ended, I really had to hit the ground running. And that's not easy to do when the condition of your soul matches your cabinet space.

I ended up taking a second mortgage out on my house and depleted myself of my home equity. Rich guy, poor guy, it is not uncommon to hear of the financial trouble a woman faces after being "dropped like its hot" and I don't know of many women who are able to focus on a career when their personal lives are in a shambles.

I found one thing to be very common in both my interviews and research, and that is a great portion of women who are having affairs with married men are having affairs with their married co-worker. In almost every one of these cases, when the affair ended the other woman found it extremely difficult to continue being forced to see him regularly in their work environment. It was too painful for her. This wasn't the only issue that she was left to deal with. A lot of these dumped mistresses also suffered ridicule and gossip from other co-workers. Her married lover was not about to leave his job. He has a family to support after all. Further, he isn't emotionally suffering as much as his tossed lover. He hasn't been left alone. He still has a wife to go home to. The standoff over who is going to leave the company really doesn't leave the former mistress much of an option. In most every case where an affair existed between co-workers, it was the other woman who was left to give up her job for the sake of her sanity.

In her book *Preventing Affairs*, Peggy Vaughan writes: "Even if she's able to keep her job, her peers' assessment of her as a worker will probably be lowered. The double standard for judging sexual behavior that exists in society as a whole exists in the workplace as well. Both men and women are likely to be more harsh in their judgment of the woman than the man when it comes to a workplace affair. Even if co-workers bring no moral judgment to her actions, they're likely to make a professional judgment that she's really not serious about her career."[10]

I interviewed a woman named Shelly, who had an affair with the owner of her company. She was very young and a single mother. The man was suffering from other failed investments and was experiencing financial ruin. She sympathized with his agony and poured a lot of her time into helping him out of a loyalty she felt while their friendship developed into an eventual affair. He promoted her to a sales manager position which really boosted her ego at such a young age. After she took the promotion, he drove her hard to boost sales and she took on the challenge with his needs in mind, desperate to save his failing business for him. He was so broke that he could not pay most of his staff and therefore many quit to find new employment. Shelly took on those vacant positions with no additional pay. She was content with this because it allowed her more time with him, she felt purpose, received a lot of praise from him and thought she was working with him as a team; they were in this together. He would tell her things like "someday, you and I will have a lot of explaining to do." Meaning an explanation about their love to his wife and employees. These things that he said to her and the praise he gave her for not only her hard work but also how she made him feel led her to believe that they would be together soon, publicly. His remaining employees became suspicious about their deeper involvement. His office manager announced in a company meeting that she was quitting because "that whore has been

---

[10] Peggy Vaughan, *Preventing Affairs*, p99

given a management position for screwing the boss." Shelly had earned her position and was keeping the company afloat by investing long hours into the company. Her hard work was not being recognized because her affair had not been as secret as she had thought it was. Eventually, he sold his company reaping a small profit based upon the client growth Shelly was able to secure with contracts. Two days later, her boss called her and told her that the affair was over. He and his wife relocated to another state immediately. Shelly had been given little pay for her management position and no pay for the several other positions she had temporarily filled. When the new company took over, they brought with them their own people and she was left with no job at all.

I could fill these pages with stories from women who have invested money they really didn't have into flying to places to meet up with their lovers. Loaning or giving them money. Paying for hotel rooms, dinners, or other expenses so that the charge would not show up on his credit card bill. Either way, there is usually an outpour of money she really can't afford to be spending.

I'll be the first to admit it. I am vain. If you aren't vain, then you must be one of those lucky ones who live in an area that has those grocery stores with the "family friendly" aisle and no *Cosmopolitan* at the checkout stand. You also must not have cable TV and you find ways to ignore the enormous cultural expectations of women today. My butt no longer looks like it did when I was twenty, and I have a hard enough time dealing with that, so when my father said one day, "He's aging you," I raced to the mirror. I had suddenly developed these huge bags and dark circles under my eyes. A few weeks later, when my bathtub clogged, I discovered there was enough hair in the drain to give my cat extensions. I was losing my hair from stress, and then I also noticed that I no longer could control my gray hairs with my tweezers. When my youngest sister sat playing with my hair one day and said, "Oh my God!" I considered starting an auto pay plan with my hair colorist. My forehead was so creased that when I wasn't wearing makeup, I called myself Steve Jr., after the son I think my father always wanted. Thank God for Botox, or I might have stayed in my jammies all day. You may think that's just a part of aging, but my affair ended many years ago while I was in my early thirties. Today, at thirty six, I look and feel far more vibrant then I did back then. Further, it's been at least two years since I ran to the local day spa for an updated Botox injection.

It wasn't just my vanity that had a severe humbling from the stress of my affair. My overall health was damaged by the time things came to an end and for sometime after. I'm one of those never-get-sick people, but during those few years of my affair and some time after, I've sometimes felt like I'm near my death bed. My adrenal glands are just now recovering from the shock they took as a result of all of my emotional ups and downs. My almost-photographic memory has evaporated, and today, if I don't write everything down this second on my "to-do" list, I'll forget it. I think I walked around for two years after my affair feeling like I was stuck in a van with Cheech and Chong, and "too much mind" left me with migraines. My chiropractor's cell phone number is stored on my speed dial in the event my neck gets stuck. I used to call him up and say, "Tim, I have whore neck again," he appreciates my humor and opened the door for me, even on his days off.

Science is finding more evidence every day that negative emotions and high states of stress are cancer causing and can contribute to some forms of heart disease. Evidence supports that women in strained relationships face greater cardiovascular risk than their male partners do. Women in contentious relationships are more likely to develop high blood pressure, high cholesterol, high blood sugar levels, or Metabolic Syndrome. Even if you have not seen the short term affects to your health in having an affair, there may be long term ones. The other woman suffers heightened anxiety, depression, and abnormal amounts of stress. When she is suffering these emotions, she is not likely to be able to eat much and probably sleeps even less. Her mental focus will usually be very fixated on her affair.

When I think of things having to do with the affects of my relationship with Blake, it seems ironic to me that the irritable bowel syndrome commercial suddenly comes on TV. I still look for "signs" from the universe. All joking aside, my health went in the shitter . . . as is bound to happen to any woman who chooses to live her life as the other woman.

Part 3

Decisions, Prevention and Healing

Of all the discoveries which men need to make,
the most important, at the present moment,
is that of self-forming power treasured
up in themselves.

~ William Ellery Channing

Chapter 20

Are You in a Toxic Relationship?

In the movie *The Thomas Crown Affair*, actress Rene Russo says the one line that causes the movie to kerplunk itself smack in the middle of my list of favorite movies: "Men make women messy." Why did that line elicit such a strong emotion from me? Because, well, *men make women messy*. Plus, I liked the character's strength and her ability to spit the truth, when sitting in a limousine with that gorgeous billionaire, Thomas Crown.

The other thing that men do is cause wonderful women to fall head over heels for them in hopes that the men will respond like Mr. Crown did. A woman wants a man to make her his utmost focal point and show unwavering resolve to love her. Almost any woman who has been in a relationship lasting for any substantial length of time can recite in detail the things that her husband, boyfriend, or lover did to sweep her off her feet.

Normally, of course, after some longevity, such acts of generosity and loving kindness fade a bit within reason. Some women are fortunate enough to never experience any change in his doting at all. But sometimes acts of generosity and loving kindness cease for good. Even worse are the unhealthy relationships that become habits and addictions where we lose ourselves and become so completely enmeshed that we forget who we really are and how we deserve to be treated. Horrible are the relationships where women end up surrendering to physical, emotional, or mental abuse.

Just because a man has an affair doesn't mean he is emotionally, mentally, or physically abusive. Some men just make horrible mistakes. Some fall out of love poorly. Others have some serious growing up to do. But there are some men who are so damaging to women that to continue our lives with them is to create a self prison with bars of misery.

What a woman should always know is the difference.

Some relationships are worth saving for the higher and better good they bring to our lives. Others are as toxic as the water around Chernobyl. Toxic water will kill you. The only way to save yourself is to swim to the shore as fast as possible, climb out, and wash away the pollution.

A toxic person can be the bitch in the cubicle down the hall or the person we choose to give our hearts to. In her book, *Toxic People*, Lillian

Glass describes a toxic person as "anyone who has poisoned your life, who is not supportive, who is not happy to see you grow, to see you succeed, and who does not wish you well. In essence they sabotage your efforts to lead a happy and productive life".[11] Glass goes on to suggest how to deal with toxic people. She adds that most psychologists agree that closing the door, letting go, and completely losing contact with the toxic person may be the only way to regain your mental health.

Toxic men are careful enough not to quickly inoculate you with their poison but slip an IV into your arm while you are asleep in infatuation. The drip is so slow you hardly notice the small effects over time as you absorb the illness.

Toxic men make us feel stupid for having dreams, desires, or goals. They don't believe we can achieve them. They think our ideas are illogical distractions from the things they think we should be putting our focus on. Toxic men make us feel like our thoughts are insignificant and our feelings are unstable. They say things that make us question ourselves while they attempt to convince us that they are the only ones who might tolerate our inadequacies. They minimize the things and people that are most important to us. "You're just like your mother," the toxic man will say, or "Yeah, but *your* family . . . ." and goes on to say that our families do things in ways that are not as good or as important as the way that theirs does things. Your job is not as important as his. Your contribution to society is not as meaningful as his. Your friends are not as relevant as his.

Toxic men also excuse their own behaviors and hurtful actions by pointing at you. *It's your fault.* You made them do it, whatever it was. "If your ex-boyfriend hadn't sent a client to your business, I wouldn't have felt insecure," he'll say, "and therefore I wouldn't have pursued inappropriate relations with the girl at the coffee shop." Or, "I was so afraid of losing you that I grabbed your throat and choked you because I was afraid that you would leave me." Or, "I didn't feel like you really loved me, and so I went to her."

You'll never find true joy and happiness with this guy, but for some reason, we still believe we are the ones who will lose when he goes.

---

[11] Lillian Glass, PHD, Toxic People, 10 ways of dealing with people who make your life miserable, St. Martins Press, 1995 p12

If you want to know if the person you share your life with is toxic or not, Glass writes, "the only thing to concern you is that you are treated with dignity and respect that you deserve." She goes on:

> Negativity can wear down your physical resistance. Anger and hostility affect the production of the hormone nor-epinephrine. A person who feels constant stress or hostility may produce an overabundance of this hormone, which causes high blood pressure as well as blockages that lead to heart attacks or stroke. There is also, as researchers have confirmed, a high correlation, in cases of cancer and heart disease, with repressing negative emotions. [12]

Glass names approximately thirty types of toxic personalities. The following seven kinds are example's of those I've found, and created based on her work. These are men we often find ourselves involved with.

1. *The Belittling Bully.* This man seems to get a thrill out of belittling you, either outright or by minimizing accomplishments, goals, perspectives, or feelings. For example, you might express your excitement for your hard work at winning a new client from a competitor and he will respond that the client switched because he likes your boobs. He is constantly analyzing everything about you and makes it a point to remark on your imperfections. To be in his presence is to be constantly scrutinized. A good example would be the story I told earlier of Blake accusing me of encouraging a man to send me flowers. He implied that I was unprofessional and flirtatious and the man sending me flowers made me unattractive to him. He often uses accusation to try to convince you that you are less than a person. He spins everything in order to keep you on the defensive. His arguments are often illogical and far fetched.

   I believe that when a man is constantly critiquing you and diminishing your self-worth, he is doing so because he secretly

---

[12] Lillian Glass, PHD, Toxic People, 10 ways of dealing with people who make your life miserable, St. Martins Press, 1995 p58

fears that you will figure out he's not as good as he wants you to believe he is. He fears that you will discover that you are actually too good for him. He thinks that if your self esteem rises, your eyes will open to his shortcomings and you will be vulnerable to being seduced by someone who will truly give you what you deserve. Therefore, the bully constantly beats up anything you say, do, feel, need, or aspire to become.

2. *The Self-Destructive Victim.* This man always wants things to go well in his life, yet every time things seem to be on track he self-destructs. As quickly as we see hope that he learned from his last mistake, he makes the same mistake all over again. I knew a man who had experienced a divorce that he said he did not want. His wife left him because she could no longer tolerate his partying. After he had settled into his new life he seemed to be on the right track. He learned his lessons. He bought a new house and was excited to see his children every chance he could, he hated to see them go and was depressed when it wasn't his week with his daughters. He wanted a family and missed having a partner to share his life with. Finally, he met a girl who he really seemed to like an awful lot. They were getting very close and she was falling in love with him. He says he was in love with her from the moment he met her. After months of romantic courting, one night he invited her to meet several of his friends at a barbeque and she joined him. She had a fabulous time and hit it off smashingly with his friends. Her blend with his friends seemed to make them both all the more twitter pated with each other and, that night, he asked her to accompany him on a vacation to meet his mother—a woman he honored greatly. Soon after inviting her to meet dear mom, he romantically told her it was time to go home. He had other things in mind now; they were both feeling very passionate toward one another. She said her goodbyes to his friends and thanked them for the invitation. She ran home to grab a night bag and agreed to meet him shortly after, at his house. But when she went to his house he wasn't there and never showed up. She worried that something had happened to him and drove back to the party to find out what time he had left and what might have happened to delay him. He wouldn't answer his cell phone and

she worried that perhaps he had been in an accident. When she arrived back at the friend's house, she walked in the door calling for him. Hearing voices, she went down to the basement where she found him doing cocaine. She left in shock. He tried to make amends and promised to never do it again but the writing was on the wall. He is alone again, still hoping she will come back. He lets her know this sometimes when he calls her late at night from bars.

Not long ago, I had coffee with this same man and he told me about his life. He spoke of how bad things always happened to him. He always seems to find himself in trouble, people always get him wrong, he's always in the wrong place at the wrong time, and it never is his fault. The victim typically banks on words more than action; talks but never does anything. He wants things a certain way, but then he acts in ways that bring the complete opposite of what he says he wants. No matter how many opportunities we give this guy, he will never change.

3. *The Problem Avoider with Ice in His Chest.* This guy is a wimp who can't confront anyone or make a decision. He is unreliable, runs away from any stressful situation, and is unable to deal with the problems at hand. He says one thing and does another. He doesn't know what he is doing and neither does anyone around him. He is often a bullshitting liar, an ultimate manipulator, and you cannot be sure if anything he says is believable. You never really can communicate with him, so you never know how he really feels about any issue. This is the guy who, when caught in a lie, hides and avoids conversation.

He also runs away from anything that may make him deal with emotions—yours or his. For example, once me and Shane were driving in minor traffic on a four lane road to a golf course. While we were stopped at a red light, I saw some small children crossing the street with a puppy. When the light turned green, the van in front of me jumped forward just as the puppy began to run back home. I knew what was going to happen. "No, no, no, no," I yelled. I watched the vehicle roll over the top of the dog and keep driving. I don't believe the driver even knew he had hit the animal. It was one of the most horrific sights I have ever seen. The dog spun and rolled, as if in a cartoon. Then I heard the children begin to scream and cry. Crying myself, I pulled up alongside the dog and saw that it was still alive and yelping. My automatic reaction was to get the dog in my car and rush it to animal emergency in hopes of saving it or, at best, putting it out of its misery kindly. I wanted to comfort the children, too. I was overwhelmed with maternal instinct and sadness. When I started to put my car in park, Shane began screaming at me. "GO, GO, GO. Drive, goddamn it, drive!" I looked at him like he was insane. The only thing to do was save the dog. But he put my car back into gear and kept screaming at me, putting his hand over my leg and pressing my foot down on the gas. I was staring at the maniac next to me as other passers-by stopped their cars. He continued to scream at me. I drove off . . . sickened and in a complete daze. I couldn't understand him. "Why?" I kept crying to him. Finally he calmed down enough to tell me that he didn't want to listen to the animal yelping in pain. It would upset him too much. I never forgave myself for letting that happen, and the scene has played over and over in my head for years. I had never left anyone or anything in need like that before in my life, and abandoning that injured dog haunts me still today. In the years that followed, every time an event major or minor transpired in my life where I needed emotional support, Shane reacted the same way.

4. *The Rabid Dog.* You never know where you stand with this guy. His emotions change like a light switch. One minute he's happy, the next he's exploding about some ridiculous thing. Once the bomb has gone off, he calms down and asks, "What's wrong?" as if you hadn't just been assaulted. You spend your life with this guy on pins and needles, never knowing if, after you've shared a fun-filled afternoon, you'll face a catastrophe that evening. He loves combat and will challenge everything you have to say, even if it's not directed at him. I once had a conversation with one of these guys about car insurance. I had slid on ice and smashed my car into a tree, causing a wee bit of damage to the front end of my vehicle. He suggested that I use his friend's body shop; perhaps we could work a deal where my insurance would cut the shop a check, and maybe I could

get some sweet accessories in addition at the expense of my insurer. When I told him that pimping my car out wasn't really my biggest concern, he turned on me and proceeded to chastise me about defrauding my insurance company. I tried to change the subject, but no matter what topic I turned it, he was still screaming at me, until finally, he hung up on me. Later, he told me that his reaction was my fault for being so difficult. When I was guarded around him afterwards, he didn't understand why I would be.

This guy wants control over every situation and picks petty fights that will go on for days. You are expected to read his mind, but when you fail, a fight erupts, not only about your inability to read the crystal ball but also about any previous failures or other crimes against him you have forgotten about. With this man, everything is a competition. Should you share any event or story or feel good about something, there is an angle in which he seeks to be superior. Everything is grounds for competitive argument.

5. *The Selfish Asshole.* This guy is all about himself. If he can't derive any benefit from you, he will discard you. He'll listen to what you say as long as you agree with him. The only agenda he has concerns himself. The only conversation he is interested in is one about himself, the only activity that suits him is one that stars him. You are expected to cater to him on every level, but he has no thoughts of catering to you in any way. He has nothing to give to others because he is empty and constantly looking for you to fill him. He denies being selfish, of course, and he'll attack you when you point out some selfish act he's committed. He has a fragile ego and constantly exhausts you complaining or yelling about the violations to his ego he feels you have committed. This guy expects you to give him your full support at all times, to be accommodating to all of his hobbies and interests. You must make every effort for him and read his mind while doing so. It is your responsibility to take care of him, but he takes no care of you. He doesn't give, he only takes. If you let him down, you will pay for it. However, on the off chance that you ask him to participate in something that interests you, he will bow out because "it's not my thing."

You make constant sacrifices for him, but he will make none for you.

6. *The Verbal Tyrant.* This guy will attack you without warning whenever things do not go his way. He is turned on by emotionally devouring you. His verbal abuse is flat out immoral and inhuman, and his words attack anything and everything that is important or has meaning to you. He will use the most intimate and sacred things in your life to abuse you. You cannot share an ounce of vulnerability with this man during good times, for in bad times he will throw the shards of your memories back at you as weapons. He will use cruel words to break you, focusing on your body, your family, your children, your capabilities, your feelings—anything that you have shared with him confidentially—to bring you to your knees. Once you're on your knees, he takes every opportunity to kick your teeth in, forcing you to wallow in defeat. Using every imaginable cruelty, he will seek to destroy your heart in order to make himself feel superior or in control. This guy's abusive words have lasting, sometimes life-long effect. In essence, his words can rob you of your life. An example would be, when I ended my relationship with Shane, he sent me text messages telling me that I was nothing special, I lacked intelligence and that he could take any woman into a doctor's office and pay to make her look as good. In other words, I was easily replaceable. My only value was in being attractive and this can be bought. I could take "that baggage you call children" and go be worthless for the rest of my life without him. He mocked my writing this book saying I was lying about writing it or that it would never amount to anything if I were. He jabbed my career as meaningless to society, my earnings as a fluke that would disappear and my family were all trash. He then bragged that he had bought a new home and other spiffy things that glorified him, he was magnanimous, better than me, and would always be wanted. He had more to offer.

7. *The Control Freak.* This guy will stop at nothing to be in control, and he'll tear you down any way he has to in order to achieve control. He'll accuse you of foul play and try to fence you in or make you submit to him. He wants to know everything you are

doing, who you speak to, what was said. Simple matters, such as laundry or which store you choose to shop at are under his scrutiny. You cannot make plans for your day, but must wait until he has advised you of his expectations. You are to be on call at all times. Once he isolates you from your friends or family, he makes you more dependent on him, using the relationship itself as a threat. Will he stay? Will he go? He uses your fear of losing him as a way to manipulate everything in his favor. Your life thus turns into a game of emotional ping pong, with him using your emotions against you, flipping the table every other minute, reverting to sweet talk and promises, even tears, when you threaten to take back control. If you do manage to gain some control, he uses his softer side to pull you back into the game

If you have found your partner to be any one (or many) of these characters, you many be suffering from a disorder that has left you paralyzed in your situation. That is, you know you are miserable, but you can't find it in yourself to let go or leave. You are not in love. You are a hostage. Stockholm Syndrome is the psychological response where a victim actually begins to feel loyalty toward her abuser. Because she has become conditioned to accept the abuse or intimidation as a method of survival, she starts to see any tokens of affection as evidence that her abuser loves her. They think that by correcting their own behavior, it will change the behavior of the intimidator. The victim walks on egg shells to forestall an outburst. Her life becomes focused on what she needs to do to keep the intimidator happy. Victims will avoid their own needs if they think it might cause problems. The victim will turn on her own friends and family with the idea that they are interfering or causing trouble and will feel protective of her abusive partner.

The tyrants in my list don't belong in our lives. Our lives are usually better off without the pain they bring, and the pain of leaving them doesn't have to exceed the pain in living with them. Cut them loose and feel pity for the next girl. You will need a great amount of support to get away, but it is probably easy to come by through family and friends, who already feel you're better off without him.

Oftentimes, a woman who stays in a bad relationship does so because she is not emotionally strong enough to leave. She is broken down mentally and doesn't believe she can live without him. Staying with him gives him too much power, and guarantees that she will live the remainder of her years in heartache.

Is that the life that you want to live? Do you truly believe that you deserve nothing more? You already know what you have if you stay. Think about what your life is like now. Is this what you want your forever to look like?

My mom once said to me when I was agonizing over letting go of a toxic relationship, "Honey, you're just worried he'll go off and be better for someone else. That he'll be everything that you ever wanted him to be for a new girl." She was right. I was convinced that he would. It took me sixteen years to get the lesson. Seldom do men change, and the new girl gets nothing different. After I realized this, I experienced growth and was able to free myself of the oppressive nature of staying with a toxic man out of fear that he would change for the better and someone else will get the reward. The real reward is in letting go of the "what if" attachment knowing that what you see is what you (or the next woman) get.

If they were assholes all of the time, spotting the toxin would be easy. I'm going to be a bit of a braggart here. Most of the men that I have had a relationship with have spoiled me rotten. Being treated like a princess has been a big part of my falling in love. My husband was excellent at doing little things to let me know that I was in his thoughts. He came home from work with flowers so often they almost stopped being appreciated. After I took my shower in the morning, I stepped out to a cup of hot coffee and ironed clothes. The man certainly knew how to treat a woman like a lady. He was also thoughtful at times when it really counted. One year he asked what I wanted for my birthday and I asked for a new robe. He bought one, and when I tried it on, acted very upset because it didn't have pockets. "Yes, it does," I said, putting my hands in the pockets to show him. My fingers touched a diamond ring safety-pinned inside.

I've had boyfriends who lavished me with jewelry right from the start. My ex-fiancé sent so many roses to my office that when the delivery man walked into the front door, the receptionist would just point her finger to my desk, still filled with vibrant flowers from the last time. My favorite kind of flower delivery is the time when it's no particular occasion, but just to say, "Hey, I'm thinking of you today." I have a garage shelf full of sentimental old vases.

But although they treated me like I was special and unlike anyone else in their life at times, the gestures didn't mask their true character. Every way that I witnessed them mistreat another was a way I was eventually treated. The bottom line is that *yes*, it is true: If he treats his mother like crap, he will eventually treat you like crap, too. And the same goes for children, employees, business associates, friends, former girlfriends, and everyone else in his life. Do I need to say that if he treats his wife horribly, his mistress will eventually get the same treatment? Gifts and showers of affection are nice, but a woman should never become so consumed by these little things she gets that she fails to recognize the bigger truth. Who cares about dead roses and a jewelry box full of apologies? I'll take the general foundation of respect any day.

Chapter 21

Identifying Authentic Love

My reason for doing research changed while Blake and I were still together and I was studying books on affairs. Initially, I had sought to figure out the psychology behind our involvement, then I began searching for statistics to support the possibility that we had a fighting chance of ending up together permanently. Towards the end of our affair, however, I was looking for the sneaky advice his wife might have found in books or on the Internet that might prevent my relationship working the way I wanted it to. I found a lot of it. I was shocked to hear so many couples speaking positively about the affects an affair had on their relationship. Later, when my friend Janet phoned me to tell me that she had learned of her husband's affair, I was glad I had done all this reading.

During one of the breaks in my affair with Blake, I went to visit Janet and her husband, Ian, and they offered me much support. It never occurred to me at that time that they would ever be in a situation like mine, that is, experiencing an affair. But a year later, while I was vacationing with my sister, I received a frantic call from Janet. "Ian said he wants a divorce," she cried, "he is accusing me of having an affair." She went on to tell me about his accusation, and she swore to me, "You know I would never do that, you know that I would never betray my husband like that!"—and I did. At that moment, I knew what all of this meant, but I didn't want to believe it.

"Janet," I said, "I may be tainted by my experience with Blake, but I think Ian is having an affair." She refused to believe me. I believe that even such a suggestion had her seething with anger. "He wouldn't do that to me," she protested. Then she hung up.

Two weeks later, she called me again. "Ian is having an affair." I was overwhelmed. If Janet and Ian aren't safe, who is? Then I recalled my visit to their home. In hindsight, I could see that the signs were all there. He had been primed for an affair, but I was just too caught up in my own emotions to recognize them. I remember thinking, *Uh oh* one afternoon at a pool party. We were all "in the spirit" after many colorful beverages, and Ian had hollered out from the pool, "Baby, come give me some! My God, it's been three weeks." Another evening, I had heard them arguing and Janet was throwing blankets on the couch, saying, "Why can't we ever just go to bed without you wanting to mess with me? Can't you ever just hold me?"

Ian's income had increased substantially in a short period of time, and I had noticed a hint of arrogance in him. Janet held her own quite well, however, and they had both become more successful than they had been when they'd first married. But while Janet was thankful for what they had built together, Ian had forgotten her part in that growth. He also failed to remember that she had loved him before he had been so successful. I had noticed his ego was out of control. Janet told me she had begun to notice changes in him. Odd events were happening around their house, like strange phone calls in the middle of the night on his cell phone, which he seemed to be hiding or stored in strange places. After trying, and failing, to dismiss what I had said to her, she cornered him. He fell to his knees in confession. My dearest friend in the world was destroyed.

I cannot tell you where I was mentally and emotionally at that moment. Here I was, the closest friend of the woman grieving over her husband's betrayal, but I also had been the other woman, and she knew every detail of my past. As I listened to her, I was afraid that she would lash out at me for the pain that I had caused someone in her shoes, that she would make me the target of all of her anger. After all, I was "one of them." I sat in silent agony as I listened to my friend's anguish. She never spoke an ill word to me. Day after day, night after night, any hour she needed me, I answered her desperate calls. Finally, I flew 6,000 miles to hold her and force her to eat something.

This was an awakening for me. I had always thought Janet and Ian had the ideal marriage. I loved their partnership. They were my hope that real love existed. Ian is not an asshole. He is a wonderful man, a good provider, and an excellent father. He is also a magnificent husband and the most intimate friend of an amazing woman. He is a man who is like a brother to me, an uncle to my children, a man who inspires and encourages everyone around him to be the best that they can be, all while keeping them in constant stitches. If you cry in this man's company, it is because he has caused you to laugh so hard you cannot help yourself. I love Ian and he messed up big time. I feared losing him from my life, and that caused me great sadness. My mother has always said, "A marriage is bigger than two people," and on the day Janet told me Ian was having an affair, I knew exactly what my mother meant. Affairs hurt more people than just the three in the entanglement.

During those nights I spoke with Janet, I wondered if I would be forced to choose a side. That wasn't an option; Janet is my best friend, and my obligation was to be loyal to her and to support her. I figured that divorce was inevitable. She and I are alike, and I knew what she was going through emotionally. I knew that she was pissed off, that her pride would be a large factor in her thinking, and that retaliation was probably next. But I hated to see this marriage fall apart. If it did, I would suffer, too, and so I begged her to not react until she had given herself some time to digest everything, see where things were going, find out what he was willing to do to save their marriage.

"Why?" she asked me. *"*Why shouldn't I leave him for doing this to me?" The pain and rage in her voice were so deep I could feel them.

And I answered her, almost thoughtlessly because my answer didn't require much thought, at all. *"Because you will be more miserable without him than you will be with him,"* I said. And in that moment I understood WHY people who truly love each other work it out.

Is This Love Authentic?

Cheri Carter-Scott is an author I have grown to admire greatly. In my opinion, her book, *If Love Is A Game These Are The Rules*, gives the most logical yet profound way of describing authentic love:

> Authentic love is choosing your partner exactly as he is; it is putting your energy behind your choice and causing the relationship to be magical, rather than searching for reasons why it cannot work. Love is supporting your partner in her choices, urging her to fulfill her hearts desire and go for all her dreams. Authentic love is honoring your partner's truth and wanting the very best for him. It is not controlling or possessing but rather respecting and trusting his unique path in life. [13]

---

[13] Cherie Carter-Scott, PHD, If Love is a Game, These are the Rules, 10 rules for finding love and creating long-lasting authentic relationships, Broadway Books, 1999 pXVI,XVII

To truly experience authentic love, couples must feel secure in their partnership and encouraged to speak the impossible. They learn to respect each others boundaries and drop their pride, reaching out even when they don't want to. They disallow themselves to assume and they ask questions in order to keep communication open. This means they will agree to work things out, even through grueling fights, without leaving. Authentic love means having the commitment not to give up, while searching for solutions. Remembering the things you love about your partner instead of focusing on the bad, and expressing your love. Authentic love is the freedom to be yourself.

Carter-Scott adds that "love can be a powerful force that sometimes eclipses reason and sound judgment" and suggests that you partner with someone who plays by the same rules you do. Are you sharing your life, she asks, with someone who agrees with the moral foundation or "rules" of what you believe a relationship should be?

Carter-Scott also discusses the importance of loving yourself first. If you do not love yourself the way that you want your partner to love you, she writes, then how is he to know how to honor you? Removing the expectation that your partner has to fulfill all your needs will not only lighten the burden of your partnership but also allow you to meet your own needs at a higher level. When you respect the validity of your own thoughts and feelings, you demand the same from others. When you know how valuable you are, you accept nothing less than to be treated with value. In other words, how you treat yourself is how others will treat you. She also reminds us that partnering is a choice. "Want leads to choice, which leads to commitment. Should leads to decisions, which lead to sacrifice."

In her book *Preventing Affairs*, author Peggy Vaughan says "After years of marriage most wives have built up a heavy load of resentment about the growing number of issues around which they feel they've done far more sacrificing and accommodating than their husbands. Over time this can erode loving feelings of all kinds, particularly sexual feelings." [14] These feelings of neglect and sacrifice are not faulted only by her husband. A lot of times, as women, we continue to sacrifice bitterly without reserving room for self love, believing often that showing love is through self sacrificing.

---

[14] Vaughan p53

I often tell women who share their heartbreak that the hardest part is losing the dream. When we listen to women recovering from relationship pain, we hear hurt and anger, we hear what they had hoped for, what they had wanted, and how things were "supposed to be." If we listen closely, we hear that their greatest pain lies in the loss of expectation. They were in love with the *idea* of their relationship, not the reality of *what was happening* in the relationship. They were so caught up in selling themselves the dream that they failed to step back and take a practical look at their partnering. We've all done this. We've all seen the little red flags that pop up and interrupt our infatuation, and we've all consciously ignored them, figuring that "love will find a way." Because we failed to pay attention, we end up wasting years of our lives and becoming far more invested than we ever should have. As the relationship begins to dissolve, we recall those signs—the signs we overlooked.

People in an authentic relationship should offer support in personal growth and encouragement to grow for each other. Support and encouragement are two of the great benefits of having a life partner. If your partner does not lovingly support you as you make your way along the path of life, why have one? Two people who are whole are a powerful combination. They enrich each other's lives. But a relationship cannot bring enrichment if either people are only looking out for themselves.

The most vital part of a relationship is the partners' ability to communicate with one another. Without communication, a relationship will lose its energy. Being able to ask for what you want and opening yourself to full disclosure without fear of judgment is what makes a relationship strong and builds sacred intimacy. "True communication," Carter-Scott tells us, "is disclosure. With each exchange, partners have a choice to draw closer to each other by disclosing truths or to move further apart by keeping secrets, refusing to share what's inside of them. Withholding builds walls, disclosing builds bridges." [15] Trusting that you are able to share your thoughts and feelings openly without judgment removes the need for a more "understanding" party later. Ideally, your

[15] Cherie Carter-Scott, PHD, If Love is a Game, These are the Rules, 10 rules for finding love and creating long-lasting authentic relationships, Broadway Books, 1999 p115

partner should be your closest friend, your confidant. Even though couples who are having an affair think they are sharing everything, full disclosure from a betraying spouse is highly unlikely.

When I was in high school, my friends called me the queen of two-week relationships. I would go gaga over the latest hottie, but then, as soon as I'd get him, he'd do something stupid, like let his stomach growl in front of me, and I'd be forced to dump him. My girlfriends always teased me about this, but no matter what, the moment he made his mistake of being imperfect, I lost the butterflies. After I left several crying quarterbacks in my wake, I started to feel bad about myself for being so picky. I tried to force myself to hang out a little longer, but then I was miserable trying to "fix" them and make them into my fantasy guy.

I remember walking through the mall one day and seeing a book displayed in the window of a bookstore called *How To Stop Looking For Someone Perfect and Find Someone To Love*. Though I was too young to understand what love really meant, I purchased it. Reading it, I learned quite a lot about the tendency women have to fall in love more with a man's potential instead of recognizing and appreciating the man himself right in front of them. We women meet a man and instantly see all he might be, but we don't recognize that our attraction is largely in how we can mold him. More relationships become issue ridden over the woman's attempt to create a *better* person out of our partner. You cannot choose a partner because of what you think he can become; you have to accept him for who he is. There is no guarantee he will become anything different, but there's a certainty that he will always be the person he is right now. When you stop trying to change your partner, you begin negotiating life as two whole people and coming to sounder agreements as to how you will deal with issues. This doesn't mean there will not be disagreements; it means they will be resolved more effectively when you both are not attempting to win or to change the person by forcing him into your way of thinking. "Disagreeing means holding opposing views," Carter—Scott writes. "Arguing means holding opposing views and investing energy into winning the other person over to your position. Fights damage the connective tissue of your relationship. If you are fighting to resolve rather than fighting to win, than arguments can be a healthy way of releasing the emotions surrounding the disagreement."[16]

One thing is for certain: relationships change. Some changes—like moving to a new city, buying a new home, or having a baby—are good and keep the energy alive. But some changes—the loss of a job, the death of a parent, the discovery a spouse is having an affair—are devastating. As Carter—Scott writes,

> Change is not a temporary thing. You do not pass through it and then return to normal. What is normal has been altered. Change is what makes life interesting and keeps people and relationships continuously evolving. Regardless of how change comes, or who brought it about, it will be a shared responsibility to process its effect on your relationship and negotiate a new game plan. When things begin to change, everything you have learned up until that point will be tested.[17]

Authentic love does not mean that life will be perfect and easy. It means that together, united and completely committed, you will face your obstacles as a team. It means that you will open your heart and break down the walls of blame and hatred. It means being able to accept your own faults when things are not smooth. It means being able to admit your mistakes without fear of being persecuted or having them pounded into you. It means being part of a partnership where both of you are able to agree to your faults and can open yourselves willingly to forgiveness. It means building each other's strengths and uniting with understanding and love. Authentic love is the encouragement to be all that you can be without ever feeling that you aren't enough as you already are.

The thought has just occurred to me that most other women believe they have in fact found authentic love in their affair partner and have

---

[16] Cherie Carter-Scott, PHD, If Love is a Game, These are the Rules, 10 rules for finding love and creating long-lasting authentic relationships, Broadway Books, 1999 p141

[17] Carter-Scott p164,173

already decided that a life without him is more painful that a life with him. She is so wrong.

Authentic love with a married man is impossible.

- Authentic love does not allow you to settle for second best, regardless how often he makes you feel first.
- Authentic love never puts you in a position to be socially damaged by being labeled the other woman.
- Authentic love does not ask you to lie, set your feelings aside, or compromise your needs.
- Authentic love would not and could not hide you.
- Authentic love postpones any involvement until the man has been completely released from the confines of his marriage, both physically and emotionally, before beginning a new life which would also take time, for proper healing.
- Authentic love is found only when both partners are whole. A married man involved in an affair is not whole. A woman involved with a married man is most likely not whole herself, nor is she receiving the whole of anything.

On the other hand, if the love in the married couple's relationship is authentic, then rebuilding after betrayal is not impossible. It is still possible for both partners to be happy. The opportunity for a dynamic partnership still exists for them. In many ways the affair ends up aiding them in making their marriage a better one. It forces them to put a lot of things they have been avoiding on the table, addressing issues that lead to an affair to begin with.

When a woman has discovered her husband's infidelity, she experiences not only pain she never thought possible but also fear she had not thought to consider—a life without him. Her world has spun out of orbit due to the emotions of betrayal. When we marry, we believe that we have partnered with the person we are going to be with forever. This is the person who is supposed to endure grueling fights with you without walking out the door for good. The mate we chose to commit ourselves to in our deepest, most sensitive places of the soul is supposed to be someone we also trust to expose our most private of emotions to. He was supposed to protect and honor those emotions loyally. A commitment we made in joy with a promise to endure the best and the worst of times was made with the belief that love conquers all. Once we walk down the aisle, we think we can stop worrying about never having any support and love in our lives. We walked into the beginning of the rest of our life, and we certainly spent each moment after our wedding investing in it.

When we are betrayed, when the center of our universe turns his affection to another, our pain is beyond comprehensible to those who have never experienced it. Then other fears enter our thoughts: The panic of does he love her? Will he leave me? And a fight to save her life begins. A fight which she is usually better armed to fight then the mistress.

Unfortunately, I have been so deeply in love with someone who I also believed loved me just as much. Then I found him in the arms of another woman. I know what it is like to fear losing my life partner, I know the sickening burn of visualizing him loving someone else. I know the devastation of emotions, the inability to sleep or eat, and the desire to have the couch swallow you. I have known no greater pain than those feelings of rejection and betrayal.

What I have also learned is that no matter how deep the pain, it does go away, even if my heart of hearts believes it never will. My only sanctuary is having experienced heartbreak before and knowing that in fact, time heals all wounds.

There is a whole new equation when it is not just your own emotions to consider, when there are other lives affected to the extreme. I don't believe in being in a relationship where there is not respect and I don't believe in hanging out and being miserable for the sake of the kids, though I do believe that children provide a great reason to work through difficulties and make a marriage work. Every parent wants their children to live in a home with both of their parents as they are entitled to. But a life with two unhappy parents is not fair for them either. Children are resilient to divorce, as ugly as that sounds. Not to say that they are not largely affected by divorce, because they are. Overall, what they are less resilient to are the lessons they learn from living with two parents who hate each other. A couple's marriage and ways in which they interact with one another are the children's example for all their future relationships.

I spoke earlier in this book about a fiancé I had in my mid twenties. I'm not sure if I have ever felt the depth of love for any one else than I did for Brock, not because I haven't loved again, but because young love tends to be less tainted. The last year that Brock and I were together was very unstable. We fought constantly. I was often an emotional wreck and felt ping ponged and never secure. When I wanted him in my life, he did not want to be with me. When he wanted me in his life, I had begun to recover from his rejection and I did not want to be there. It was a constant state of tug of war. My children were fairly young then, and Brock was a father figure living in our home. One night, while I was kissing my daughters goodnight, I suddenly knew it was time to let Brock go. The thought hit me like a two by four—"If not for you, my God, then do it for them."

I knew I wanted my daughters to experience more solid, deeper relationships in their lives. I wanted my daughters to learn how to demand the respect and love they deserve, not to tolerate constant heartbreak. It was not that Brock and I were having arguments that led me to this decision. I am not one of those who think that fighting should not occur in front of children. Contrary, I believe that a healthy argument isn't such a bad thing for children to hear. It can teach them truths about relationships and also show that even when people argue sometimes, it doesn't mean that the relationship is ending. What led me to break if off with Brock was the emotional turmoil, the depression, negativity, and pain that filled our home and affected my daughters.

I believe in marriage. I believe that marriages can survive an affair and go on to be a happy relationship. I've seen it happen more than I've ever seen a divorce over an affair. The ones who stay successfully married are the ones who decide to stay together based upon what they *want* for their life, not what they *don't want*. In other words, "I want us to find the love we once had," not, "I don't want to have to divide the assets." "I want to live with my best friend," not, "I don't want to have to change the way I've been living." "I want us to continue working toward the dreams we have," not, "I don't want someone else to have what I've dreamed of." The ones who stay out of fear will only repeat the pattern. Fear is a weak reason to stay and offers little love, while love can, in fact, move mountains.

Chapter 22

Will He Really Leave Her?

Despite all of the very bleak odds I've shared, if you desperately love your married man, you're hoping against hope that I'm wrong or that you are the third of the three percent that will end up happily ever after. I'd even bet that you've done as I did and searched for examples of relationships that began as an affair and ended in a seemingly happy marriage.

I was actually pretty successful at that. Every time I mulled over the negative odds, I always seemed to find a "what about Paul and Karen?" And suddenly successful affairs appeared to be everywhere.

I would let my friend Tony know about these fine examples while in dispute over my relationship. He was always a bit of a juggernaut, saying something meant to be profound like "Ya, you kind of remind me of that scene in Dumb and Dumber where the guy asks the girl what his chances of her dating him are and she says one in a million." Then he'd put his arm around me and pull me into his chest for the final delivery "So, you're saying I have a chance!"

Nonetheless, there still *is* a chance. So, do you have one?

Power and self-esteem change according to the stage of an affair. The expectations change or vary with women who are involved with a married man. Some do not expect or even want a commitment. Most eventually do. Some are not sure what they want, while most decide they do know what they want after getting to know him. What they want is for the men to leave their wives.

What you need to know is, are you experiencing the affair the same way he is?

Some men are serial lovers and have many one night stands or short lived affairs. A serial lover doesn't have the ability to sustain an emotionally intimate relationship with anyone, even his wife. Being able to have lovers keeps him from getting close to either woman. His affairs keep him distant and aids in his need for the excitement of living in the moment. This person is self centered and narcissistic and has no concern about how any of the women in his life feel. Those who continue a relationship with an individual like this need to discover why it is they tolerate such inconsiderate behavior. The man who has serial affairs will not be committing to anyone. He is not going to change his ways when the "right girl" comes along. His right girl could never blend into one human. Has he had affairs before? If the answer is yes, then you are his Right Now girl, nothing else. Harsh but true.

Other affairs are flings with little or no emotional connection. Misinterpretation as to what kind of affair is taking place happens frequently in the fling. Often the partners feel there is more of a connection than there really is. The passion and excitement is really intoxicating, making each person feel heightened self-esteem and devoid of everyday responsibility and problems. An oasis exists where the lovers can escape to adoring arms. Sometimes the fling will evolve into an actual love affair but most of the time a fling is just a fling characterized by passion. To assess whether or not your relationship is just a fling, you need to ask yourself if sex is the most important aspect of being together? If sex were sparse, would he still want to spend time with you? Is he reluctant to talk about the future? If he does talk about the future, does it sound like he is making promises instead of plans? How deep is the relationship really? Is he there for you when it's *your* emotional crisis time?

Affairs where the individuals have developed feelings of love have much more intensity but assessing whether both partners feel the same way is much more difficult. Determining what is really happening is essential to understanding what to expect of the relationship. Often a woman believes she is involved in a love affair because of his excitement to see her, the passion, the lovely words she carries with her. A romantic love affair usually includes conversation about what to do, how to handle things, and leaving his marriage because he has an emotional connection. Conflicting however, is the emotional connection he also has to his family. This is usually the type of affair where he cannot make a decision and cannot leave his lover. Ultimately, the love affair develops into a long-term affair. Affairs have an intense passion with a longing to see each other. The passion, which is like an addiction, becomes the motivational component to the triangle. There is much intimacy and they are able to open themselves and still be accepted. Commitment is the only thing missing. Are you maintaining your affair by making personal sacrifices? Do you have anxiety about sharing your weaknesses? Does he care about your overall wellbeing? Does he support your growth? Is the relationship harmful for you or does it move you toward your goals? Are you tricking yourself? Have you minimized the affect the affair has on you, allowing your thinking to be distorted?

A woman involved in an affair really needs to assess herself carefully and try to understand how she got here—what is it that lead her to have an affair? Is there an emotional need that you are satisfying through the affair? What other ways could this emotional need be met without causing yourself pain? Is the affair a way to help you cope with loneliness? Is your affair happening with someone you had a past relationship with? Are you trying to relive old memories that compete with the reality of today? Is he an important person who flatters you by his interest? Do you rely on him to lift your self-esteem by his pursuit and attention? Is the affair something you rely on to feel better about yourself? Do you have a history with unavailable men?

There are many reason far more related to a woman's past than her present that bring her to an affair. For example, a relationship with an unavailable man could be a result of the childhood experience of winning a competition with mom for dad's attention.

What about what's going on in his life? Has a new child arrived? Has he suddenly become an empty nester? What changes are happening in his home that perhaps has not gone smoothly? Sometimes when couples are having difficulty working through problems, instead they reach out for another. This will typically result in only a fling, not a committed relationship with his affair partner. Is he reacting to aging? Has he gone through any difficult transitions? Is there an ongoing problem in his marriage? An affair is usually just an escape and nothing more.

If your affair has more to do with his trouble negotiating turmoil and life changes, you need to ask yourself if the affair will comfort your needs or bring anxiety and pain into your life?

Are you clinging to his negative comments about his wife? Do you believe that the problems in his marriage strengthen your chance of being together? It is to his advantage that you think his marriage is issue ridden. You will work harder to make your time together beautiful, pleasing him and removing any concern about being in a permanent relationship with you. Every complaint he has about her, you will work hard to be the opposite. If you are working so diligently to be the opposite, are you really being yourself? Humans have other emotions besides happy. Positive and negative feelings are to be expected in any person. Being with a partner, in an authentic love relationship, allows the freedom to be yourself with the support and acceptance that comes with real love.

You have probably come to believe that his wife is not a good lover and that you are sexier. Interestingly enough, studies show that men who have affairs were not necessarily looking for better sex, just different sex. You have probably come to believe his wife does not understand him. She probably understands him better than anyone. So is it her fault he is having an affair?

Because men and women view sexual involvement so differently, most women believe they are having a romantic love affair, while the man is having a fling. So many affairs are off balance due to this difference in thinking. The man may have no plans to end his marriage, while the woman is planning her wedding.

So will he leave her? The wife has more power. They have history, emotional investment, children, families, friends, accumulated memories of great experiences and overcome adversities. They have an attachment. He also has fear of exposure. Disappointment of friends is a big deal if it is someone whose opinion he values. His wife also has the most power when he feels remorse. He may not realize all that he has until he contemplates leaving her. Most husbands are reluctant to cause their wives the pain of leaving them. Many times the men are in shock over their wives reaction after an affair is exposed. They just cannot believe how badly she is hurt. They feel extreme remorse and guilt and would do anything to reverse their action.

A man, who refuses to end the affair after his wife's discovery, will continue on in the limbo stage as long as both women are willing to hang on. There are many wives who handle the situation by blaming the other woman. She has no respect for her and she bears the burden of fault. Sometimes, if the wife does leave him over an affair he refuses to end, he will break off the relationship with his mistress when he sees his wife is serious. He only breaks off the affair in this case because it suits his own purpose. The man who refuses to end either relationship is narcissistic and only cares about how events affect him.

Does he keep indicating that he is going to end his marriage but doesn't? Does it seem to you that he really wants this but there is always an obstacle? Does he give you time frames that pass with no action and then follow up with avoidance? He probably has no intention of leaving her but telling you this increases the risk that you will leave him. For him, having both of you is the perfect scenario. From his standpoint, you are enjoying the affair just as much as he is.

It is easy to hang on to empty promises and imagine a future together when in a relationship that is devoid of reality. Both of you are tricked by the glitter of the affair, and your affair has become a safety valve that makes his marriage more tolerable.

If he continues to make plans with his family, his future plans do not include you. If you are not comfortable asking him for answers and he cannot answer specific questions about leaving her, such as when and how, you might want to ask yourself why asking for the specifics of your future together frightens you so much? When you put your plans and desires aside waiting for something to happen and they are not, you're getting your answer. If he changes the subject, or wont talk about it, it's because he doesn't want to be pinned down to a definite answer. Things are good for him as they are.

He is serious about his relationship with you only if he is open to discussion and tells you the truth about what is really going on, what he is going to do, how he is going to do it—and then does. He should seek counseling to help him deal with his guilt so that later it doesn't resurface as hostility towards you. He then separates and is open to counseling for the two of you, keeping in mind that the best predictor of the future is the past. You have every reason to be worried about his potential to cheat on you and this is a concern he should be willing to address.

You really need to think about these questions because you will be putting your life on hold for this man. Every dream, hope, and plan for the future may be sacrificed as you become a lady-in-waiting.

Affairs have a pattern. First, obviously, is the attraction stage. Next comes the honeymoon phase where you enjoy the intoxicating passion while trying to forget he is married. After the honeymoon comes the turbulence. Arguments arise, promises are made, promises are broken, and he tries to pacify you. Finally, comes the answer to shit or get off the pot. The marriage may end but more likely the affair. If neither occurs, indecision is still an answer. You should now be prepared to go on with the understanding that he isn't going to leave his wife. If this is not acceptable to you, prepare yourself to end things. He has two women, they each have half of a man.

When things shift from his loving pursuit and lavished attention, which made you feel loved, you become uncomfortable, worried, and afraid. You begin to pursue him wanting back the good feelings and power you felt, in turn, handing over all of your personal power to him.

Is your time respected? Have you given him control over the direction of your life? Does he make all of the rules? Do your needs go unmet because he is the priority? Do you give up all of your plans to be with him? Does he bail on your needs to meet the needs of his family? Will he leave you if you tell him what it is you really want? Is your life influenced by the fear that he will leave you? Is your self-esteem tied to his opinion of you? Do you have any power in making decisions about your future together? Are you willing to give up a relationship with someone who can meet your needs because you remain committed to a married man who cannot commit to you? Can you accept all of the limitations this relationship presents, as it is? Because believing thing will change is foolish.

If you have really contemplated each of these questions and answered honestly to yourself, and with love for yourself, I believe that everything will become very clear to you and you will know what you need for your life and what you should do about your relationship with your married man.

Please use all of your strength for follow through. I promise you a beautiful life is out there waiting!

Chapter 23

Tid Bits

I was able to discover one true positive thing that came from my affair with Blake: Based on my experience, I was able to help my friend Janet through the difficult time of confusion and devastation after her husband Ian's affair. I was able to offer her the insights that I had gained as the other woman. Ian, who is also my dear friend, came to realize the hurt that he not only caused his wife but also the pain that he had caused the other woman by selfishly misleading her. In my conversations with Janet and Ian, I learned much about the marriage side of things, things that I had never understood before as the other woman. Because of what I learned, I became passionate about sharing my experience. I feel that I have valuable insight that I can share with husbands and wives. But even more valuable, are the insights I wish to expose the other woman to. I felt compelled to open the curtains not only to all parties involved in the messy business of an affair but also to those who judge them. In essence, I wish to close the door on the opportunity for affairs to create destruction.

As I spoke regularly with Janet during that difficult time of her life, I recalled all the reasons that Blake had given me as to why he was unable to let go of our relationship and return to his marriage and give his wife one hundred percent effort. I shared with Janet what Blake had told me. What she had the most trouble understanding was my advice to not constantly revisit the affair and to stop continuously mentioning Kelly's name. Ian was being honest with Janet about his affair and how he had succumbed to temptation. He had spilled the beans, falling to his knees in confession. He remained contrite for months, enduring endless nights of interrogation by Janet, who felt she had to know every detail. She couldn't get the affair out of her mind, and even in moments when they would begin to share a bit of joy, her anger would quickly resurface and she would bring the subject up again.

It wasn't just my experience with Blake that told me dwelling on the affair and the anger was dangerous. I also remembered my mother telling me about an affair my father had, after which she spent a number of years running it through her mind and torturing him with questions and blame. She was so angry, filled with so much self-inflicted pain because she kept reliving that time over and over in her mind, that one day she just got sick of herself. She could no longer go on. She was making herself and my father miserable. Finally, she concluded, "Either I let go and move forward today or I have to leave him to spare the both of us." Like other women I've talked to, my mother also discovered that interrogations about details (What restaurant did you go to? What shirt did you wear? What sexual positions did you use?) only created the desire to learn more. Each question led to more questioning. Wives want all the details so that they can actually feel present in moments where they were left out. They want to know *exactly what happened*, but each new piece of information is a new imagined visual. Continual interrogation is self-torture. It destroys our mental health. I had to remind Janet that she was working on a future, not living in the past. What was done could not be undone, I told her; she had been given enough honest detail for now.

Blake told me that when he reconciled with Beth, she bombarded him with questions, references, and pot shots pertaining to our affair. "Every time I had committed to working on the marriage and felt resolved to put effort in rebuilding our relationship," he said, "she brought you up again. She never allowed me to forget about you." Each time Beth mentioned my name, he was catapulted back to a time we shared together. I knew that if Janet wanted Ian to forget Kelly, then *she had to*. It had to stop, not only for her sanity, but also for the marriage to move forward. She had to focus on her marriage, not on the other woman. Talking about Kelly specifically, gave her power and let her into the marriage. I told her to shut the gate.

The next important thing was for Ian and Janet to date each other again, to go back to sharing those moments together that are just for them. No children, no work issues, none of the distractions that take their focus away from rebuilding the connection. Life has to go on, of course, and with it come the everyday responsibilities that are required of us, but one day a week (or once a month, if that is all that can be squeezed in) there must be special time for just the two of them to remember what it was that brought them together in the first place. Taking time to renew their relationship is vital. They need to instill new life into their relationship. They need to remember to laugh, reinvent their shared life, embark on new journeys together. Janet needed to recognize the wonderful qualities in her husband. She needs to focus on positive issues, not on his flaws and his history.

I remember that Blake also complained about feeling neglected by Beth. "She wanted me back," he said, "but when I was back, she didn't want to do anything together." The last time I spoke to him, he was still complaining. "I cannot tell you when the last time Beth and I actually had a date together." This was a major bone of contention with him then, and it still is. It is also one reason why he still strays today.

I also told Janet that she needed to remember that Ian's sexual needs are very important. This is how a man connects with his lover. He has to have sex in order to feel loved and to give love. Without sex, the wife has no security that the husband will want to faithfully stay in the marriage. It's not simply that he isn't getting laid as much as he thinks he should. It's that without sex he cannot connect with her. He cannot express himself, and he is left to feel not only sexually frustrated but also emotionally frustrated. Without sex, he feels neglected, rejected, and unloved. This is the other woman's greatest purpose in an affair. She is not there to replace his spouse entirely, she is there to fill in what is lacking in his marriage.

During my study about why men cheat, I found some very blunt and profound insights. For example, one man compared a woman's need to talk about things as a man's need to have sex. He said that he needed to feel respected and loved to have the incentive to do the right thing. "The other woman "needs" him with a respect and adoration that happens when he is primed to have an affair after feeling neglected,." He said.

Let me break it down like this. I'm a woman. I like my sex with butterflies and romance. Bring me sweet words and thoughtfulness. Add a glass or two of wine. And animal planet can't bring as much passion. However, when I am dog-ass tired and stressed to the max and my brain cannot shut off, the last thing I feel like doing is crawling all over my mate like some porn queen. To me, it is down right rude and disrespectful to focus on his throbbing member when I'm dealing with the latest crisis in my family. I recall Blake wanting me to "get up on it" while the early morning news was broadcasting the Space Shuttle explosion that killed everyone on board. I was listening in shock as he was groping me. Am I the only one who thinks this was a tad inappropriate? Can I just have a minute to mourn what just happened? Even a second to take this in? But even though I believed we were headed toward marriage, deep inside I knew "no" was not an option for the woman in my position. Deep inside, most mistresses will relate and therefore, deep inside she knows where her place is in his life.

All that being said, unfortunately, if a married woman can't get her husband to comprehend when sex is appropriate and when it is not, and she refuses him too many times, she's opening the door, or leaving it open, to problems. The number one complaint from every man I've ever spoken to who has strayed was that their wives do not give them enough sexual attention. By the way, my fellow other woman, sex and love are two very different things to a man. I love being with you is not the same as I love you.

Janet took my advice. She already knew about Ian's sexual needs, though it didn't hurt to hear an affirmation. She wanted to start dating him because she felt their connection was disappearing and they needed those moments now more than ever. But my advice not to mention the "bitch's" name was, she admitted, both the most difficult and the most valuable thing I told her. She took my advice, and it worked. It helped to make Kelly history.

Ian had reached a threshold. He loves Janet. He wanted their marriage to work, but after months and months of ceaseless groveling every time Janet mentioned Kelly, he was becoming convinced that the marriage was over and all was lost. He felt that Janet would never forgive him enough to let them move forward and heal and be happy again. He was getting angrier and angrier. As she berated him and barraged him with more questions about Kelly, he found it harder and harder to stuff his feelings. He was beginning to accept that they would have to divorce because he had lost faith that either of them would be able to withstand the hatred that plagued their marriage. Then, suddenly, she gave him a break. Kelly's name evaporated from their conversations. He was able to stop feeling defensive and focus on giving his wife the love and affection he wanted to give her. Janet thus received what she really needed—his reassurance that he truly loved her.

Janet and Ian attended marriage counseling and found it very helpful. They also attended a marriage workshop from which they gleaned a great deal. I'm surprised at how openly they are able to discuss their past. It is not a taboo subject in their home. His affair is something that happened, something they worked through successfully. What is important is that they *both* wanted their marriage to work and they *both* put forth the effort to make it work. A marriage like this, where both parties love each other and work hard not to lose each other is, in my opinion, the one that not only can really be saved, but is even worth saving.

But what about the circumstances where the affair does not end after it has been exposed? Circumstances such as my affair, where Blake remained confused, and in a constant state of vacillation. What should wives do then? Where does either woman find power? The answer; by being strong and willing to walk. His ability to play the game lies in the tactic of fear. Each woman is afraid to lose him, so neither of them let go. Thus, he never has to suffer any consequences for his actions because no one is letting him. They're both protecting him. He's getting a free ride, no one gets off of a free ride. What he is avoiding is pain. He doesn't want to feel the hurt of losing either woman. He will not feel the totality of his loss until he really loses one or both of them. When someone walks away, he awakens to the fact that she, also, will be free to move on with her life, another factor he has been avoiding. He will end up with the one he hurts the most in losing. Nine in ten times that person is the one he is already married to. It is when his wife is gone that the other woman begins to reveal her imperfections and the apple of temptation starts to rot. If he doesn't return to the marriage, it's doubtful he will remain with the mistress over time. As painful as that is to accept, why would anyone want a man in their life who preferred to be somewhere else? In reality, his departure saves years of torture and the opportunity to find healing and real love by letting him go.

Women in risky circumstances should always be prepared and have an escape plan. My father had an affair when I was young. I was not aware of what was going on, only that we moved "back home" to where my mother had grown up and that he did not attend my fifth birthday but sent me two stuffed puppies with Velcro arms hugging each other. Later, we moved back to our house, which had a few new items of furniture in it that my Dad had bought while we were gone. Sometime later, we moved to a home at least double the size. I learned as an adult that my mother had always been responsible for maintaining their checking account and paying the bills. Each time that she sat down to pay a bill, she would write a check to herself and put it in the bottom of a drawer. Finally she said to my father, "Let's move and start over," to which he replied, "We can't afford it." My mother ran into her bedroom, took all the checks out of the bottom of the drawer, and laid down enough money to make the down payment on our new house. I took this story and applied it to my own life when I was living during rocky times with my fiancé. I knew that if he left, I could not afford to pay the rent on my own. I had two small children and a small, inconsistent income. Each time I went to the grocery store, therefore, I wrote a check for $50 over the amount and opened a private account. Occasionally, I received bonuses from my employer, and those too went into the account. When my fiancé left, I had saved a few thousand dollars. This bought me time to pull myself together and implement a new plan.

If he leaves you, do NOT be a victim. If you are the wife, make him shoulder all joint responsibilities, including child support and care taking. Take a vacation, go out on the town. Under no circumstance should you give him the satisfaction of believing that you are sitting weepily at home, lost without him, and doing nothing but awaiting his return. Save your tears for your girlfriends, who will inevitably be there to support you. *Success is the best revenge.* Do all of the things that you dreamed of doing. This is your life now. Be selfish about living it. You deserve it! Focus on yourself and what is most important to your life.

Believe in karma or fate and let Dame Fortune do her job. Incidentally, I have learned that "what goes around, comes around" comes only when you stop wishing for it to happen. It happens that way as not to earn yourself a little bad juju of your own for wishing ill will on others. By the time it does come around, it is when we are almost able to feel sorry for them . . . almost. I have witnessed this fact of life so many times that I have become a devout follower. As you reap, so shall you sew, is a universal law. Trust it and move on.

Keeping a journal is an excellent way to work through emotions. Seeing your thoughts in writing can change your life. I can tell you right now that the woman who began writing this book is not the same woman who is ending it. I've learned a lot by writing down the events as they played out. Putting things in black and white is one hell of an eye opener. Patterns in my life were revealed to me in ways that I could no longer deny, and that was extremely empowering. I grew stronger. I found that I was fed up with things I had allowed myself to wander into, not only my affair with Blake, but also things in the relationship that came next. There my life was, staring me in the face, repeat, repeat, repeat, and my eyes were opened. I never want to experience any of these emotional traumas again, and I see that many of my choices, even some made with good intent, have all contributed to my wounds.

I had never been one to journal until a friend called me for some support and advice regarding her troubled relationship. As we talked, she said, "You know, I used to journal all of the time, but recently I stopped. I read everything I write about things with Terry, and I become sick with myself for putting up with this stuff." Her comment struck me profoundly. I said, "Angie, why are you shutting off your wisdom?" At my suggestion, she began journaling again, and we agreed that I would do the same. Within two months, she was seeing the reality of her relationship. She realized that she wasn't ever happy and that the things that she needed and wanted in her life would never be found in her relationship. Having a journal to write in made the grief in letting go less painful.

Either woman should never, never, ever, ever give their power to "her." Never let her feel that she is doing this damage to you, causing this circumstance, or that she has any power to affect your happiness. The harder the fight between the wife and the mistress, the more the mistress and husband come together. And so on with the wife and husband. He's playing both sides, remember? Each wants the other to retaliate so that she can gain his sympathy for how terrible the other is to her. This only reinforces all of the lies he has told his mistress about his reasons for straying and gives him reason to coddle his spouse.

We can waste a lot of years being bitter, but the only years we've lost are our own. Now that's something to feel bitter about! My mother used to vent that "he knew when he married me that all I wanted was to stay home and take care of my husband and children." For many years after my parents divorce, my mom went to work and struggled to take care of her children, all the while harboring bitterness and resentment because her dream hadn't come true. Life changes. The only guarantee is that someday we get out. The only thing we can do as women is take control of our own outcome, for the only person truly in control of the life we live is us.

My father, on the other hand, offered me these words of advice when I was young: "If all her life, she never drove or fueled a car, if her husband drove and filled the tank, what does she do on the day he dies?" A woman should always know how to take care of herself and be prepared to live on her own. She should never be in the position of needing a man for her very survival.

People are so afraid to be alone. I've felt this fear myself, especially when I knew a relationship was coming to an end. We start thinking we will never find someone to live our life with. We live awhile, and then suddenly one day we are used to doing things our own way. Then we wonder how we'll ever fit someone else into our lives. They might alter our patterns. I find being alone a lot easier. For example, it's after 4 a.m. and I'm sitting at my computer writing this paragraph. This would pose a big problem for some of the men in my past, as would the two hours of hitting "snooze" that will inevitably follow later this morning, and the dirty house I am sure to ignore all day.

What exactly would I miss about having my ass chewed for my screwball schedule? Oh yeah. That love thing. I suppose there's give and take. I do think, however, that people who are afraid to be alone might need to try it for a while. Being comfortable in your own skin is a must, lest you spend the rest of your life finding partners that mirror your inadequacies. The next man who enters my life will find me in the study when he wakes up in the morning. Before he goes to work, he will bring me a cup of coffee and a kiss, and should he ever find himself in the arms of another woman, I'll drive to Starbucks in my jammies.

Chapter 24

Keeping the other woman out

There are times, of course, when even the strongest marriages become vulnerable. If a man feels that his needs are not being met at home, he becomes vulnerable to a fleeting moment of passion eventually or potentially. Many fleeting moments of passion create a need in him for more fleeting moments of passion, and finally the meaningless sex becomes a relationship he never planned. Obviously, I'm not the marriage survival lady. What I do have to offer are things from the other side of the spectrum, the ones married men share about their reasons for having an affair with us "understanding" types. The bottom line is, if you're not growing together, you're growing apart. This doesn't mean that you are required to spend every waking moment together. Actually, healthy couples are able to find creative outlets that allow them to safely get away from stress. For example, Sasha's significant other finds relief on a golf course. She'd much rather he abandon her for a round of eighteen holes and hang out with the guys for a sandwich and beer in the club house afterwards than feel as if he had no escape, which can later lead to troubles. In her book *Preventing Affairs*, author Peggy Vaughan says, "You and your partner don't need to avoid change or grow in the same direction in order to avoid growing apart. You simply need to stay in touch, to keep each other informed about your changes, and to support each other in the changes you choose to make. Don't worry about growing apart; that's unlikely if you clearly communicate on an ongoing basis." [18]

Couples who nurture safe friendships with other happy couples are able to find support for their marriage. Like my mama used to say, a marriage is bigger than two people. When couples are faced with inevitable troubles, having friends who support the union of marriage to confide in can help bring back mental and emotional clarity. Having happily married couples as friends are like accountability partners when it comes to maintaining solid boundaries. Friends who have successful marriages are a great support network when things don't feel so hot in a relationship. Likewise, associating with people who do not honor their commitment to marriage can be detrimental. Never underestimate the power of influence, even amongst adults.

My step-son and his wife had an argument once where in the heat of the moment, his wife threatened divorce. I sat her down afterwards

---

[18] Vaughan, *preventing affairs*, 2008 p16

and spoke to her about the danger of speaking that word. Once a couple starts throwing the "D" word around it is usually only a matter of time before it happens. Eventually someone's going to call the bluff and a stand off begins. The connective tissue begins to deteriorate as each party begins to prepare themselves for the possibility. Likewise, learning how to fight by establishing ground rules for engagement can make fighting a healthy way to save a marriage. Other basic ground rules would be the agreement to only speak positively about your spouse to other individuals. Co-workers and acquaintances are not the appropriate persons to vent marital frustrations to. Another agreement would be to not communicate or behave in ways that you would not want your spouse to behave or communicate. I call it the fair and square commitment.

Couples should never forget that lust can be like a drug. Feeling the spark of butterflies can make just about anyone silly brained. Knowing that eventually all of us will find ourselves experiencing forbidden intrigue can help the sudden rush of feelings to not be such a shock when it is finally felt. Remembering that the newness of those feelings won't last can stabilize wondering thoughts. But more than anything, being free to be honest with your spouse that you have experienced the sudden rush of attraction to another can be the life support system in your marriage. Most women experience panic feelings or insecurity upon first hearing this advice. "My God, I can't imagine my husband coming home one day and telling me that he is having feelings of attraction toward another woman." But the fact of the matter is, he has and he will. By not being able to share these feelings with you, he begins to hold inside himself a secret. He wonders, what does this mean? What is it about this woman that I feel drawn to? And as he wonders, he dwells. In the absence of being able to talk about it, he is left with only being able to think about it. As he continues to do nothing but think about it the fantasy continues to grow, as does his curiosity. When he is able to share with you that he has felt an attraction toward another woman, as he speaks of his feelings, the air in his head begins to evaporate and soon his feet are much closer to the ground. He isn't going to tell you, obviously, about an attraction he has had for another if he knows you are just going to freak out. Therefore, an agreement for radical honesty and safety in being honest is necessary in affair prevention.

"When thoughts or feelings about someone else are kept secret, the very process of keeping the feeling secret tends to make them stronger," says Vaughan in *Preventing Affairs*. "It allows for focusing *only* on the positive aspects and blinds people to the reality of the consequences of acting on the feelings. So talking about it (in whatever way can bring into reality without creating additional problems) can help cut through the fantasy. This "talking" can be with a professional or a friend or family member who can be totally trusted. There's something about discussing your feelings out loud (and seeing it through the eyes of someone else) that allows you to view it more realistically."[19]

Sometimes we forget the simplest things such as love and affection. Often time's affairs begin after the birth of a child. Once we have given birth to our bundle of perfection, we discover that there is no greater love than the love we have for our infant. When I gave birth to my first daughter, just the thought of not holding her brought tears to my eyes. My husband kept asking me, "Honey, are you ever going to put the baby down?" I loved to watch her eyes look into mine. It was like looking at the innocent part of my own soul. Holding her and watching her sleep was my favorite pastime. I wanted to do nothing else. Putting her to bed at night brought paranoia of Sudden Infant Death Syndrome, and I started to imagine my life without her. Worry about losing her brought bursts of tears at random moments.

Men feel left out when facing a new mother. What used to be your undivided attention for him now belongs to this child. Your husband no longer holds the key to your heart; it has been given over, a betrayal often felt by him subconsciously. Suddenly he needs to feel like he's the most important one. This makes him vulnerable to an affair if he continues to feel forgotten. He needs to be reminded that he remains an integral part of your life. To keep the life-changing event of having a baby from causing issues you never dreamed possible, remember to take time out for daddy. Do not forget to save a little room for the other number one in your life.

Maybe your children are older now and though through the years you have made their wants and needs the focal point of your life. Perhaps you have a demanding career. Somewhere in the mix of things, your husband has begun to feel as if his whole life is just "going with

---

[19] Peggy Vaughan, *Preventing Affairs*, 2008 p26

the flow." Everything that connects the two of you revolves around the children or he is off on his own enjoying his interests without your participation. Soccer games, dance recitals, plays, slumber parties. Every day between you both consists of running the business of raising children or just managing life without feeling like he has a lover. Where's the fun in that? Where is the lovey dovey stuff?

Don't think for one minute that because he handles the duties of fatherhood well, and even enjoys them, that he does not feel need for affection. The minute another woman offers him some admiration, your guy is tempted. That's when he begins to daydream about life "out there." He isn't thinking about having an affair and leaving his family, but he is swayed to experience a brief life of butterflies and infatuation. This is the beginning of trouble. It's trouble that takes wings of its own and lands in places he never thought it would. The silliest thing a couple can sell themselves is their immunity to being capable of having an affair. Understanding that every couple will be susceptible to an affair at some time during their married life is crucial for preventing the action from actually occurring.

"Like most things related to a long term marriage, no one time statement or one time intent is sufficient to sustain a marriage as people change through the years," says Peggy Vaughan, "It's essential to invest time and energy into the commitment implied by the vows—rather than relying on the words spoken at a wedding ceremony. It's unreasonable to expect the vows to be central to long term protection from affairs." [20]

When you first fell in love, I'm sure, you filled each other with loving compliments and gushy, sappy sweetness. Over time, however, we begin to realize our "better half" isn't quite as "better" as he could be. Compliments and affection turn into nagging and bitching about all the things he doesn't do right. Is having to put the toilet seat down really that big a deal? If all he hears are your *petty* complaints (I'm not suggesting real concerns are left to the way side), he is sure to be tempted by a nice, fun girl who "understands" him. When he receives attention from others who make him feel appreciated and worth more than mowing the lawn, a man gets the urge to stray. If you treat your relationship with appreciation and respect, it will remain strong. But you need to pay attention to it for it to grow. Hold him dear to you by

---

[20] Vaughn, Preventing Affairs, p27

reminding him that he is important and special to your life. If you want to keep a man from straying, he must feel needed, loved, appreciated, and respected. That's not to suggest that he should receive unearned attention, but you should remember and focus on the good things that you love about him too.

Over the years, we become way too comfortable. "As time passes," Carter-Scott writes, "you may view your mate as being as familiar and comfortable as your old jeans, and rarely do old jeans inspire passion."[21] Comfort is good. After all, why else would we choose to settle down with a partner if it were not for the comfort they give us to be ourselves? But don't let comfort turn into "she isn't what she used to be." You can't stop caring for yourself. If you do, he might be tempted by riper fruit.

I remember asking my mom when I was young, "Mommy, why do ladies still buy new stuff and get pretty every day after they get married? They already have a husband." Her answer did not make sense to me at say, the age of seven, but today it sure does. "Honey," she said, "after you get married, you do it for yourself." I used to think that the whole purpose for dolling up was to attract your Prince Charming. Sure it is in the beginning, but don't trick Prince Charming, catch him, and then give him something different later. Even more so, don't stop wanting to feel good for your self. It just feels good to feel good, and sometimes that means wearing a damn hot matching bra and panty beneath your clothes on a day no one will ever see them.

Go on a date and converse. Setting time aside for the two of you is crucial. A couple should continue to date well after they are married. This means time away from the kids, the family, and friends. Going to dinner together, taking a walk, enjoying a movie together, whether at the theater or snuggled up on the couch, whatever you choose to do, do it alone together. Take the time to hold a real conversation, just like you did when you were getting to know each other. Spend time in recreation together, spend time adoring one another. Be fully present in the moment. Going on a date gives you the opportunity to check up on your relationship. If you find time for open communication, it can be a wonderful time to repair emotions or soothe feelings of neglect.

---

[21] Cherie Carter-Scott, PHD, If Love is a Game, These are the Rules, 10 rules for finding love and creating long-lasting authentic relationships, Broadway Books, 1999 P211

A couple that chooses to be honest will prevent a lot of hurts in the future. Having a designated time alone gives you the opportunity to release negative emotions and reconnect positively. One of the things many cheaters say is that their wife doesn't understand them. They say she is caught up in her own life and is not taking the time out to recognize him. As one man said, "Perspective is everything. You may see your issue and it looks like a boulder, but your wife sees the issue as a pebble. You have to communicate that the issue is a boulder to you."

One major reason that men have affairs (and the number one reason that women do) is that their emotional needs are not being met. Emotional needs are met best by sharing, listening, and being fully present while in conversation with one another.

Dr. Willard Harley, Jr., coauthor of the book *Surviving an Affair*, suggested in an interview with CBN's Terry Meeuwsen that we are all wired to have an affair and that if we do not take precautions to avoid it, we will generally succumb to the temptation. He said that people start out assuming that it's not going to happen to them, so they don't take precautions. "We get inoculated for various diseases that we're likely to get," he said, "but we don't bother to get inoculated for an affair." [22] We go to the altar thinking we're going to make it, but statistics show that a majority of marriages go through an affair. Dr. Harley says that one of the most important precautions is to be radically honest with each other about everything and agree that your husband or wife will always be your best friend, the one you spend your leisure time and travels with.

Finally, whatever you do, don't stop having sex. Guys think of sex and love as two totally different things. They believe that they can love their wives and still want to have sex with other women. Once passion wanes in the marriage, he starts to think about having sex with other women and eventually he takes the step. If you want to be sure you're not vulnerable to an affair, you had better find a way to charge up your libido.

Men cheat because they want to escape reality and play out their sexual fantasies. If you are not open to exploring at least some of his

---

[22] Dr. Willard Harley Jr, Surviving an Affair, www.cbn.com
Interview by Terry Meeuwesn http://www.cbn.com/family/marriage/affairproof.aspx
Accessed September 9, 2007

fantasies, those within reason, he is going to be tempted by someone who is open to them. If nothing keeps him faithful, however, don't blame yourself. If you're already doing all of those things and you end up with a man who is a serial cheater, then maybe it's time to think about moving on. It's not about you; it's a problem within him.

Affairs generally happen when a husband feels that his needs are not being met. He feels bored, lonely, deprived, or lacking companionship. It is impossible for a wife to satisfy all of these needs all the time. The bottom line is this: If many of your husband's needs are not being met together, over an extended duration of time, you'll probably find yourself dealing with an affair. What to do? Stay connected and involved with his life, be open to radical honesty, and don't give up sex. These are the best things you can possibly do. After those suggestions, the only person who can prevent an affair is the person who is contemplating having one.

Chapter 25

Letting go and Moving On

Letting go of pain from relationship finality can seem almost impossible. Much of this feeling has to do with our female brains being hardwired to build strong, solid, lasting relationships through our Stone Age instinct for survival and our ancient dependency on a man to ensure that survival. The rest has to do with the female brain chemistry recording our being in love in the deepest parts of our neurological sensors.

Studies by Robert Joseph at the University of Texas concluded that a woman's self esteem is maintained by her ability to sustain relationships. One of her greatest sources of stress, therefore, can be the fear of losing an intimate relationship. When a woman suffers the loss of a relationship, her brain behaves as though it's in a drug—withdrawal state. Women who suffer through the end of a relationship can undergo serious depression. They cannot concentrate on anything other than their loss. They cannot sleep, cannot eat, and spend their hours in constant tears.

I suffered the unbearable pain after Brock and I split up. It was the most difficult break up I've ever experienced in my life. We were engaged and had been living together for five years. I spent the last year in a constant state of internal fighting to keep my relationship together. He would leave and a piece of me would die (more and more each time), but then he would decide that our relationship mattered to him and ask me to work it out again. Because my love was so deep, I turned into a puddle every time (first, second, third, fourth . . . you get the picture) he asked for reconciliation.

At the same time, however, I found myself becoming a little stronger with each parting. I started delaying his return, each time a little longer than the last. And each time he came back a new man, at least temporarily, and gradually my heart would open again. The relationship ended with my discovery of another girl in his life. I was devastated. I couldn't understand how he could move on from "us," how he could enjoy time with another woman, knowing that I was suffering such deep pain. How could he smile and laugh with her while I was dying?

My sanity was toast. I would think about them together, imagine him touching her, hear him saying the same things to her he said to me, see him sharing with her the bond I thought we had. I saw her as the one living my dream. I felt like I'd been robbed. I could think of nothing but him and her together until I was so sick of my own thoughts that I wanted to bang my head against a wall. (I literally did that once.)

I tried everything imaginable to make him regret losing me. I got breast implants. I tried several new hairstyles. I bought new clothes I couldn't afford. I went out on the town trying to bury myself in a "good time" that I wasn't really having. I went on dates with men whom I otherwise had zero interest in, were it not for the fact that I thought it might bother *him*. My dates were either drop-dead gorgeous (and sure to have no brain) or loaded with success (and sure to only be looking for an arm charm). The only reason I dated these men, of course, was because I hoped that Brock would hear about them and get jealous. But nothing worked the way I wanted it to. My whole life revolved around decisions I thought might bring him running back to me and actions that insured he wouldn't. I couldn't think of anything else.

He consumed my thoughts so much that I remember once going to my kitchen sink to get a glass of water and the faucet had a slow drip. The water drops didn't have a patterned fall. One drip, pause, three drips, pause, two. If three drops fall together, then he will want me back. I thought to myself and allowed my kitchen faucet to become an oracle. Eventually, I collapsed on my couch, unable to move, and cried until there wasn't a drop of water left in my body. Lying there, all I wanted was to die. My life was over. I could actually imagine dirt being tossed on top of me and my body sinking into the ground. It was too painful to be awake and it was impossible for me to sleep. My skin was gray, and I lost so much weight that I looked like one of those starving youths in the "feed the children" commercial. I wanted to be done with my life, except I had those kids to take care of, and I wasn't doing a good job at being a parent because my mind was absent. I did not see how my depression could ever lift.

But it did lift. Things did change and eventually the only part of the pain that was left was its memory. I suffered other heartbreaks over the years and though I always felt deeply hurt, no pain was ever quite as deep as the pain that I felt with Brock. Getting up again always required great strength, but knowing that if I could survive my experience with Brock, I could get through anything, I was always able to go on with my life trusting that eventually the pain would pass.

Ending my affair with Blake, while different, was almost as difficult. I felt more mental pain than I ever had because that breakup offered a new set of challenges that I wouldn't wish on my greatest enemy.

After Blake, I fell into one final disastrous relationship. This one was the one that made me figure out how to stop the emotional cycle. Having experienced so much tumult, by now I was tired of the emotional wear and tear these relationships were taking on my soul, my body, and my mind. (Free rent of the brain, my dad calls it.)

Late one afternoon, I arrived at Shane's house to pick him up and drive us to dinner. He opened the door wearing his standard grumpy face, left over from an unsatisfactory day at the office, said hello, and walked upstairs to finish getting ready to go out. I immediately felt rejected. There was no warm greeting, no kiss, no "Hi, honey, it's good to see you." I plopped down on his couch and waited for my girly boy to spend thirty minutes getting ready, even though he had already had plenty of notice to be ready when I walked in the door. I sat there, thinking about my children, who were home alone eating leftovers, about clients I had not followed up with earlier in my busy day, about all the useful things that I could be doing with my time instead of waiting for this guy to get dressed. When I hollered up to him, "Are you about ready to go?" his reply was in a tone that only furthered my frustration. Too much time to think on his couch got me to ponder an irony.

I had been reading a bunch of books about the Law of Attraction. You don't have to be a New Age guru to believe in the basic psychology that your own feelings about yourself draw in or allow for certain types of partners to enter your life. I was really getting into the theories presented in these books. So there I was, sitting on Shane's couch, and suddenly it came to me—"My God," I thought, "I've been nothing but an asshole magnet!" And then I further contemplated these ideas about the laws of energy and like attracting like, etc. I thought, "Well, if I'm an asshole magnet, then I gotta figure out how to shut the magnet off." It sounded like a good theory, and I joked about it with a few of my girlfriends until one day I got curious enough to do some serious research. Maybe it's not so far fetched, I thought. How do you demagnetize a magnet? I Googled.

There are two ways to demagnetize a magnet. The irony is that I can see how these very steps are applicable to demagnetizing an asshole magnet as well.

1. **Heating, hammering, or jarring.** When you hammer, heat or jar a magnet, you cause the molecules in the magnet to rearrange. When you heat a magnet, you cause the energy to free the magnetic pull.

   Heating is akin to sweating out the discomfort of taking a hard look at what's in front of you. It's boiling out the bacteria of daydreams and fantasy, separating illusion from reality and forcing yourself to accept pure truth. Heating builds up a healthy sort of anger. It's anger at yourself for accepting less than you really deserve; anger at the nerve of a man who treats you in any way that is less than respectful. Heating is reaching the boiling point that says, I've *had enough*. It's building up your passion and getting to the point of being really, really sick of dealing with assholes.

   Next, you have to hammer reality into your head. You have to see the things present in your relationship that aren't good for you, and pound yourself until you believe that you deserve better. You have to hammer in the belief that you deserve to share your life with someone who treats you with respect. You have to hammer into your belief system the fact that you are valuable, significant, and worth having a partner who will love you with as much love as you give him—exclusively. You have to hammer the commitment into your heart; *To thine own self be true.*

   Until you can be happy with yourself, you cannot be happy with someone else. Hammer that into your head.

   If relationships create the same brain chemistry reaction as drug addiction, then jarring is like suffering through the withdrawal, white knuckling your way through the separation. Jarring is just that: Forcefully shaking your fingers loose from the asshole you're holding onto. Shaking loose and letting go. To let go means "to liberate, disengage, and set free."

2. **Alternating Current.** AC Current is also used to demagnetize. By using an alternate current, you produce a magnetic field of changing direction. When magnetic dipoles switch direction, the magnet will align with the new direction and it will reduce the magnet to almost zero. The magnet field is eliminated.

   Applying Alternating Current is changing the direction of your life through will. Using alternating current means bringing new energy into your life. You have to turn your focus and change direction. As a woman, if you've been in a relationship for any length of time, you have probably focused on your partner so much that you have neglected yourself. Using alternating current in this sense means staying busy, focusing on things you enjoy. If you don't know what it is you enjoy, that's even better. You're prime for new adventures and self-discovery. It's time to get out there and explore new things in your quest to learn what it is that *really* makes *you* happy.

Shane and I had several break ups before the final one. In one of our splits, we were on vacation with two other couples. Before we broke up, we ate at restaurants every night that were not my taste, serving hamburgers, chicken wings, or (my least favorite meal in the world) Mexican food. Breaking up on a lovers holiday wasn't the vacation of my dreams, but instead of being miserable and wasting the time off and the expense to get there, I chose to make the best of that vacation. The first thing that I did alone after we broke up was walk into a restaurant serving Thai food, which gave me a little piece of *me* alongside my spring roll. Shane and the other two couples were more interested in golfing, shopping, and night life than in seeing historical monuments. After our breakup, I grabbed a map of the area and made it a point to visit several historical sites. I grabbed brochures and made a list of everything that I would like to do and I did them. Before I hammered my way out, I was stressing about coordinating our activities and making sure that whatever we did with our day pleased not only Shane but everyone else in our group, too. Afterward, I lay on the beach and soaked up a lot of sun. I listened to waves crashing against the rocks, instead of an asshole yelling in my ear.

When Shane and I finally broke up, I flew to Maui to center myself, thinking that time relaxing on a beach would soothe my soul. I planned to "Ohm on a rock" and spend all of my time alone in contemplation. It was time to take care of *me*, and I called this trip my honeymoon following my marriage to myself. Every morning, I walked to a coffee shop several miles from my hotel. The exercise gave me a much needed endorphin rush, relieving stress and creating positive energy. On the way back, I walked along the beach, appreciating the scenery. I sat on rocks and stared at the ocean while I sipped my breakfast, making sure

I also breathed in deep breaths of the air. When we feel appreciation and gratitude in the moment, our thoughts shift out of negativity. Next, I decided to allow myself to grieve instead of forcing myself either to stuff the pain inside of me or try to not feel it. Resistance to pain only prolongs it. So I didn't resist the hurt, and my nonresistance allowed it to pass away much more quickly. When my muscles were tense, I bought myself a massage on the beach. I catered to *my* needs, not anyone else's, and focused on loving myself. It worked. This is why I said earlier that the easiest way to fall out of love with a man who is bad for you is to fall in love with yourself.

What was even more helpful to my healing was that I opened myself to new experiences. Initially, I was adamant that this was *me time*, and I refused to let anyone get in the way of my date with myself. My mission was to do only *what I wanted to do*. What I thought I wanted was to be alone. To my surprise, however, I met several people on the beach at Maui and shared many delightful dinners with them. I learned by being open that I also wanted new people in my life. These were the kinds of people I admire and would like to model in my own life. One couple stole my heart. They were a refreshing match vacationing with her mother-in-law in tow. I noticed how connected this couple was and I commented on how pleasant their relationship seemed to his mother while the couple were off swimming. "They complement each other very well" she said "I am really blessed to have her for a daughter-in-law." I lay on the beach talking to the wife after she came back from her swim with her husband and she revealed to me her age, which was at least fifteen years older than she appeared. "I guess I'm really lucky to have a husband who keeps me active," she said after I expressed my shock. Later they invited me to join them on several ocean dives.

I spent some time with them on their balcony before dinner one night and I had the sense of peace. They were warm, real, (not phony people) who were enjoying life. They were present in the now and enjoying each moment of it with their very best friend. By connecting with these new people, I found my wounds healing. Clarity followed healing. The last night on the island, I said to the wife of this beautiful couple, "You know, it's strange. Meeting the two of you has truly been the highlight of my trip. I'm so glad that I was able to spend so much time with you and that I didn't just sit alone like I had planned, thinking that solitude was what was the healthiest thing for me." She replied, "Maybe this is what you *really* needed." She was right. Sitting home alone, all by yourself, is healthy for only so long. It is vital to healing to get back out in the world and connect with people. Connecting with people who are aligned with themselves can be a great reminder of the values you hold inside, and when you observe happy people, your thinking will become clear with regard to how you want your own life to look.

When I returned home, I was eager to be around my family. It wasn't that I *felt* like being around them as much as noticing that I was distracted enough by my nieces and nephews and their innocent laughter and demands for attention to pull me out of my pity party. My family, who had been observing my life, offered valuable outsider perspective about my strengths and weaknesses, my talents and abilities, which is irreplaceable when it comes from people who know you so intimately. And even though it was difficult for me to go to the trouble of getting dressed and pulling myself together to meet with friends, getting out of my pajamas was always rewarded. Once I was in a group of people, I felt connected again and release from sadness.

When Brock and I broke up, I did not have the financial ability to jaunt off to a tropical location. When I was feeling consumed by feelings of despair, I took a long drive along an inlet until I found a place to pull to the side of the road. Then I hiked out onto the rocks and sat and watched the water, praying, crying, and releasing.

When Blake and I ended our affair, I found myself in the very same place along the inlet as I had after Brock. I searched for new places to hike too, so I could be alone, get some exercise, breathe fresh air and appreciate the life all around me. I poured myself into my work and also spent time writing the rough draft of this book, hoping to make a difference in peoples' lives. In essence, I found new places to pour my passion.

A woman having an affair with a married man has no choice but to demagnetize herself from him. If she doesn't do it on her own, it will eventually be done to her, forcibly and much more painfully. When she chooses to let go and cut the ties herself, she leaves with more of her self-respect intact than if she is tossed. If she stays with him, she is bound to remain filled with negative energy. Even if she becomes one of the three percent of lovers who marry, and even if she survives as one of the third who stay married, she will have cheated herself of a better life that awaited her.

A woman who suffers divorce after experiencing adultery also has to struggle to find direction in her life. She resists the change of direction her life has taken. She is angry, confused, and afraid—no, scared shitless. The process of letting go is easier said than done, but the process is really just a brain shift. If a woman suffering relationship finality chooses to view the divorce or breakup as a new beginning, rather than an end, she is several steps ahead in her emotional battle. Sometimes the most painful experiences turn out to be the most rewarding.

There are two kinds of women who survive divorce after infidelity. When I was interviewing women for this book, I could tell immediately which of the two types I was talking to.

The first spends the rest of her life feeling angry, bitter, and robbed. You can see it on her face. She looks grouchy, negative, and dejected. When she speaks, she is guarded, and her answers are brief. When she speaks of her ex-husband or her life, hatred and blame are evident and her tone is sarcastic. She is miserable because she resists letting go. She does not accept her "fate." She lives one day to the next, just getting by, anxious for her day to be over, but dreading getting out of bed the next morning. Her bitterness toward men guarantees that she will continue being alone, if she doesn't fall into another unhappy relationship. She's an Ice Maiden on the outside, but inside she is a sorrowing woman. She lives in the past, she is disconnected to the present, and she blocks any progress or future happiness.

For example, one woman I spoke with, Mattie, had divorced several years earlier. She had married her high school sweetheart, Kevin. He had started a contracting business that experienced substantial growth, and they had two children. They lived a very comfortable lifestyle. She kept a part-time job and was involved in many charities. She and her husband had several couples they spent a lot of time with, traveling and getting together at home. But Kevin was seeing another woman. He didn't tell Mattie this of course, but he began acting very strange. He became a distant jerk. Eventually, the marriage had so many problems and they argued so much that Kevin moved out of the house. They tried to work on their marriage (at least, she did). They went to counseling and set time aside for dating and activities with their boys, but still they could not restore the marriage. Kevin kept stringing her along, leading her to believe they would work through things. This lasted for a year. Mattie was miserable, but she remained hopeful. Finally, Kevin made a clear decision. He wanted a divorce. It was then that Mattie discovered that Kevin's affair had been going on for two years and he was moving in with his mistress.

When I met Mattie, she had been divorced for almost six years. We sat on her patio as we talked. Her body language was stiff, but her shoulders slumped. Her eyes, indeed, her whole face, was filled with distrust. When her young sons interrupted us to ask if they could go visit a friend, she asked them many questions as if they were set on lying to her. When she spoke about Kevin, she found much bitter humor in relaying rumors she had heard about his not being happy in his new relationship. Every time our conversation turned to any man, she had a snide comment to make. She spent most of our conversation bitching about all of the things that Kevin wasn't doing. Every small incident with the boys came up, including things as minor as his forgetting to repack their toothbrushes. It all meant he was an awful father. Every contribution of his toward an expense they shared sent fire out of her mouth. Every friend that had turned their back on Kevin made her happy. She had gone on a few dates since her divorce, but every man was a loser, and she nagged about their imperfections to the point of being annoying. And it wasn't just men that made her unhappy. Her job sucked. Her house was always lacking something. All she spoke about her friends was negative gossip. She was harshly judgmental and made back-handed comments about them. Mattie was an unhappy woman.

Another woman, Betty, has found *herself* through her pain and likes the woman she has become much more than the woman she was before. She shines with inner power. She sees her life as an adventure and has enjoyed so much personal growth that she enjoys quality *me* time, her relationships are enriched, she is more self-assured, and she is always seeking new ways to discover self. She is whole.

Betty's husband, John, had left her for another woman. Actually, by the time he left her, he'd had several affairs. Betty, of course, was devastated. She had spent more than twenty-five years married to him. He was the only partner she could remember. They raised a child together and lived quite handsomely. She was anticipating retirement when he dropped the bomb that he wanted a divorce. At first, she was bitter and angry. They had planned to buy a retirement home in the country near his family, and she'd had visions of them spending time together on a golf course, relaxing and enjoying the fruits of their labor together. Now that dream had been ripped from her. She knew that retirement for her was in the distant future and that she would possibly spend it alone.

Though Betty had suffered all the insults of divorce and another woman's presence, when I saw her she was no longer unhappy. She liked to call herself the New Betty. She told me that she'd had an awakening. "I could either cry every day, and be resentful and miserable," she said, "or I could get on with my life." She realized that she had always put John's needs above hers. It hadn't really been her idea to buy a country home near John's family. Though she didn't mind the idea, she now wondered what it was *she* really wanted. She discovered that she was already home. She didn't want to move. She had enjoyed golfing with John because it gave them time together, but she really thought it was a pretty boring sport. What did *she* like to do? Betty tried various things until she joined a kayaking class, something John would never have done. After meeting interesting new friends, she started entertaining in her home more often, something else John hated. Next, she joined a book club, but she soon got bored with it. She thought she should stick to it because she had committed, but then she realized that was John's voice in her head, not her own. She took cooking classes, joined hiking groups, and went on a Club Med cruise where she made lasting friendships.

Betty realized that she didn't need a man in her life to be happy. Once she found happiness in herself, she met Carl. She's not quite sure what to do with Carl. He's so kind and attentive, "It takes some getting used to," she told me, "but I like trying." And so Carl remains her companion and very best friend while she decides if there is any need to move the relationship to the next level. "My life is perfect as it is," she said. I can't argue with her. I've yet to see her without a smile.

We have two choices when a relationship ends. We can be a Mattie or . . . . be a *Betty*!

Chapter 26

The Caboose

As I closed out this book—this chapter in my life really—I struggled to find the proper ending. I had initially thought that I would end things with a letter to Beth saying heartfelt apologies and announcing my realizations to her and other married women recovering from their husbands' affairs. But no matter what I wrote, nothing seemed good enough. I wanted to tell her how sorry I was for the part I played in causing her pain. I wanted to explain to her that one of the toughest realities for me to embrace was that she was not the Ice Queen I had come to believe her to be and the ugliness this caused me to feel about myself. I realized that I had been very selfish and that Blake was a fool. I wanted to tell her that I know she is an excellent mother, a beautiful woman, and a better wife to Blake than I'm ever capable of being. I hoped she would understand that I realize now what I thought I offered him, he already had and if he was not satisfied in his life with her, he would never have been satisfied in a life with anyone else. I hoped for her own sake that she would also know this about herself and not allow the affair to beat at her self confidence or self worth, or affect her ability to believe in all that she truly deserves. But how many apologies can one say and would they even matter?

I could not find the right way to place those revelations in an apology. I began searching for inspiration and methods by calling people I had previously interviewed. I asked them if they were to have the opportunity to tell their former lovers wives anything, what would it be. Most struggled just the same as I have with a loss for words. They only said how sorry they were and how awful they felt for his wife—each of them. Next I called Janet and asked her if there were anything that she needed to hear from Kelly, the other woman in her husbands affair. Was there anything that Kelly could possibly say to her that would ease her pain? For the first time in the duration of my project, she changed the subject.

A few days later, I attended a seminar with a girlfriend of mine and we were joined by another friend of hers. I was acquainted with Sherry, and my friend had spoken to me often about her over the years. Sherry's husband had an affair and left her for his pregnant lover. Sherry has recently remarried. After the seminar had ended, I asked Sherry questions about her new life, hoping to hear that time had healed her wounds and that she was happier now, that she had let go of the past—I was hoping she was a Betty. Eventually she brought up the topic of her ex-husband. I knew instantly not to ask her if there were any words that her husband's lover could ever say to ease her bitterness or hurt. But she did enlighten me about the effectiveness an apology from the other woman would have—none. She told me that all she really wanted was for her husband to regret his decision. I understood her feelings and they weren't entirely unusual for a woman in her shoes. Even in the fifth grade I wanted Keith to feel like he made the biggest mistake of his life when he asked his friend Robby to call me up for him and do the dirty deed of dumping me. I certainly wanted Blake to feel the same regret over our end and I even secretly hoped my husband would never remarry someone *better* than me, even though I asked for the divorce. I think what Sherry said was completely human, at least for a woman.

But my friend said something very logical to her that has stuck with me. She asked her why it *mattered*. Sherry had remarried. She has moved on with her life. If her husband called her tomorrow and said "I regret leaving you." What good would it do her now? Besides having a few feelings of revenge, there was no ability to turn back. My friend continued to probe Sherry, "What do his feelings have to do with you?" she asked, "Why are you wasting energy on the past?" Wow, that was really—real to me. So much dwelling and emotion was being spent on hoping that she would receive an outcome *that really didn't matter*. I'd even bet that if the outcome of his regret played out, it would offer her less gratification than she hoped for. I suspect this because I've received the "regret" phone call in my life and it's anti-climatic, bitter sweet at best. It's not necessary to move on.

You see, we seem to fixate our thoughts on this *thing* that could make us feel better outside of ourselves, leaving our happiness at the mercy of another's hand. What's even more profound is that when you ask these women who are emotionally devastated to identify this *thing* that could happen to make them feel better about their husband's affair, they don't know for certain what it really is or why they believe it will work. That's because there isn't any *thing* that can be done to change the past. Would his regretful feelings about having an affair cause her own feelings about it to disappear? In my experience, his announcement of regret generally restarts the bitter return of questioning *why*. Why now? Why couldn't he have figured this out before he hurt me? The thing they really hope for is the ability to turn back the hands of time. A hope that is as possible as grasping the wind. The only rest from fighting to hold the wind, is to realize the wasted struggle, open the palm, and feel the breeze. Surrender. *Let go.*

To the wives who read this book and are working on restoring their marriage, I'd like you to think about your pain from another perspective. You are not Sherry, Betty, Mattie or any married woman whose husband walked out the door to start a life with their mistress. You have been through hell (that I'm not minimizing) but you are not left to pick up the pieces alone. Your earth shattered, but the shards still exist by which you may still piece the shatters together. I'm telling you this because if you picked up this book, it is safe for me to assume that you have some letting go to do. Though no one wants to experience what you have, you're struggles are less than the wife who was abandoned or the mistress left to shame herself. He has stayed because you are the woman he values life with. You are the woman that he loves. May your wounds heal quickly. May you find release of negative emotions and may you find strength in rebuilding your marriage, because behind all of your hurt there is more hope and that should be where your focus lies. My prayer for you is that soon . . . . all of this *doesn't matter.*

I leave you with the wisdom of my mother: You can hold onto this affair everyday and make both of your lives miserable or you can *let go* from today on, focusing on how to build a future.

Last night I shut down my computer feeling that I had said all that I possibly could on the subject of affairs and being the other woman. Before I dozed to sleep, I prayed to God or my muse—whomever it was that inspired me to write—and I asked, is it done? Have I completed this book? I worried that I might have left something out.

As I slept, I dreamed that I drove my car into a small town in search of a little toy caboose for a train set my nephew has. The set has a wooden track with train cars that hook together magnetically. My father is a railroader and so I always think there is more significance to train dreams for me than the average dreamer. But no matter what, a caboose belongs at the end of the train.

While I was driving Beth called me and my heart softened when I heard her voice. I told her that I had been thinking of her a lot and forewarned her that I had written this book. I was worried about how she was going to feel reading the details of my affair with her husband. She started to cry and asked me once again if Blake and I were over and I assured her that it had been over for many years. She sobbed some more and seemed uneasy about the publication. She asked me what I said in the book, and I explained to her that Part One was the story of our affair. Then I told her that Part Two was a culmination of a great amount of research; Part Three, prevention and healing. I interjected that I had thought many times to call her and ask her if she would like to write a chapter about her side of things (the thought had crossed my mind a few times in waking life) but that it was too bold of a request and I never found the nerve. I told her what I had wanted from her in that chapter (I had wanted her to write what was happening with them while he and I were in the affair) and she told me that she had done much of her own research and had things to say that maybe weren't exactly what I was looking for, they were less personal, she had more statistics to include and additions to Parts Two.

While I spoke to her, I had walked into a toy shop and was approached by a shop keeper offering help. I told him that I was looking for a caboose and he left me to go search for one. I was still perusing the little toy shop as Beth and I spoke and the shop keeper returned and placed a wooden caboose in my hand. The toy was very elaborate, hand painted with shiny primary colors and more detailed than what I had been looking for. I had been holding the caboose in my hand when Beth told me that she wanted to contribute to my book, negotiating writing what she wanted to, rather then what I had wanted. I looked at the toy and saw that it wasn't what I was looking for, but thought about buying it anyway. I was frustrated that I had driven so far to find this toy, and felt that I shouldn't leave without what I came for. But in the end, I decided that speaking to Beth was more important and so I thanked the shop keeper and set it down. As I drove back toward the city, I was still talking to Beth on my phone and agreed to hold off with publishing my book until she wrote her pages and then I woke up.

As much as I would like to believe that my higher conscious has whispered an important message to me and as tempted as I am to pull up next to her in the Junior High parking lot after our children are dismissed from school today, I also dream that I can fly on occasion. I know that dreams can also be wishes from the subconscious. Things in life don't always turn out as we dreamed they would. Sometimes we can lose our way by trying to second guess outcomes and hold back from living our lives by consuming our thoughts with *what if*, more so in real life than in dreams. In my dream, I delayed my life some more while

I waited for someone else to be ready for what I wanted. I waited for her to align with me and join me in putting the mess behind us. I *waited* and delayed sticking the caboose on the end of my train and sending it down the track because I wanted Beth to say something that might make me feel release. Maybe Beth has already spoken in this book, in some way, I think she has. Right now, the significance of my dream will whisper to me . . . . *let go.*

Though the caboose wasn't the one I was looking for, the one the shop keeper gave me was actually better than the one I wanted. So often is the case with endings. And so frequent do we dismiss the better by fixating on what we want. We backtrack the way we came, putting our lives on hold hoping that someone else will make things better, ... when better was set in the palm of our hands; if only we believed we should buy it.

Bibliography

Alexander, S. (n.d.). *www.womansavers.com/why-men-cheat.asp*. Retrieved September 8, 2007, from www.womansavers.com: http://www. womansavers.com/why-men-cheat.asp

Bercht, A. (n.d.). *www.beyondaffairs.com/articles/questionsfromotherwoman.htm*. Retrieved November 25, 2007, from www.beyondaffairs.com: www. beyondaffairs.com/articles/questionsfromtheotherwoman.htm

Carter-Scott, C. (1999). *If Love Is a Game, These Are The Rules*. New York: Broadway Books.

Glass, L. (1995). *Toxic People*. New York: St. Martins Press.

Hartley, G., & Karinch, M. (2005). *How To Spot A Liar*. Franklin Lakes: Career Press. *http://www.cbn.com/family/marriage/affairproof.aspx*. (n.d.). Retrieved September 9, 2007, from www.cbn.com: http://www.cbn. com/family/marriage/affairproof.aspx

Louann Brizendine, M. (2006). The Female Brain. In L. Brizendine, *The Female Brain*. New York: Broadway Books.

Vaughan, P. (2003). The Monogamy Myth. In P. Vaughan, *The Monogamy Myth*. W.W Norton & Co Inc.

Subotnik, Rona B. Will He Really Leave Her For Me? Avon: Adams Media, 2005.

31483092R00180

Made in the USA
Lexington, KY
21 February 2019